REDISCOVERING
NEW TESTAMENT PRAYER

Other Books by John Koenig

Charismata
Jews and Christians in Dialogue
Philippians and Philemon
New Testament Hospitality

Rediscovering
New Testament Prayer

BOLDNESS AND BLESSING
IN THE NAME OF JESUS

John Koenig

HarperSanFrancisco
A Division of HarperCollins*Publishers*

FIRST EDITION

Library of Congress Cataloging-in-Publication Data

Koenig, John
    Rediscovering New Testament prayer : boldness and blessing in the name of Jesus / John Koenig.
        p.   cm.
    Includes bibliographical references and index.
    ISBN 0-06-064755-8 (alk. paper)
    1. Prayer.   I. Title.
BV210.2.K58   1992
248.3'2—dc20   91-50500
                                                                     CIP

92 93 94 95 96 RRD(H) 10 9 8 7 6 5 4 3 2 1

This edition is printed on acid-free paper that meets the American National Standards Institute Z39.48 Standard.

*To the seminary communities in which
I have been privileged to teach,
especially Princeton, Union, and General.
May our study be guided by praise and thanksgiving.*

Contents

Preface

ALL THINGS CONSIDERED, the surgery turned out to be quite routine. I was on the table for only forty minutes, blissfully detached from the scene by a mild solution of Valium dripping into my veins. The hospital had classified me as an ambulatory patient, and so I was. Barely two hours after the operation, with Elisabeth grasping my arm to keep me steady, I eased into a cab on Third Avenue for the short trip home to lower Manhattan.

The lump on my tongue had developed suddenly, toward the end of a much-needed sabbatical leave in Los Angeles. It was too large to ignore and showed no signs of diminishing. How odd that it should appear at just about the time the first draft of this book was completed. I was praying then with some regularity, mostly to give thanks for a special time of refreshment, and for the end of a long project. In hours the whole landscape of my inner life was transformed.

From a medical point of view my recovery proceeded normally. But I was filled with distress as I waited for the results of the biopsy. Strange mixtures of high anxiety and stoic resignation became the order of the day. Only by offering all of them up to God did I find something like peace. Two weeks after the surgery I learned, to my huge relief, that the tumor was benign. I was lucky, as they say, although for me the word *spared* rings truer. This time, it seems, I escaped from a major showdown with death. I know much younger people who have not been granted such a reprieve, and in fact I continue to work through a kind of survivor's guilt about my healing.

All over the country family and friends were praying with me that the lump would prove not to be cancerous; but I shall never know, in this life, exactly what role their requests played in God's providence. What I do know is that early on in the long process of diagnosis and treatment a few words from the psalmist became startlingly real: "[God] shall give his angels charge over you, to keep you in all your ways. They shall bear you in their hands, lest you dash your foot against a stone" (Ps. 91:11–12, Book of Common Prayer). Well, of course I did dash my foot in the sense of incurring a physical ailment, but not in the more important sense of tripping over that stone of offense and falling into a pit of despair. I knew I was being buoyed up by a strength that far exceeded my own.

And now I have returned to gratitude, especially for the simple pleasures of eating normally and speaking clearly. Scripture contains a host of warnings against the misuse of the tongue. Mostly they serve to accent its proper vocation, which is the articulation of God's praise (Ps. 35:28; 50:19–23; 71:23–24; 126:1–3; Lk. 1:64; Acts 2:4, 11; Rom. 14:11; Phil. 2:11). Indeed, praise and thanksgiving form the very soul of New Testament prayer. It makes sense to me that now I can honestly say I enjoy singing hymns to God. Perhaps that is the lesson I needed to learn before sending this book on its way. Perhaps it will be a lesson to relearn and teach for the rest of my life.

The music of thanksgiving continues to swell as I reflect on how the present study came into being. I began my research with considerable reluctance. I had to be persuaded over a period of years by editor Roland Seboldt and others that such a book was needed and that I might be the right person to attempt it. Now I want to express my thanks for their persistence. Even before I began writing in earnest, several people came forward to announce that they were praying for the project. Exactly what this means, or will mean, I cannot say. No one would believe me if I reported that the writing went altogether smoothly. (It didn't.) But I can say that I was not consumed by it, as I sometimes have been by previous assignments. Instead, I felt mostly enriched, and sometimes even led.

Special words of gratitude must be directed to a number of people and groups without whose support there would be no book: to Professor Elisabeth Koenig, my wife, for depths of sharing that cannot be put into words; to the Reverends Valarie Whitcomb and Carol Anderson, along with their congregations, for mighty intercession and good humor; to the history department at UCLA for granting me the status of visiting scholar in the fall of 1990; to Professor Scott Bartchy of that department and his spouse Nancy Breuer for many words and acts of welcome; to Nancy and Linc Field for probing conversations over many sumptuous meals; to Melissa and Michael Hentges for constancy in their caring; to the Board for Theological Education of the Episcopal Church for a generous sabbatical grant, awarded through the Conant Fund; to Dr. Mary Tanner, Moderator of the Faith and Order Commission, World Council of Churches, Chaplain Emeritus

F. W. Dillistone of Oriel College, Oxford, and Dean Charles Elliott of Trinity Hall, Cambridge, for their ongoing words of encouragement. Alice Madden, faculty secretary at the General Theological Seminary, deserves much praise for preparing several "final" copies of this manuscript. I also want to pay tribute to my editors at HarperSanFrancisco, Roland Seboldt and Ronald Klug. Throughout this project our relationship has been far more than business as usual. Both at the beginning and the end they guided me into better forms of expression than I myself could have imagined. In the final stages of the book's production, editors Hilary Vartanian, Holly Elliott, Caroline Pincus, and Terri Goff also provided indispensable help of the highest quality. Senior seminarian Rebecca Brown produced the biblical index with grace as well as efficiency.

And what shall I say to God? Some words by an obscure librettist come to mind, perhaps because I heard them sung in concert just a few days before my surgery. They live on in the collective memory of Western culture through the great music that was composed for them by Bach. But they also have a value of their own, and in many ways they tell the central story of New Testament prayer.

> Lord of the heavens, give ear to our stamm'ring,
> Scarcely our faint alleluias can praise you
> When by your angels with psalms you are lauded.
> Yet hear the hearts that rejoice in your glory;
> We would to you our devotion be singing
> In whom alone our salvation can stand.[1]

CHAPTER ONE

Communion
with God
at the Turn
of the Ages

DO WE NEED YET ANOTHER BOOK ON PRAYER? One could make a good case for answering "no." In recent years the great devotional classics of both the Eastern and Western traditions have become available to the reading public on an unprecedented scale.[1] Many contemporary works are also of excellent quality. The popularity of retreat centers for prayer and meditation continues at a high level, and there is no shortage of people ready to offer their services as spiritual guides. In addition, the various twelve-step programs emerging from our national anguish over addictive behaviors have helped tens of thousands find their way to a lively relationship with a Higher Power. A whole new body of writing on spirituality has developed from such programs and from other groups and movements that are best identified by the term *New Age*.

Yet there is a difficulty with this recent upsurge in devotional practice and literature, for much of it seems to reflect and foster a diffuse kind of religion in general, only marginally related to the biblical forms of faith.[2] While I empathize with people who find the worship life of their local churches and synagogues to be less than inspiring, I cannot quite believe that the present growth of non-institutional or para-institutional religion signals a real deepening in our communion with God. I mean that religion without a solid base often falls prey to peculiar romanticisms, which in turn lead to the very opposite of spiritual truth and freedom. Moreover, religion in general, as I perceive it, frequently lives in deprivation. Always standing just outside the houses of the ancient traditions, it does not get properly nourished at any one of their tables. Religion in general often searches for esoteric experiences but turns away from daily sustenance.[3] Such a tendency, I believe, nearly always proves to be self-defeating. And it is far from necessary.

One simple truth about the spiritual life just now coming into focus for me as a result of work on this book is that careful reflection on the fundamentals of our prayer tradition—which means, for Christians, the New Testament—pushes us very quickly beyond conventional distinctions between the esoteric and the ordinary. Or, to put it a little differently, even the most rudimentary practice of what the earliest believers meant by prayer turns out to include what we now think of as extraordinary encounters with the Holy.

But here is another paradox. Most of us Christians today are not well schooled in the basics of New Testament faith, and even those of us who devote long years to learning or teaching them often fail to connect with them at the level of our prayer life. I admire the candor of Loren Halvorsen, who recently wrote: "Though I have taught for many years at a theological seminary, I am very much in need of instruction in prayer. I am not alone."[4] I know exactly what he means. As a doctor of theology, I must admit to being just a novice at prayer; and I have even taught a course on the subject for men and women seeking ordination!

I am not much comforted by the knowledge that many of my parish-based colleagues also suffer from difficulties with personal prayer. The Reverend Donna Schaper observes that pastoral leadership often "has to do with turning our bodies, minds, and souls into an instrument through which others may turn to God."[5] But in Schaper's experience, which may well be typical, this necessary public stewardship all too frequently becomes a false substitute for the minister's personal communion with God. Here many of us who are clergy will feel called upon to make embarrassing confessions. Yet our honesty can also be a way toward health. To speak of our deficiencies before God is a prayer of repentance; and Jesus promises that whenever we attempt it, "there is joy before the angels of God" (Lk. 15:10), which means in God's own heart.

I suspect that a good number of laypeople who read these lines may be feeling a similar blend of honesty and penitence about their prayer lives. I hope they will find this study speaking as much to their condition as to that of their clerical sisters and brothers. More and more, I am convinced, biblical specialists need to be writing for the general public of the churches, and for those on the ecclesiastical boundaries. It may well be that we should discern in the current popular fascination with religion a genuine desire on the part of many for a more disciplined, life-transforming communion with God. If so, Christians of all types and self-definitions will find no better guide toward the fulfillment of that desire than the New Testament.

But laypeople and clergy alike may harbor certain doubts about the value of a text-centered approach to prayer like the one presented here. In leading Bible classes on this topic, I encounter occasional skepticism about whether research into the basic documents of our faith can help very much when it comes to something as nonrational as prayer. The point is well taken, but it loses force if we begin to conceive of textual study as something more than an intellectual enterprise. For me, true literary investigation always involves listening for the reasons of the heart that have produced a given passage. Why, I want to find out, would anyone say, "I pray that you may . . . know the love of Christ that surpasses knowledge, so that you may be filled with all the fullness of God" (Eph. 3:18–19)? What sort of relationship with the Divine has prompted these words? What I think I have discovered is that when Jesus and the New Testament authors offer their teachings on prayer or allow us to overhear their prayers, they wish not only to instruct our minds but also to renew our spirits and change our behaviors. Behind and within the biblical text is the real prayer experience of the One we name as Christ and of his first followers. It reaches out to us, inviting us to share in its richness.

Here a small item from the annals of publishing should also be noted. As far as I can tell, the last treatment of our topic produced by a biblical specialist for the English-speaking public appeared in 1967. It is a fine volume called *The Prayers of the New Testament* by Donald Coggan, later Archbishop of Canterbury from 1974 to 1980.[6] The present study in no way attempts to replace Lord Coggan's, but it does try to take advantage of whatever progress New Testament scholars have made over the intervening years. And I think we can in fact point to a few breakthroughs.

The Holy One Seeks Our Company

"This afternoon, while you were in class, a dragonfly sailed through the window of your study and circled around the room for a while. It seemed quite friendly." Dragonflies are uncommon in lower Manhattan, but that was not the real reason Elisabeth's announcement over dinner hit me like a snowball in the face. As noted above, I had some years ago taught a seminary-level course on the practice of prayer in the New Testament. One of the assigned readings came from a remarkable little book by H. A. Nielsen called *The Bible— As If for the First Time.*[7] In it Nielsen retells an incident, barely noticed by most of us, from the first chapter of John's Gospel. It concerns the call of Nathanael, who had initially countered his friend Philip's enthusiasm over Jesus with the cynical quip, "Can anything good come out of Nazareth?" (1:46). Eventually Nathanael was persuaded to "come and see," but before he could even form an opinion about this strange prophet, Jesus reached out to him with a greeting: "Behold, an Israelite indeed, in whom there is no guile" (1:47). Nathanael was startled. Did Philip tell Jesus about his cynicism? Perhaps, but Jesus did not actually accuse him of that vice. His words might be an ironic compliment—or a joke. Nathanael responded, warily: "How do you know me?" And Jesus answered: "I saw you under the fig tree before Philip called you" (1:48). *Before* Philip called you? But how, Nathanael must have thought, could he be watching me then? And how could he have gotten to know me in that private moment? The text itself does not spell out these reflections but instead tells us that at this point Nathanael just broke down and blurted out one of the loftier christological confessions in John's Gospel: "Rabbi, you are the Son of God! You are the King of Israel!" (1:49).

What is going on here? Nielsen thinks that Nathanael was doing something unusual under the fig tree: "solitary prayer perhaps, but something that tied in with a temptation to deceive." In any case, "humanly speaking, Jesus *could* not have seen him under the fig tree, a haunt chosen by one who took pains to be alone."[8] Nielsen helps us enter this mysterious story by means of a modern one. He asks us to imagine ourselves alone, rowing out onto a quiet pond we know in order to struggle through a problem of conscience, a temptation perhaps, to misrepresent ourselves so that we can stand first in line for an attractive new job.

4

Out in the middle of the pond you are isolated. Everything is so still that a dragonfly finds rest on the blade of your shipped oar. Only your thoughts are busy for that quarter of an hour. Finally you think: "What if I don't land that job? It won't be the end of the world."

On the way back to the house you meet a bright-eyed stranger and trade greetings. He knows your name, surprising but not impossible, and tells you his. Then out of the blue he says, "I appreciate someone who can't tolerate lies." . . . How could he know? "Have I met you somewhere?" you manage to ask. "Not exactly," he replies, "but I was watching you through the dragonfly's eye."[9]

Perhaps the reader will already have guessed that Elisabeth had no inkling of this story or of my fascination with it when I first read it years ago. (I notice now that most of it is underlined in my copy of Nielsen's book.)

Prayer is like this. God visits us and knows us in our most private places and then seeks us out for a conscious encounter with the true Source of our being. It has been happening ever since creation. The Lord God, "walking in the garden in the cool of the day," was not looking for Adam and Eve's sin but for them, for their company (Gen. 3:8–9). Marjorie Thompson writes: "Some of us remember the first article of Westminster Catechism, which asks: 'What is the chief end of Man?', to which the resounding response is: 'The chief end of Man is to glorify God and enjoy Him forever!' I am firmly convinced that God delights in our companionship. . . . I am equally convinced that God yearns for us to delight in the Divine Presence, to love God for who God is, not merely for what God can give us or make of us."[10] When the psalmist lifted up his voice in prayer to God, it was because he had first heard a voice within: "'Come, my heart says, seek his face'" (Ps. 27:8, NRSV). The New Testament confirms this in words of Jesus that seem to convey both promise and command at the same time: "You shall love the Lord your God with all your heart, and with all your soul, and with all your mind, and with all your strength" (Mk. 12:30). "The hour is coming and now is here when true worshipers will worship the Father in spirit and truth, for the Father seeks such to worship him" (Jn. 4:23, NRSV).

True worship means approaching the throne of grace (Heb. 4:16) to acknowledge God's primacy and transcendent otherness. At the same time, however, it also includes making ever-new discoveries of God's loving presence with and in us. I chose the word *company* for this section of the first chapter because it seemed appropriate to describe the New Testament's way of telling us what God wants from us and for us. Only then did I think to check out the several meanings of this word in the *Oxford English Dictionary.* Here is the substance of what I found.

"Company" comes from the old French word *compagnie,* which literally means "an eating of bread together," an everyday relationship in which ordinary things are intimately shared. In Chaucer the word sometimes denotes a sexual connection, and this is consistent with the Hebrew verb for knowing, which can also refer to physical intercourse. More often, however, the desire for someone's company implies a guest-host relationship that is characterized by a wide range of social interaction. A company can also be a group of people assembled for some common purpose. We may think of a band of actors or a medieval trade guild. In the United States our first image of company is likely to be a corporation established for the purpose of economic gain. Finally, a company can mean a formation of soldiers or a ship's crew, that is, a group of individuals efficiently deployed for battle.

If I have understood the New Testament correctly, virtually all of these meanings are present, at least by implication, in the communing with God that we call prayer. The larger company that God wants to keep with us through prayer is the church. Here society and economics are being revalued, first of all in the depths of the human heart. In addition, the church is a school where we are trained and set in formation for quasi-military encounters with the principalities and powers of this age. And these clashes, as we shall see, are experienced chiefly through prayer.

But what about God's knowing of us? The New Testament is restrained in its use of overtly sexual language to describe this dimension of prayer.[11] On the other hand, it does speak graphically of God's intimate and exclusive claim upon the whole of our selves in ways that suggest the erotic. Here are some relevant texts from Paul's letters:

> Do you not know that your bodies are members of Christ? Should
> I therefore take the members of Christ and make them members
> of a prostitute? Never! Do you not know that whoever is united
> with a prostitute becomes one body with her? For it is said, "The

6

two shall become one flesh." But anyone united to the Lord becomes one spirit with him [1 Cor. 6:15–17]. Anyone who loves
God is known by him [1 Cor. 8:3]. Now I know only in part; then
I will know fully, even as I have been fully known [1 Cor. 13:13].
Formerly, when you did not know God, you were enslaved to beings
that by nature are not gods. Now, however, that you have come
to know God, or rather, to be known by God, how can you turn
back again to the weak and beggarly elemental spirits? [Gal. 4:8–9]

It seems clear that in all the texts cited a close prayer relationship
with God or Christ is taken for granted as the mode of our knowing
and being known (see Gal. 4:6). Moreover, Paul assumes a certain
degree of consciousness on the part of his readers regarding God's
intimacy with them.[12] For most believers, however, this consciousness needs to grow. In all his letters the apostle's goal is to promote
an "undivided devotion to the Lord" (1 Cor. 7:35).

We may conclude, then, that a large part of New Testament prayer
has to do with a dawning awareness of God's loving closeness in
Christ (Eph. 3:14–21) and with our response to this in a variety of
forms (e.g., praise, thanksgiving, petition, intercession, confession,
self-offering). Then faith begins to work through love toward others
as a natural expression of our communion with God (Gal. 5:6,
16–20).[13] An old collect (short liturgical prayer) sums it up nicely:
"Make us love what you command and desire what you promise, that
amid the changes of this world, our hearts may be fixed where true
joy is found." This joy comes not from commands and promises as
such but from knowing the God who draws near to reveal them. If the
New Testament is correct, the Holy One seeks our company, indeed,
makes us into a company worthy of the Holy (Eph. 2:13–22). And so
we discover what it means to worship in spirit and truth.

In the Rush of a New World Coming

According to the New Testament, God's persistent search for our
companionship now takes place within a context of unique urgency.
We see this early on in the Gospel tradition when Mark describes the
beginning of Jesus' public ministry as follows: "Now after John was
arrested, Jesus came to Galilee, proclaiming the gospel of God, and
saying, 'The time is fulfilled and the kingdom of God has come near;

repent and believe in the gospel'" (1:14). The claim being made here is that with Jesus' advent a decisive shift in the cosmic order has occurred. Jesus and the apostolic writers use a variety of language to interpret this novelty. The nearness of God's kingdom, which refers, among other things, to a special form of God's ruling presence, becomes the hallmark of Jesus' preaching and teaching in parables. But he also refers to the "new wine" of his ministry (Mk. 2:22), insisting that it can only be contained by new wineskins (concepts? communities?). Jesus' first followers continued to use kingdom language to express their experience of God's nearness. But in the light of their Lord's death and resurrection they felt compelled to supplement it with other images, such as "new creation," "the present moment," "the day of salvation," "the ends of the ages," "the fullness of time," and "the judgment of this world."[14] Most of these phrases were drawn from the apocalyptic traditions of Judaism, where it was expected that God would someday bring an end to the world order as we know it in order to reestablish the peace and righteousness of Eden.

There was no rigid uniformity among the early believers about exactly when this would happen (Mk. 13:32), or about the extent to which it was already beginning to transpire. Paul seemed to think that the end of all things was imminent and could occur within his own lifetime, although he also placed great stress on the presence of the Holy Spirit as a generous "first installment" of what was soon to be completed (2 Cor. 1:22, NRSV). The author of the Fourth Gospel, on the other hand, shows almost no interest in speculating about the date of the world's final transformation, since he was convinced that believers even now enjoy full access to eternal life in communion with the risen Jesus (6:41–59).

Yet on one point all the New Testament authors—and Jesus—agree: with the coming near of God's kingdom in the early decades of what we now call the first century, something unique was happening to the world order. An extraordinary infusion of God's goodness had occurred, and this was bringing about a new kind of warfare against evil—not only in the human heart but also in "the heavenly places," where it was thought to operate through superhuman principalities and powers (Eph. 6:12).

I use the word *rush* to describe a distinctive feature of what the New Testament means by life at the turn of the ages. A rush is a forward movement characterized by an unusual force or eagerness that sometimes approaches the violent. We find this usage in Luke's account of the first Spirit-led prayer of the church: "When the day of Pentecost had come, [the followers of Jesus] were all together in one place. And suddenly a sound came from heaven like the rush of a mighty wind, and it filled all the house where we were sitting. . . . And they were all filled with the Holy Spirit and began to speak in other tongues, as the Spirit gave them utterance" (Acts 2:1–4). Luke goes on to explain how the words of these earliest disciples issued in a combination of praise and prophecy. That is, the tongues were addressed directly to God as a type of adoration (see Acts 10:46). But they were also intelligible languages, announcing to onlookers that God's mighty acts of the past were now happening once again, this time in their final form (Acts 2:11, 17–21).

Throughout the New Testament we have the sense that prayer is an urgent matter because it grows out of God's decisive acts at the end of conventional time. Prayer is never casual, for it takes place in the midst of a great cosmic flux. What we do or do not do in our communion with God *now* matters in some very real way for the life of the world. What we do or do not do, along with our praying neighbors, can tip a secret balance in the course of history.

It may be hard for us contemporary believers to enter into the rush of expectation that pervaded virtually all the prayers of the New Testament. But I think we can at least open ourselves to its viability and allow God's Spirit to educate us in its nuances. Today we need not include within our articles of faith a confession that the world will come to an end in our lifetime (though that could happen through an ecological disaster). What does seem essential for Christians to affirm is that we are living at the juncture of the ages, when both good and evil are coming to their ultimate expression. This interim period has obviously lasted for two thousand years and may last for many thousands more. The key issue is not time as we reckon it in weeks and months but time as it intersects with eternity.

Does this happen in a new way—and continue to happen— through the person of Jesus? That is what the church has always confessed; and if it is so, our prayers will be shaped accordingly. Here, perhaps, we can understand Evelyn Underhill's definition of Christian prayer as "the substance of eternal life."[15] She does not mean, I think, that we who pray will become timeless or lose interest in the affairs of the present but rather that we will be joined together with the Incarnation, which is God's way of granting the earth its greatest possible reality. The cosmic fullness of time experienced by the earliest believers was inherently linked by them with what they came to call the Word made flesh (Jn. 1:14). And this event, they felt, was being replicated among them again and again through prayer: "Because you are [God's] children, God has sent the Spirit of his Son into our hearts, crying 'Abba! Father!'" (Gal. 4:6; see also Jn. 1:12).

Kyrios Iesous

The Greek words above are thought by many scholars to be the earliest of all Christian confessions (see 1 Cor. 12:3; Rom. 10:9), although they were probably first uttered in Aramaic as *Mar Jehoshua*.[16] Paul says that only the Holy Spirit can move people to make such a confession from the heart. But what does it mean? To call Jesus "Lord" is to name him as the one whom God has raised from the dead and given divine authority to rule over the turn of the ages (Rom. 1:1–6; 1 Cor. 15:20–28). This naming also becomes a cry of emancipation, because the advent of God's governance through Jesus spells the defeat of every oppressive power. Indeed, the reigning of God's Son is the very opposite of oppression, because he consistently and decisively overcomes evil with good, not with retaliation. To name Jesus as Lord means to praise God for all the blessings of the new creation and at the same time to defy every other force that claims control over human destiny. With just two words we articulate God's will that "at the name of Jesus every knee should bend, in heaven and on earth and under the earth" (Phil. 2:10).

Kyrios Iesous. Perhaps these words (or their Aramaic equivalent) were even spoken by the stunned disciples at the first resurrection appearances. In any case, believers used them not long afterward in responding to visions of the Risen One (Acts 7:59; 9:5); and the apostle Paul refers to his call as a seeing of "Jesus our Lord" (1 Cor. 9:1). This evidence suggests that almost from the beginning the expression "Lord Jesus" constituted a prayer. In fact we find such a prayer at the very end of John's Apocalypse in the weighty little sentence "Come, Lord Jesus" (Rev. 22:20; see further Mt. 7:21–23; 1 Cor. 16:22; 2 Cor. 12:8, where the words are implied). It may well be that Jesus' name was also spoken as an act of devotion during prayers to God, for he was often felt to be present alongside petitioners (Mt. 18:18–20) or in heaven at God's right hand, interceding on their behalf as they themselves approached the throne of grace (Heb. 4:14–16; 7:24; 8:1).

In other words, saying "Lord Jesus" was never just a matter of declaring one's thoughts about his identity. It was always, in addition, a cry of the heart, expressing or longing for communion with him. It was also a personal claim upon the fruits of the promise bestowed on all disciples at the end of Matthew's Gospel: "All authority in heaven and on earth has been given to me . . . and lo, I am with you always, even to the close of the age" (28:18–20).

Down through the centuries the simple words "Lord Jesus" have remained a primal element in the common worship of the church. They are not the only basis for our prayer life—we shall learn that the name of Abba for God is more fundamental still—but they are nevertheless indispensable. And they tend to gain prominence when the church is experiencing a renewal. Psychiatrist Gerald May recalls this moment of resolution during a hard period in his life: "One evening . . . I was diligently practicing a form of yoga meditation that encourages the free coming and going of all thoughts. It is a method that might be described as the opposite of repression. In the freedom I gave my mind, one of the thoughts that came was prayer. It was, in the beginning, the prayer of a nine year old, embarrassingly immature. 'Dear Jesus, help me.'"[17] May refers to his prayer as a "sad and painful thing," presumably because it made him feel so young and incompetent. But if the New Testament is correct, we shall never outgrow our childlike (and childish) need for Jesus' help. Nor is this incompatible with growth. The prayer tradition of the Eastern churches speaks of a great maturity that emerges from the meditative uttering of Jesus' name. Jesuit William Johnston, a pioneer in the Christian-Buddhist dialogue and veteran spiritual director, predicts that the next general council of the Roman Catholic Church "will treat mainly the person of Jesus Christ. It will be an ongoing conversion of the Christian people to the historical Jesus of Nazareth, who died for our sins and rose from the dead."[18] I have no idea whether Johnston's words will prove to be a true prophecy, but his intuition about the need of believers throughout the world for an "ongoing conversion to the historical Jesus" seems to me an accurate reading not only of the present situation but also of what New Testament prayer holds out to us as command and promise.

According to the apostolic witnesses, Jesus is our way to communion with God at the turn of the ages (1 Cor. 1:4–9). When we acclaim him Kyrios or address him as such, we are already speaking from an experience of the power, presence, and praise of God. But we are also asking, in his name, to enter more deeply into God's new creation, to take our own unique part, through prayer and action, in the final act of the divine drama.

The Plan of This Book

Readers will notice, from the table of contents, that this study is not arranged according to what the various writers of the New Testament teach about prayer. My aim is, wherever possible, to present a unified view of this teaching, along with the message of Jesus undergirding it; and so I have tried to devise chapter titles that reflect the major issues as they are treated by the whole of the apostolic record. I believe that despite their diversity on numerous other matters, the canonical Scriptures exhibit an almost seamless quality when it comes to articulating our prayer relationship with God. This shines through in the ministry of Jesus and all its subsequent interpretations by the Gospel and epistle writers.

Some of our chapter titles more or less dovetail with the concerns people have always had about prayer, concerns about petition, praise, intercession, healing, and individual versus corporate worship. In other cases, distinctive features of the New Testament, which would not necessarily enter into discussions of Christian prayer, have emerged to shape the titles, especially those having to do with the imminence of God's kingdom and the special roles assigned to prayer in peacemaking, spiritual warfare, and the progress of the new creation. The first three chapters are designed to emphasize the trinitarian character of New Testament prayer; and every chapter, I trust, will provide a clear witness to the centrality of Jesus' name in the devotional lives of the earliest believers.

I have come to believe that the distance between us and the faith of the New Testament is not nearly so great as it is sometimes imagined. Of course, times change and human consciousness evolves—to some degree. But especially when we seek to understand prayer, we shall often discover (and find ourselves compelled to use) a language of the heart that spans the centuries. In fact, it is probably fair to say that modern people are increasingly open to the possibility that ancient sources might guide them toward a fuller communion with God. But then, of course, questions about who God is and what kind of communion God desires become paramount.

I have never put too much stock in tidy definitions, which is probably why I have not been able in this book to fashion two or three sentences that capture everything worth knowing about New Testament prayer. (On the other hand, chapter 12 does set forth a composite picture of our results, and some readers may wish to turn to it now.) Although this study contains many historical observations and textual analyses, its chief purpose is not to excavate the past. Instead, my goal is to present the biblical material in such a way that we can enter it, begin to participate anew in the extraordinary first-century movement that gave rise to it, and then work out our own definitions, as needed.

In Walt Whitman's *Leaves of Grass* one finds a short poem entitled "I Hear America Singing." I think, in the course of producing this study, that I have actually heard the New Testament praying. My hope is that what follows will help us all to discern those praying voices and join them, with high expectation, at the throne of grace.

Jesus, Our Teacher and Priest

IN THE FOUR GOSPELS we find not only Jesus' teaching on prayer but also a number of personal prayers attributed to him. We can meditate on these passages, or we can analyze them for their literary and philosophical merits. We can set them aside for a while, as with any material printed in a book. We can (and do) forget them. But if we have begun to follow Jesus' way of discipleship, even tentatively, we cannot hold his words and the words of his Gospel interpreters at arm's length. Once we have read them, they work away at our inmost selves, calling us through prayer to a deeper companionship with our Lord.

One Gospel writer furnishes a quite literal picture of this process. Matthew records a prayer in which Jesus thanks God for his vocation as revealer of divine truth to "babes," that is, those who are thought by society to be lacking in power and wisdom. But then, quite suddenly and without any transitional statement from the evangelist, Jesus turns to us, the readers, with these breathtaking words of invitation: "Come to me all you who labor and are heavy laden, and I will give you rest. Take my yoke upon you and learn from me; for I am gentle and lowly in heart, and you will find rest for your souls. For my yoke is easy and my burden is light" (11:25–30). In effect, Jesus tells us: "You are the infants in my prayer. If you linger a bit to hear me conversing with God, you must be ready to take the next step of entering into the renewal of discipleship that I offer. As I pray, so I teach, and so I call you to myself."

The call of Jesus in the words of Scripture proves especially forceful when it comes to prayer, for here our Lord not only teaches us by saying and example but also vows to be with us, personally, as we learn. Thus he promises that wherever two or three gather in his name he will be present in the midst of them (Mt. 18:20). Indeed, it is the communal experience of the earliest Christians that Jesus prays for us and even in us through the guidance of the Holy Spirit (Rom. 8:26–27, 34).

Jesus the risen Christ is our priest as well as our teacher. He comes to us through the Gospels; he lives in our minds and our hearts; he intercedes for us at God's right hand so that wherever we are, spiritually or emotionally, we too may approach the throne of grace, offering our petitions and praises with his help. For those who pray (or want to pray) in Jesus' name, the study of his teachings is nothing less than a step into fuller communion with him and his ongoing mission of redemption.

He Too Sought God in Prayer

"And in the morning, a great while before day, he rose and went out to a lonely place, and there he prayed." This is the earliest reference to prayer in Mark's story of Jesus' life (1:35). The incident occurred after Jesus had spent a very taxing evening in the village of Capernaum healing people afflicted with illnesses and evil spirits. According to Mark, this was the first time a great throng had pressed upon him for help. We can almost hear the evangelist telling us: "Yes, my readers, even he, the Son of God, sought refuge in prayer when his work overpowered him. And what about you? Aren't your needs still greater?" Mark then relates that Simon, at whose house Jesus had been staying, searched for him with some friends and finally located him. The little group prevailed on Jesus to return with them to Capernaum, no doubt urging him to keep up the good work for them and their neighbors. But in prayer Jesus had come to another conclusion. "Let us go on to the next towns," he said, "for that is why I came out" (1:38). The impression we get here is that Jesus had found both renewed strength and clarity of vocation. At a crucial point near the beginning of his public ministry he decided, with God's guidance, to become an itinerant messenger of the kingdom. And now he challenged his disciples to join him on the road.

Luke adds significantly to our picture of Jesus' need for conversation with God, especially in moments of great transition. Only the third evangelist tells us that Jesus was praying immediately after his baptism. It was then, apparently, that he saw the Holy Spirit descending in the form of a dove and heard God's sovereign assurance: "Thou art my beloved Son" (3:21–22). Luke also notes that Jesus spent an entire night in prayer before choosing his twelve closest disciples from a larger group of followers (6:12–13) and that he was praying on a high mountain at the moment of his transfiguration (9:28–36). Furthermore, Luke's special source included descriptions of two turning points in Jesus' ministry prior to which he prayed by himself, but not far from his disciples. On the first of these occasions he ended his prayer by approaching his followers to ask them, for the first time, that question which all of us must answer: "Who do you say that I am?" (9:18–20). On the second occasion one of Jesus' disciples, moved by his master's devotion, blurted out (on behalf of us all): "Lord, teach us to pray." And Jesus responded with the words Christians have come to cherish ever since as the Lord's Prayer (11:1–4).

Matthew, Mark, and Luke all tell of Jesus' private struggle with God in the Garden of Gethsemane just before his arrest. John, while noting Jesus' troubled state, emphasizes his prayerful conformation to the divine will (12:27–28). In the longer version of his passion story Luke offers this poignant account of Jesus' last wrestling with his destiny: "And he withdrew from [his disciples] about a stone's throw and knelt down and prayed, 'Father, if thou art willing, remove this cup from me; nevertheless not my will but thine be done.' And there appeared to him an angel from heaven, strengthening him. And being in agony he prayed more earnestly; and his sweat became like great drops of blood falling down upon the ground" (22:41–44).[1] Like any fearful human being, Jesus prayed for release from his approaching death, and part of him believed that God might still grant this request. But at the same time he asked that he might freely embrace the divine will, no matter what. The conflict in Jesus was real and painful; it could not be resolved in an instant. No divine action could simply make Jesus obey. The strengthening angel was a sign of the Father's compassion and respect for Jesus' struggle. Whatever our convictions about the reality of angels, we may learn from this vignette that God honors and helps those who offer up their battles in prayer.

Even on the cross Jesus revealed himself as a teacher of prayer. Matthew and Mark record our Lord's tortured address to the God who seems utterly gone ("My God, my God, why have you forsaken me?" Mt. 27:46; Mk. 15:34, NIV). This cry, both anguished and faithful, serves to remind us of Jesus' true humanity, for he really felt God's absence as he prayed. But he *did* pray, which means that his words can encourage us to reach out for the distant God from the worst of our personal desolations.

True to form, Luke adds to our knowledge of Jesus' praying, even at the hour of his death. The third evangelist knows of a tradition according to which Jesus finally experienced such inner peace in his dying that he could intercede for his executioners ("Father, forgive them, for they know not what they do"; 23:34) and yield up his last breath in total confidence ("Father, into thy hands I commit my spirit"; 23:46). We do not know how all of Luke's special information on Jesus' prayer life found its way into his Gospel, although he does tell us in his prologue that he has gained access to reports from "eyewitnesses and ministers of the word" (1:3). What can be established without doubt is that each of the Gospel writers, working from diverse sources, felt constrained to portray Jesus as an exemplary man of prayer because this was the collective memory of him in the earliest church.

One intriguing aspect of this common tradition is the frequency with which Jesus prayed alone. This is not to say that he neglected common worship. He regularly visited synagogues, and so he must have joined in the corporate prayers of his people. Moreover, he typically taught his disciples to pray as a group (Mt. 5:44; 6:5–15; Mk. 11:22–25; Lk. 11:1–4; 18:1–8) and promised to be with them whenever two or three gathered in his name. Some few days prior to his arrest he pronounced a judgment upon the temple in Jerusalem because, in his view, it was not fulfilling its God-intended purpose as a "house of prayer" (Mk. 11:15–17 and parallels). Nevertheless, the distinctive mark of Jesus' own praying in all four Gospels is his solitary stance before God.

In part, this uniform picture is meant to accent Jesus' unique relationship with his heavenly Father. That is especially true in John's Gospel (1:18; 12:49; 14:16). But Jesus' individuality in God's presence must also be understood as a model for every believer. Thus, he teaches his followers: "When you [singular] pray, go into your room and shut the door and pray to your Father who is in secret; and your Father who sees in secret will reward you" (Mt. 6:6; see also 5:23–24). So there is something about our praying too that requires intensely personal and private conversations with God. These conversations do not suffice for maturity in discipleship; but they are absolutely necessary, and they will not go unrewarded.

Who is this God who sees and rewards in secret? Another strikingly consistent element in the Gospel tradition about Jesus' prayer life is his name for the God of Israel. With one exception—his cry of abandonment from the cross quotes directly from the Hebrew of Ps. 22:1, where *Eloi* means "my God"—Jesus himself always prayed to God as "Father" and almost always called God "Father" or "Heavenly Father" when teaching his disciples.

The word for Father in these passages is the ordinary Greek term *pater*; but again there is one exception, and it tells us a great deal about the personal qualities that Jesus associated with his favorite divine name. In Mark, the earliest of our four Gospels, we are told that when Jesus went off to pray in Gethsemane, he began with the word *Abba* (14:36). *Abba* is Aramaic (the language Jesus grew up speaking in Galilee), and it means not just father-in-general but one's own dearest and closest father. In fact, Abba comes close to our English word "Daddy." If Jesus' special name for God was Abba, and this seems undeniable in the light of its widespread liturgical use even by Greek-speaking Gentile believers (see Gal. 4:6; Rom. 8:15),[2] then every time we encounter the word *pater* on Jesus' lips in reference to prayer, we must mentally translate it back to the more intimate term of address. Other teachers in Judaism at the time of Jesus may have used this prayer name for the Holy One of Israel, but as yet we have no evidence that they told their disciples to envision or invoke God in this way.[3]

So the God to whom Jesus prayed is closer than any earthly parent. But this does not mean that God was always hovering about, implanting the divine will directly into Jesus' mind. Despite Jesus' extraordinary intimacy with his Abba and his knowledge that this Dear One had pronounced him beloved (Mk. 1:11; 9:7), he had to seek God's will repeatedly and enact it creatively when he simply did not know the whole divine plan (Mk. 13:32). Jesus suffered frustration (Mk. 8:11–12) and sorrow (Jn. 11:35–38) and anger (Jn. 2:13–17). Things did not always go his way (Mt. 11:16–19; Lk. 7:31–35). He experienced temptation and betrayal (Mk. 1:13; 14:43–72); and at least once, in Gethsemane, when he *did* know the will of God, he struggled with his Abba to alter it.

A remarkable passage from the Epistle to the Hebrews counters any suspicion that Jesus' prayer life was mostly a privileged relationship with an indulgent parent: "In the days of his flesh Jesus offered up prayers and supplications, with loud cries and tears, to him who was able to save him from death, and he was heard for his godly fear. Although he was a Son, he learned obedience through what he suffered" (5:7–8). These words suggest that Jesus had to strive with God on a number of occasions, not only to hear answers from on high but also to receive the power to live them out. It would be naive to expect that our own conversations with God will be chiefly peaceful and pleasant. If serenity in prayer becomes a matter of routine for us, we can be almost certain that we have more maturing to do.

The Consequences of Prayer

As the four evangelists make clear, Jesus' suffering in prayer bore abundant fruit for his contemporaries in Galilee and Judea. Among the choicest of these fruits was Jesus' power to heal. We should always remember that in the Gospel accounts of his ministry Jesus' wisdom most often attracted people after they had first come to know him as a great physician. Thus the Sermon on the Mount, which contains several of Jesus' best-known instructions on prayer (including the Lord's Prayer itself), is framed in Matthew's Gospel by stories of healing (see 4:23–8:17). Mark in particular links Jesus' power to heal with his praying. This is implied in the early morning prayer we have already examined (1:32–39) and is stated directly in two other passages.

First, in Jesus' healing of a deaf man with a speech impediment, Mark notes that the Lord "put his fingers into [the man's] ears and he spat and touched his tongue; and looking up into heaven, he sighed, and said to him 'Ephphatha,' that is 'Be opened.' And his ears were opened, his tongue was released and he spoke plainly" (7:33–35). Second, when Jesus healed an epileptic boy after his disciples had failed in the attempt, he told them that "this kind [of unclean spirit] cannot be driven out by anything but prayer" (9:29). In other words, Jesus revealed that he himself had to ask God for unusual power in this case. We shall have more to say about our own ministries of healing in chapter 8, and it will come as no surprise to learn that prayer plays a central role (see Jas. 5:13–18).

In the Gospels Jesus is also known as one who pronounced the forgiveness of sins on individuals (Mk. 2:5; Lk. 7:48). Ordinarily this power to absolve resided only in the priests of Israel. From Jesus' behavior we can surmise that although he did not belong to any of the priestly families in his day, he nevertheless felt called on to restore people with assurances of God's forgiveness. We can surmise that this unusual vocation came to him through his prayer relationship with his Abba.

Another facet of Jesus' priestly identity during his ministry on earth can be seen in his many words of blessing. Blessings are a curious mixture of prayer and pronouncement. Sometimes one directs them to God, as in Paul's phrase, "Blessed be the God and Father of our Lord Jesus Christ" (2 Cor. 1:3). In Jesus' ministry, however, blessings occurred most frequently as gifts from God conferred upon and recognized in people. When Peter first confessed Jesus to be the Christ, Matthew records this response from our Lord: "Blessed are you, Simon bar Jona, for flesh and blood has not revealed it to you but my Father who is in heaven" (Mt. 16:17). But such discernments remain a form of prayer, for the one who recognizes a blessing speaks out of an intimate communion with the divine will. Even to call forth a blessing one must be thinking prayerfully. Charles Dickens illustrates this in his *Christmas Carol* when he has Tiny Tim say: "God bless us every one!" These words represent both a petition for God's favor and, through the innocence of a crippled child, the beginning of an answer to that petition.

Jesus announces God's special presence and power to all sorts and conditions of people, above all in his now-famous Beatitudes:

> Blessed are the poor in spirit, for theirs is the kingdom of heaven. . . .
> Blessed are the meek, for they shall inherit the earth [Mt. 5:3, 5].
> Blessed are you poor, for yours is the kingdom of God. Blessed are
> you that hunger now, for you shall be satisfied. Blessed are you
> that weep now, for you shall laugh [Lk. 6:20–21].

Those whom Jesus names here are not necessarily to be distinguished for their piety. They are not blessed because they deserve the blessing but because God is merciful and takes the part of those in need.[4] Scholars tell us that these sayings, which appear to be so simple and even innocuous, would have been heard in the first century not as vague promises that things will get better some day but as actual transferrals of divine grace. In the ancient world blessings from a holy person were *felt*; they conferred immediate and concrete benefits.

According to Matthew, some of those who heard Jesus brought young children to him "that he might lay his hands on them and pray" (19:13). Mark's version of the story tells us that Jesus took the children "in his arms and blessed them, laying his hands upon them" (10:16). Perhaps the children needed healing, or perhaps their guardians had previously experienced the power of Jesus' Beatitudes and wanted these youngsters to share in it as well. In any case, Jesus accepted his caring role and seized the opportunity to tell both the guardians and his disciples, "Truly I say to you, whoever does not receive the kingdom of God like a child shall not enter it" (10:15). So we too must become those "babes" who alone understand God's wisdom (Mt. 11:25). We need to be blessed as little ones by the priest who learns from his Abba in prayer.

Jesus was also the priestly head of household for his followers, and as such he blessed God for the food they ate together. On one numinous occasion (the only miracle recorded by all four Gospel writers) he somehow hosted more than five thousand people with only five loaves and two fish. Mark tells the story this way: "And taking [the food] he looked up to heaven and blessed and broke the loaves and gave them to the disciples to set before the people; and he divided the two fish among them all. And they all ate and were satisfied" (6:41–42). We may wonder about what really happened that day, but given the solid place this tradition holds in the church's memory, we can hardly doubt that Jesus' earliest followers found his blessings over food to be materially transforming.[5]

Less spectacular, but no less mysterious, was Jesus' blessing over the bread and wine at his last supper with the disciples. Here he identified everyday nourishment with his own body and blood, soon to be offered up in God's service (Mk. 14:22–25). In a moving echo of this event, Luke tells us how two of Jesus' disciples met their risen master on the road to Emmaus but could see him only as a stranger until they invited him to dinner that evening. Then, "when he was at table with them, he took the bread and blessed, and broke it, and gave it to them. And their eyes were opened and they recognized him" (Lk. 24:30–31). The disclosure of Jesus' true identity in the breaking of bread found its place early on in the church's celebration of the Eucharist. But it originated earlier still, in the ministry of Jesus himself. He was the teacher and priest who hallowed all meals with his blessing.

Need and Perseverance

As we reflect on the centrality of healing and blessing in Jesus' life and begin to see how this activity grew out of his intimacy with his Abba, his teachings on prayer take on a fuller tonality. Two major notes, which sound forth brightly from these instructions, are his absolute confidence that God will answer every prayer and his passionate concern that our praying must serve the cause of reconciliation with our neighbors. We shall treat these matters in some detail in chapters 5 and 8, respectively. Here we shall do well to look at two other themes that stand out in Jesus' sayings on prayer: neediness and persistence.

Many of us today find it difficult to acknowledge our personal neediness. Unless we are devastated by poverty or illness or tragedy or severe addiction, we mostly subscribe to the secular gospel of self-reliance. To the extent that this is so, Jesus' teaching on prayer catches us up short, for he understood human beings to be exceedingly dependent on their heavenly Abba. This meant, for him, that the form our prayer most often takes is that of petition. We are in need, and so we need to ask—frequently. This is not to deny the high value that Jesus placed on honoring and glorifying God's name (Mt. 5:16; 6:10) as a necessary expression of our love (Mk. 12:30). But overwhelmingly his special guidance on prayer has to do with asking, seeking, and knocking (Mt. 6:31–33; 7:7–11; 19:18–19; Mk. 11:22–24; Lk. 11:9–13; Jn. 16:24–26). The Lord's Prayer itself consists of about 80 percent petitionary material.

And it is surely no accident that in the only three parables on prayer spoken by Jesus, the exemplary figures turn out to be vulnerable people expressing their need. The first of these is a man who awakens his neighbor at midnight, explaining that he must trouble him for bread at this most inconvenient hour because a friend has arrived unexpectedly and he has nothing to set before him (Lk. 11:5–13). The second figure is a widow, whose few rights are threatened by a legal action against her. In desperation she badgers an indifferent judge for help until he finally acts to vindicate her against her adversary (Lk. 18:1–8). Third is a troubled tax collector who approaches the temple in Jerusalem with a simple penitential cry: "God, be merciful to me a sinner." Jesus contrasts this prayer of humble access with another man's thanksgiving for his own virtuous behavior. For Jesus, authenticity in prayer clearly resides with those who offer their shame and need to God (18:9–14).

Closely related to Jesus' emphasis on petition is his strong encouragement to persist in prayer. This forms the real center of his parable about the importuning widow. From her story we may infer that God, who is far more righteous than any human judge, will "vindicate his elect, who cry to him day and night." Indeed, God "will vindicate them speedily" (18:7–8). An incident from Jesus' ministry amplifies this teaching. According to Mark, a Gentile woman from the region of Tyre and Sidon accosted Jesus with the urgent request that her daughter be cleansed of a demon. At first, Jesus refused on the ground that he had been sent for service to Israel, not the nations. His words are anything but subtle: "Let the children [of Israel] first be fed, for it is not right to take the children's bread and throw it to the dogs." Today we can hardly hear these words as anything but an insult, but perhaps they were also meant as a playful incitement. In any event, when the woman matched Jesus' barb with wit and faith ("Yes, Lord; yet even the dogs under the table eat the children's crumbs"), he gave in, perhaps with a hearty laugh, and performed the healing (Mk. 7:24–30). One wonders if the people who first heard this story were able to draw parallels with their experience of God in prayer and whether we ourselves are up to dealing with God as an adversary who must be won over to our point of view.

Ultimately Jesus' own life of prayer furnishes the supreme model of persistence. We have seen that throughout his ministry he prayed frequently, sometimes for many hours and especially in times of crisis. In the terrible long night of his arrest and trial he struggled with God on three separate occasions. It is as though he needed to act out his own admonitions to ask, seek, and knock. In fact, these commands to his disciples always appear in the Greek present tense, which means that they are best translated *"Keep* asking, seeking, and knocking." The message is clear: no matter how hard it is, no matter how fruitless it seems, we must keep up our contact with the heavenly Abba.

But now comes an odd turn. In apparent opposition to his single-minded stress on petition and persistence, Jesus also taught that when we pray we should not "heap up empty phrases as the Gentiles do, for they think they will be heard for their many words. Do not be like them, for your Father knows what you need before you ask him" (Mt. 6:7–8). How are we to deal with this tension in Jesus' precepts? First, in the passage just cited, Jesus seems to be speaking against mechanical rituals, magical formulas of petition that make some kind of automatic claim upon God's ear. Of course we all use some of these stock expressions in our prayers from time to time. We learn them from liturgies or pious people, or even from the Bible. Often we creatures of habit are simply too busy or exhausted to come up with "creative" ways of asking for what we want. Yet we also know those moments of grace in prayer when we just let go of our tired old cries for help or laugh at them with God because they sound so pathetic or pretentious.

But Jesus' saying against verbosity tells us something else: we can let go of piling up words in prayer, because God already knows what we need. This must mean that in petitionary prayers, even long and frequent petitionary prayers, something other than our asking, seeking, and knocking makes up the core reality. Probably we should call that reality communion or touching or, as Tilden Edwards puts it so beautifully, just "living in the Presence."[6] True, there are many legitimate requests to be made and great needs to be expressed. But somehow God's presence frees us from the compulsion to spell them all out in great detail, as if we were teaching our Abba.

I Am with You Always

Here we reenter the mystery of prayer with which we began this chapter. If the bold claims of Jesus' first followers hold true, we needy disciples are never alone when we come before God with our prayers. Jesus is there too, as high priest, supporting us and interceding for us at the throne of grace. This conviction emerges so frequently in early Christian literature that it must reflect a widespread experience among first-century believers.

John devotes an entire chapter in his Gospel to what we now call the "high priestly prayer." It is an ambiguous scene. Jesus seems to be at table with his original followers as the last supper draws to a conclusion. The disciples overhear Jesus' request that his Abba would guard them from all evil and grant them a strange, Godlike unity, "that they may be one even as we [Jesus and the Father] are one, I in them and thou in me, that they may become perfectly one" (17:22–23). But we also learn in the course of this prayer that Jesus is offering his petitions for *us*, even as we read John's Gospel ("I do not pray for these only but also for those who believe in me through their word"; 17:20). And eventually we discover that this Jesus, who has yet to suffer death, no longer resides only on earth but has already entered somehow into God's heavenly presence ("Father, I desire that they also . . . may be with me where I am, to behold my glory which thou hast given me in thy love"; 17:24).

An earlier passage in John's Gospel, which resonates with this one, strongly suggests that in the worship of the evangelist's congregation people had actually seen a vision of Jesus as a gigantic ladder stretching from earth to heaven, with angels ascending and descending upon him (1:51).[7] These celestial figures may well symbolize the requests that believers make in prayer and the answers God grants. Jesus is the priestly mediator for both.

The author of the Letter to the Hebrews reminds us that whatever heavenly visions may reveal to us, our basic trust in Jesus' intercession must rest on his true humanity:

> Since then we have a great high priest who has passed through the heavens, Jesus, the Son of God, let us hold fast our confession. For we have not a high priest who is unable to sympathize with our weaknesses, but one who in every respect has been tempted as we are, yet without sin. Let us then with confidence draw near to the throne of grace, that we may receive mercy and find grace to help in time of need. (5:14–16)

A similar message comes to expression in Romans 8:34, where Paul writes: "Who is to condemn? Is it Christ Jesus, who died, yes, who was raised from the dead, who is at the right hand of God, who indeed intercedes for us?"

What is being said here, with one voice, by John, the author of Hebrews, and Paul carries tremendous weight for our life of prayer. Essentially these early believers are insisting that what we learn about Jesus from the Gospels is no past event. What he did and said in first-century Palestine he does and says now. He is the risen teacher and priest who fulfills his mission also in our time. And he calls us, continually, to join him in his gracious work of healing the world. Prayer is the unique time and place before God where this joining comes most sharply to consciousness.

CHAPTER THREE

How *the Spirit* Leads Us *in Prayer*

PAUL CLOSES THE LETTER known to us as 2 Corinthians with a gemlike blessing: "The grace of the Lord Jesus Christ and the love of God and the communion of the Holy Spirit be with you all" (13:14, NRSV). This apostolic benediction, which has enriched the lives of millions over the centuries in the liturgies of the church, teaches us two important lessons about New Testament prayer. First, it shows that from very early times Christians thought of their prayer experience along trinitarian lines. Paul's triad of Christ, God, and the Holy Spirit did not introduce a new thought to his readers but rather connected with their already existing devotional life. Second, the special mark or work of the Holy Spirit within God's threefold nature was assumed to be that of "communion" (*koinonia* in Greek). Again, Paul did not argue this point as if he were presenting something novel. Instead he simply expressed what he and his congregations had known ever since their conversions, that a divine force called the Holy Spirit repeatedly brought them, with varying degrees of consciousness, into the saving presence of God and the Lord Jesus.

Anglican Bishop John V. Taylor has aptly named the Holy Spirit "the Go-Between God." He notes that while *koinonia* is usually translated "communion" or "fellowship," it really means something closer to "in-between-ness." In fact, it stands for a whole network of relationships that faith allows us to see and feel. Furthermore, "what *causes* [this *koinonia*] is the gift of awareness which opens our eyes to one another, makes us see, as we never saw before, the secret of all evolution, the spark that sets off most revolution, the dangerous

26

lifegiver, the Holy Spirit."[1] It may seem odd to call the Holy Spirit dangerous, but as we shall see, there is much to support Bishop Taylor's use of this adjective. Some readers will know already what he has in mind.

How does the Spirit bind us together with God and Jesus? Paul was convinced that some palpable sense of the Spirit's power comes to believers at baptism (1 Cor. 12:13) and usually even prior to baptism when they first hear the preaching of the gospel and respond with faith (Rom. 15:19; 1 Cor. 2:1–5; Gal. 3:1–5). But the steady laboring of the Spirit at all times is to create in us a deep inclination toward calling upon God as Abba and Jesus as Kyrios.

These thoughts from Paul surely derive not only from his own prayer life but also from that of his readers:

> For you did not receive the spirit of slavery to fall back into fear, but you have received a spirit of adoption. When we cry "Abba! Father!" it is that very Spirit [of God] bearing witness with our spirit that we are children of God [Rom. 8:14–16, NRSV]. And because you are children, God has sent the Spirit of his Son into our hearts, crying "Abba! Father!" [Gal. 4:6, NRSV]. No one can say "Jesus is Lord" [*Kyrios Iesous*] except by the Holy Spirit [1 Cor. 12:3].

These passages show us the very wellspring of New Testament spirituality. We may pray, indeed we are impelled by the Spirit to pray, with the same love word for God that Jesus used. And we are led to address Jesus as the true ruler of our world. Because Jesus' life before God in his ministry is vindicated by the resurrection, and because the God who raised Jesus graciously unites us with him through the Holy Spirit, we are caught up into nothing less than the dynamism of the Trinity itself.

New Testament writers express such mysteries in a variety of ways that are not always strictly compatible with one another from a logical point of view. But taken together they reveal a discrete set of convictions about the threeness and oneness of God that arises from real experience. Thus we are told that the Holy Spirit is truly God's Spirit, sent by the Father to dwell in our hearts. But this same Spirit is also the Spirit of God's Son, the Spirit of Jesus or of Christ (Gal. 4:6; Acts 16:7; Rom. 8:9). This is so because Jesus himself prays for God to send the Spirit (Jn. 14:16); and at Pentecost it is the risen Jesus who receives the Spirit "at the right hand of God" and personally

pours it out on his followers (Acts 2:33). The Spirit is "another Counselor," like Jesus, who will remind his followers of "all that he has
said to them" (Jn. 14:16, 35).

Language like this may tempt us to imagine the Spirit as an
impersonal power, a kind of force field emanating from Jesus and the
Father. If so, our notions are challenged by these thoughts:

> The Spirit searches everything, even the depths of God. For what
> human being knows what is truly human except the human
> spirit that is within? So also no one comprehends the thoughts of
> God except the Spirit of God [1 Cor. 2:10–11, NRSV]. . . . That very
> Spirit intercedes with sighs too deep for words. And God, who
> searches the heart, knows what is the mind of the Spirit, because
> the Spirit intercedes for the saints according to the will of God
> [Rom. 8:26–27, NRSV].

Here we learn that the Spirit retains a kind of personhood of its own,
somehow distinct from God's. God and the Spirit interact; they search
each other out, and always in a way that brings the person and work
of Jesus close to believers (Jn. 14:15–23; 16:14). For the earliest Christians there was never a spirituality separate from the Jesus of the
Gospel tradition. Even when New Testament prayers are not explicitly offered "through Jesus" (Rom. 1:8; 16:27; 2 Cor. 1:20; Col. 3:17;
1 Pet. 4:11) or "in the name of Jesus" (Mt. 18:20; Jn. 15:16; 16:24; Acts
4:30; Eph. 5:20; Jas. 5:14), his presence with believers is assumed.
When Paul asserts that we are all beholding the glory of God as in a
mirror (2 Cor. 3:18), he means "the glory of God in the face of Christ"
which we "see" in our hearts, prayerfully, through the action of the
Holy Spirit (3:18c; 4:6).

Few of us can wrap up these conceptions of God's threefold nature
into a tidy, rational package. Even fewer of us, I suspect, have actually
felt through all the claims that ground them in our own meditation
and contemplation. And yet, to the degree that we know ourselves to
be called by the living Jesus of the New Testament, we do sense a real
communion with him, and we empathize with his first disciples as
we see them struggling toward intelligible expressions of their faith.
Thus we also know something of that life-giving Spirit who leads our
prayers to our Abba.

Today a number of Christians feel they must downplay the lord-
ship of Jesus in their praying, some for reasons of ecumenical dialogue,
others for the purpose of setting limits on the use of hierarchical terms.

Sometimes these believers want to minimize or eliminate that portion of the Christian tradition in which prayers are addressed directly to Jesus as the risen Christ. But such prayers were very dear to the writers of the New Testament, most of whom learned their acts of devotion from Jesus' earliest Jewish disciples. Examples of this are Stephen's prayer to the Lord Jesus, whom he sees in a vision "at the right hand of God" (Acts 7:55–60); Paul's wrestling with the risen Lord over an affliction he calls his "thorn in the flesh" (2 Cor. 12:7–9); and the early Aramaic prayer word *Maranatha*, which means "Our Lord, come!" (1 Cor. 16:22; *Didache* 10:6; see also Rev. 22:20, where John prays, "Amen. Come Lord Jesus!").

One can find much evidence to show that New Testament believers typically addressed Jesus as a divine figure "exalted to heavenly glory and legitimated by God himself as an object of their devotion."[2] It was "in the Spirit" that the earliest Christians formulated their prayers and hymns to the risen Christ (Acts 7:55; Eph. 5:18–20). The creating of communion with God and Christ in prayer was understood by New Testament writers to be the very hallmark of this Spirit. For many contemporary believers, it still is.

Renewer of the Heart

For other Christians today, however, an emphasis on the work of the Holy Spirit in prayer is extremely disturbing. We (I number myself in this company more often than I care to admit) do not regularly feel ourselves to be "led," in our prayers or our lives as a whole, by an inner voice from God. Doubtless a large part of our problem can be traced to the frantic pace of modernity. It simply takes time to pray. We need quiet spaces during the day to discern the movement of the Spirit within us. It humbles me to recall that Martin Luther, who produced the equivalent of a hundred book-length manuscripts (by hand) and fathered six children in his relatively short life (1483–1546), is reported to have spent an average of three hours a day in prayer.[3]

Moreover, nearly all of us need to expose ourselves more frequently than we do to what classical theology calls the means of grace, the hearing and reading of God's scriptural word along with regular participation in the Eucharist. Through these channels Christians without number have received the Spirit's ministrations.

In addition—and this sounds so elementary as to be comical—we largely neglect to pray for the Spirit's guidance *in our prayers*. Yet Jesus spoke a definite word on this matter to his followers: "If you, who are evil,[4] know how to give good gifts to your children, how much more will the heavenly Father give the Holy Spirit to those who ask him!" (Lk. 11:13). Here we may hang back because we fear that our prayers will be answered, that the "dangerous lifegiver" will actually visit us and direct us into words and deeds of mission that we would very much like to avoid.

It is risky to pray for and in the Spirit. Can we do it at all, in the New Testament sense, without losing our everyday "selves"? The answer is both yes and no. Because our God is profoundly "courteous," to borrow a term from Dame Julian of Norwich, a major part of the Holy Spirit's work in our prayers has to do with the renewal of our hearts. A passage that holds immense meaning for me in this connection is a word of encouragement from Paul, written to the Christians at Rome: "Hope does not cause us to be ashamed because the love of God has been poured out in our hearts through the Holy Spirit which has been given to us" (Rom. 5:5, my translation). The context for this passage indicates that (1) "hope" refers to "sharing the glory of God" (5:2), something that has already begun at the level of knowing (2 Cor. 3:18; 4:6); (2) the potential shame consists of exposure in the eyes of others for trusting in an ineffective or unreal God; (3) the love of God means God's love for us; and (4) the event of outpouring is baptism or one's first conscious apprehension of the Spirit's power.[5] The image that simply overwhelms me in this passage is that of the Holy Spirit as life-giving water, rushing through the parched landscape of my body, beginning with the very core of my self. Moreover, as Rom. 8:14–16 clearly implies, Paul expects this irrigation by the Spirit to happen again and again. In a quite somatic way, we may feel the love of God spreading out from our center to assure us, repeatedly, that we really count in the creation and redemption of the world. This onrush of loving refreshment is what the New Testament elsewhere refers to as being filled with the Spirit (see especially Acts 4:31 and Eph. 5:18–20) or what some charismatic Christians today call the "release" of the Spirit (Jn. 7:38 is usually cited).

I am convinced that for the earliest believers a regular, though not constant, part of their prayer life consisted of experiences like this. It is to remind the Romans of something he and they held in common that Paul writes, "All who are led by the Spirit of God are children of

God. For you did not receive a spirit of slavery to fall back again into fear, but you have received a spirit of adoption. When we cry 'Abba! Father!' it is that very Spirit bearing witness with our spirit that we are children of God" (8:14–16, NRSV). Being led by the Spirit means first of all the renewal of our identities as God's daughters and sons, which we sense as we "cry"—the word is charged with emotion—to the most Holy and Intimate One who adopts us in Christ.

I do not think that the Spirit will always lead us today to call on God with an ancient Aramaic word, or even with vernacular terms for the male parent. Many appropriate names for God rise up from the Scriptures, and some of them have yet to be fully acknowledged. Sandra Schneiders urges on us a biblical image for God that may offend some but will surely uplift others. If, as she says, we are born anew "of the Spirit" (Jn. 3:3–6; see also 1:1–12), does this not suggest that we may be led to address our Birthgiver as "Mother"?[6] I think so, though admittedly such a practice will take some getting used to for most of us. Nevertheless, this prayer name fits with several pictures of God in the Old Testament (Deut. 32:18; Isa. 42:14; 49:15; Jer. 31:20)[7] and in no way contradicts the New Testament's trinitarian teaching. Moreover, it coheres with the particular experience of the Spirit's leading described in Rom. 8:14–16, namely an expressed dependence on the personal God who makes us joint heirs with Jesus Christ. In this passage the word *cry* denotes both need and urgency, and we can all remember running to our mothers in just such circumstances. The Spirit (in its feminine mode) may well lead us to throw ourselves into the (feminine) Everlasting Arms.[8]

Strangely, this leap of faith results in a strengthening of the self, the true self or human spirit, alongside whom the Holy Spirit "bears witness." In the Abba prayer we and the Spirit speak together in the presence of God. Our communion is so close that Paul can name the Spirit as the one who cries "Abba" in our hearts (Gal. 4:6), although later, in our passage from Romans, he states that we humans utter the prayer. In any case, the real center of our individual being is not diminished or absorbed into Deity but built up in its integrity. That is, "we" (understood as inner self, human spirit, heart, or mind)[9] are being renewed.

Much of the language about renewal and inner strengthening used by our New Testament authors seems to grow out of prayer experiences like the one alluded to in Rom. 8:15–16. Here are some notable examples:

The one who believes in me, as the scripture has said, "Out of that person's heart shall flow rivers of living water." Now this [Jesus] said about the Spirit which those who believed in him were to receive [Jn. 7:38–39, my translation]. I appeal to you, brothers and sisters . . . to present your bodies as a living sacrifice . . . [and] be transformed by the renewal of your mind [Rom. 12:1–2]. I bow my knees before the Father . . . that according to the riches of his glory he may grant you to be strengthened with might through his Spirit in the inmost self [Eph. 3:14–16]. Put off your old nature . . . and be renewed in the spirit of your minds [Eph. 4:22]. So we do not lose heart. Though our outer nature is wasting away, our inner nature is being renewed every day [2 Cor. 4:16].

The last two passages cited make it clear that for renewal to happen, something false and superficial about us, the old or outer nature, must be stripped away. That is why true prayer must also involve a *loss* of "self," the grasping, domineering self that rules so much of our everyday life. This paradox will reappear as we move on to explore other dimensions of our basic training in prayer under the Spirit's direction.

Guide to All Truth

As we have seen, the Spirit's first and abiding lesson, communicated to us through prayer, is how dearly God loves us. According to John, Jesus says that the Father even seeks out our company so that we may worship in spirit and truth (4:23–24). But what is the content of God's searching love, and what are the contours of the knowing through which we receive it? To these questions the New Testament provides surprisingly definite answers.

In a farewell address to his disciples on the evening of his arrest Jesus promises that "the Holy Spirit, whom the Father will send in my name . . . , will teach you all things and bring to your remembrance all that I have said to you. . . . When the Spirit of truth comes, that One will guide you to all truth . . . [and] will glorify me by taking things that are mine and announcing them to you" (Jn. 14:25; 16:13–15, my translation). Above all, the Spirit transmits knowledge of Jesus, who is the way, the truth, and the life. Originally such knowledge would have included concrete memories of Jesus' words and actions, and perhaps even how he looked as he said and did these things. But the memories would have been enlightened ones, revealing the deeper meanings of the incidents recalled (see Jn. 2:18–22; 12:12–16). I suspect that much of the Jesus tradition from which our four Gospels emerged came into being through the prayerful telling and retelling of things remembered. Likewise, in our prayers today the Spirit often grants us vivid sensations of Jesus' words and deeds that address our immediate needs with awesome precision. The love of God incarnates itself not only in the historical Jesus but also in us, through memories of Jesus revived by the Spirit.

Sometimes the guidance of the Spirit results in an experience more intense than memory. In the normal process of recall, images routinely form in our minds, but on certain occasions a particular image looms before us with such power that we must call it a vision. In the New Testament, visions of the risen Jesus and of other people or objects occur with some frequency. (In addition to the Gospel accounts, see Acts 1:3–11; 7:55–60; 9:3–11; 10:1–20; 18:9; 22:17–21; 27:23–24; 2 Cor. 12:1–9; Rev. 1:10–20). Nearly always they are treated as experiences of worship during which believers respond to the image revealed with prayer language. If we were to poll all the Christians alive today who admit to praying with some regularity, my guess is that the majority would report at least a few visionary events associated with their prayers. And I suspect that even Christians who find such a statement astounding might, with a little effort, recall something close to a vision from their personal moments of worship. Our biggest problem in the West is that we simply do not pay attention to these things.

In this connection spiritual director and teacher Flora Slosson Wuellner gives us an account that developed out of a prayer meeting at her home, which was distinguished by a number of healings and verbal testimonies to God's presence:

> The day after the meeting, one of the group members telephoned me. A woman in her mid 80s, she was a person of great common sense and a delightful sense of humor. . . . "I didn't want to talk about this right away to the whole group," she told me, "but last night, during the silence, before so many of us experienced healing and inner transformation, I *saw* the Lord coming through

the closed door of our room, bringing an intense warm light with him. Then he slowly walked around the circle, pausing before each person there. Some he embraced. He held the hands of others. To yet others he seemed to be giving something. He laid his hands on the heads of a few. Then he stood in the center and his light expanded until it filled the whole room. Then I couldn't see him any more.

Wuellner also relates her response to her friend's story. She writes: "I listened to her, honoring and believing what I heard. Though I do not experience such visions, I had seen the reality of Christ's transforming presence through our changing lives."[10] Whether we actually see visions or not is unimportant. What does matter is that we pray with an openness to "all truth."

Especially prominent in the New Testament are references to the face of Christ (Mt. 17:2; Lk. 9:29; Acts 3:20 and probably 7:55; 2 Cor. 4:6; 1 Pet. 3:12; Rev. 1:14); usually this is sensed devotionally, as a disclosure of God's power and glory. Several New Testament writers also affirm that a major blessing conferred by the Spirit is an ability to "see" how we too will someday take on the luminous appearance of the risen Christ (Jn. 16:12–14; 17:21–22; 2 Cor. 3:18; 4:18–5:5; Eph. 1:17–18; 1 Jn. 3:2). We can hardly doubt that these passages stem from visionary experiences of some kind; and it seems quite plausible that this prayer tradition was chiefly responsible for the development of crucifixes and icons as points of focus for our devotion.

All of this is well worth pondering in the image-dominated consumerism of our North American culture. Perhaps our prayers can become opportunities for the Spirit to grant us an alternative system of images so we can stand at a critical distance from the escalating hype of our viewing screens. Or perhaps the Spirit will help us to detach from the images of this world by leading us into quiet, empty spaces where the love of God can be savored with other senses.[11]

The Spirit guides our prayers toward truth in many ways (e.g., dreams, prophecies, glossolalia, and audible words of counsel). But at this point we need to highlight one aspect of that guidance, for neglecting it here might well result in a distorted picture of everything that precedes and follows. The issue is this: Although the Spirit frees us again and again from ultimate oppression by sin and death and from the terror they instill, it also reminds us that complete restoration remains in the future.

We know that the whole creation has been groaning in labor pains until now; and not only the creation, but we ourselves, who have the first fruits of the Spirit, groan inwardly while we wait for [the final event of] adoption, the redemption of our bodies. . . . Likewise the Spirit helps us in our weakness; for we do not know how to pray as we ought, but that very Spirit intercedes with sighs too deep for words. And God, who searches the heart, knows what is the mind of the Spirit, because the Spirit intercedes for the saints according to the will of God. (Rom. 8:23–27, NRSV; my interpretive comment added in brackets)

Because we are created beings, we still share in the "bondage to decay" (8:21) that is suffered by all parts of God's world until the final day of redemption. One obvious piece of evidence for this is our vulnerable body, subject to aging, illness, and death. Paul sometimes calls our bondage "the flesh," but he does not mean by this term our physicality, which is inherently good.[12]

In prayer, or rather in our failures at prayer, the Spirit lovingly but forcefully exposes our flesh. "For the Spirit opposes the desires of the flesh; for these two are placed in conflict lest you act out 'whatever you want' in the mode of the flesh" (Gal. 5:17, my translation.) Prayer is not simply to be equated with serenity. It can be, and often is, an occasion for Spirit-initiated warfare. The flesh causes weakness, frustration, and rebellion against God. It is not something we escape or transcend in prayer. Instead, through the ministry of the Spirit, the flesh is brought to consciousness and faced and offered up to God with groaning. Every pain we feel in ourselves or on behalf of others, plus every malicious act or thought we generate, comes to light in the Spirit's presence. We are searched and known by the Holy and Immortal One. But because the Spirit lives within us, interceding, God's judgment comes in mercy and does not revoke the promise of our inheritance. Indeed, judgment by God through the Spirit and the renewal of our hearts finally amount to much the same thing. We come to know ourselves as God knows us: beloved children who are destined for glory but also sinners who, left to ourselves, distort or reject God's love. This is an indispensable part of the truth that the Spirit grants us in prayer.

> Eternal Spirit of the living Christ,
> I know not how to ask or what to say;

I only know my need, as deep as life,
and only you can teach me how to pray.

Come, pray in me the prayer I need this day;
help me to see your purpose and your will—
where I have failed, what I have done amiss;
held in forgiving love, let me be still.[13]

Sanctifier of Offerings

Paul's words about our inward groaning (Rom. 8:23) and the Spirit's intercession for us "with sighs too deep for words" (8:27) may point to his own experience and that of his Roman readers with speaking in tongues. My friends who practice this gift of the Spirit today tend to think of it as a prayer language that cuts through our personal blocks to communion with God. This is one reason they commend it so enthusiastically. But those of us who do not pray in tongues are hardly excluded by this passage.[14] In fact, the entire spectrum of Christian devotional literature testifies to God's compassionate outreach toward our poor efforts at prayer, with or without glossolalia. And this outreach is the special task of the sanctifying Spirit.

The New Testament presents us with a rich fund of sacrificial imagery. As in the Old Testament prophets, it applies overwhelmingly to people and their behavior. This is particularly true of Jesus, of whom it is said that he offered himself without blemish to God "through the eternal Spirit" (Heb. 9:14). From several other passages in Hebrews we learn that the writer does not think of Jesus' self-sacrifice as needing any sort of purification. Yet the Spirit was required as "Go-Between God" to make this earthly sacrifice a heavenly one, effective for the redemption of all humanity.

In our case, the work of the Spirit engages us at a much more elementary level. Here are some New Testament texts that help us picture the Spirit's role in our sacrificial life before God:

Do you not know that your body is a temple of the Holy Spirit within you, which you have from God? You are not your own; you were bought with a price. So glorify God in your body [1 Cor. 6:19]. [You are] members of the household of God . . . Christ Jesus himself being the cornerstone . . . in whom you also are built into it for a dwelling place of God in the Spirit [Eph. 2:19–22]. Come to [Christ] . . . and like living stones be yourselves built into a spiritual house, to be a holy priesthood, to offer spiritual sacrifices acceptable to God through Jesus Christ [1 Pet. 2:4–5]. I appeal to you therefore, brothers and sisters, by the mercies of God, to present your bodies as a living sacrifice, holy and acceptable to God, which is your spiritual worship [Rom. 12:1, NRSV]. On some points I [Paul] have written to you very boldly by way of reminder, because of the grace given to me by God to be a minister of Christ Jesus to the Gentiles in the priestly service of the gospel of God, so that the offering of the Gentiles may be acceptable, sanctified by the Holy Spirit [Rom. 15:15–16].

As we come to terms with the powerful images emanating from these passages, we do well to remind ourselves that when our New Testament authors use the adjective "spiritual" (*pneumatikos*), they never mean simply the natural inwardness that characterizes all people but rather our guidance by God's Holy Spirit as it deepens our communion with the crucified and risen Christ.

From the collection of texts cited above, it also follows that we believers are to treat ourselves as temples for God's presence, even in our physical being. The Spirit works to make us worthy of such an honor, but we must cooperate with its sanctifying power by offering up our entire behavior, both inner and outer, to God's purposes. Paul refers to our sacrifice as a yielding of our "members" (all our human faculties and natural capacities, psychic as well as physical) as instruments of righteousness (Rom. 6:13). Clearly this is an act of prayer, which takes place repeatedly, and most likely with some conscious modeling of the ways in which Jesus himself fulfilled God's will.

Our yielding is also part of a larger process of conformation to Christ, which is never completed in our lifetime (2 Cor. 3:18; Phil. 3:10–11). The "spiritual sacrifices" we are to offer as a community of priests (see 1 Pet. 2:5, where no distinction is intended between laypeople and clergy) may be words of praise and thanksgiving or intercession. But they might be right actions as well. In any case, they are to be rendered so that they "declare the wonderful deeds of him who called you out of darkness in to his marvelous light" (2:9). This means that they have a public character that is visible to those who are not Christians. Here we discern the echo of a familiar saying by Jesus: "Let your light so shine before others, that they may see your good works and give glory to your Father who is in heaven" (Mt. 5:16 NRSV). According to James Dunn, the phrase "offering of the Gentiles" in Rom. 15:16 is left purposely ambiguous by Paul. It derives, at least in part, from Isa. 66:20, where the worshipers of God themselves constitute the offering. But the phrase could also mean "the offering made *by* the Gentiles (cf. Rom. 12:1), conjoined to Paul's priestly ministry as evangelist."[15]

Our efforts to interpret these sacrificial images could go on and on, and still their many layers of meaning would not be exhausted. Nevertheless, when we bring them together as a collage, several distinct elements of prayer come into focus. Under the Spirit's leadership early Christians felt themselves to be (a) literal, physical temples for God's habitation; (b) priests offering up sacrifices to God; and (c) personal self-offerings, surrendered repeatedly to God's holy purposes. Moreover, the shape of this prayerful interaction is distinctly trinitarian, because God, Christ, and the Spirit are all felt to be at work simultaneously in the believer. And finally, offerings of prayer are sanctified by the Spirit, for we are constantly pushed and pulled toward Christlike action even as we utter them.

This last point is amplified in Gal. 5:25–6:2, where Paul writes: "If we live by the Spirit, let us also walk by the Spirit. Let us have no self-conceit, no provoking of one another, no envy of one another. Brothers and sisters, if someone is overtaken in any trespass, you who are spiritual should restore that person in a spirit of gentleness. . . . Bear one another's burdens, and so fulfill the law of Christ" (my translation; see also Eph. 2:10). Living by the Spirit refers chiefly to the inner life, to the renewal of our hearts and the growth of our knowledge. Walking by the Spirit means loving behavior that develops from prayerful communion with God and Christ. Both are essential to the life of discipleship. The author of Hebrews underscores this point with his unique double use of the Greek word *thysia* (indicated by italics): "Through [Christ] then let us continually offer up a *sacrifice* of praise to God, that is, the fruit of lips that acknowledge his name. Do not neglect to do good and to share what you have, for such *sacrifices* are pleasing to God" (13:15–16).

On most weekdays during the academic year students, teachers, and visitors gather in the chapel of the General Seminary at 5:30 P.M. to chant the service of evensong. One of the fixed parts of this liturgy is an ancient prayer I have come to cherish. It is called the Collect for

Peace, and it begins this way: "O God, from whom all holy desires, all good counsels, and all just works do proceed . . . " Whether the anonymous framers of this collect were thinking specifically of the Holy Spirit I do not know. But I would be hard pressed to come up with a better portrait of that most subtle and forceful Leader of Prayers.

CHAPTER FOUR

Thy Kingdom Come

"OUR FATHER, WHO ART IN HEAVEN;" "Padre nuestro, que estas en los cielos;" "Vater unser, der du bist im Himmel." Every day, in countless languages, in public and in private, in virtually every country of the world, this prayer ascends to God. It could be argued that no single minute passes when it is not being uttered. Paradoxically, one could also argue that very few of us who pray this prayer have a clear notion of what we are asking for, especially when we reach the second petition: "Let your kingdom come." Yet in many ways this is the central focus of the only prayer Jesus taught us, just as it was the central focus of his entire ministry. Even if we render the word "kingdom" (*malkah* in Hebrew and Aramaic; *basileia* in Greek) with more contemporary terms like "sovereignty" or "reign" or "reigning activity," all legitimate translations, the situation is not much improved. Doesn't God always reign? For what special manifestations of the divine rule are we asking? And in our very asking, do we not declare ourselves ready to take some active part in the appearance of God's reign? Daily bread and the forgiveness of sins seem closer to our ordinary lives than the kingdom of God. But if, as I believe, the kingdom petition really shapes all the others, we shall do well to pay close attention to our Lord's broader teachings on this matter.

Jesus and the Kingdom

In our four canonical Gospels the word *basileia* occurs some 123 times. In the vast majority of cases it refers to God's kingdom, and

Jesus himself is the speaker. Occasionally the Gospel writers use *basileia* to summarize Jesus' ministry, as in Mt. 4:23: "And he went about all Galilee, teaching in their synagogues and preaching the gospel of the kingdom and healing every disease and every infirmity among the people" (see also 9:35 and Lk. 8:1; 9:11). The term *malkah* has a long history among the people of Israel and was probably used in the synagogue prayers of Jesus' day. Yet it does not occur very often in the Jewish literature of the first century known to us; and we have no record of a Jewish teacher from any period who used it, like Jesus, as the chief image for his instruction.

Jesus employed the word "kingdom" most frequently in his parables, which often turned out to be word pictures of what God's reign "is like" (Mk. 4:31–32; Mt. 13:24–50; Lk. 13:18–21.) But *basileia* also surfaces in Jesus' Beatitudes, his explanation of his healings, and his teachings about the future. Thus he predicts that "many will come from east and west and sit at table with Abraham, Isaac, and Jacob in the kingdom of heaven" (Mt. 8:11) and that some of those who hear him "will not taste death before they see that the kingdom of God has come with power" (Mk. 9:1). Moreover, speaking at his last supper with the disciples, he vowed: "I shall not drink again of the fruit of the vine until that day when I drink it new in the kingdom of God" (Mk. 14:25). These and several other pronouncements imply a final establishment of God's rule over the universe in which all evil will be conquered and celebration will be the chief activity.[1]

During his ministry, however, Jesus did not simply look forward to this idyllic time. He boldly announced a situation in which the kingdom of God "has come near," and he sent his followers out with the same message (Mk. 1:15; Lk. 10:8–11). Did he mean that the final reign of God was imminent in time and space? His hearers could have understood both or either of these possibilities within the Judaism of their day. More difficult to comprehend, however, are a few sayings in which an actual presence of God's kingdom in the everyday affairs of humans is presupposed. Thus, in responding to objections by religious leaders that he was exorcising demons in the name of Beelzebub (a variant term for the prince of evil or Satan), Jesus reversed the charges: "If I cast out demons by Beelzebub, by whom do your sons cast them out? Therefore they shall be your judges." And then, heightening the tension, he confronted his critics with an alternative view of his healing: "But if it is by the Spirit of God that I cast out demons, then the kingdom of God has come upon you"

(Mt. 12:27–28). This assertion is put into the form of a hypothesis, but it is really a truth claim. According to Jesus it is not God's constant, providential reign but something more tangible, linked with the power of the Holy Spirit to heal, that has broken in on human life through his ministry. The claim is odd because as far as we know, Jews of the first century did not consider healings to be signs of an inbreaking kingdom, and the Holy Spirit was seldom invoked to describe God's redemptive work in the present.

What kind of kingdom was being announced? In another enigmatic reference to what seems to be a new state of affairs for the world Jesus said: "From the days of John the Baptist until now the kingdom of heaven has suffered violence, and violent people take it by force" (Mt. 11:12). However we construe the full meaning of this aphorism, Jesus must have been saying that the kingdom was present during his ministry in such a way that it could be injured, or even raped.[2] Despite its great potential for world transformation, it remains extremely vulnerable.

Yet it never departs altogether from everyday life, as we see in a passage from Luke's Gospel that has sometimes been taken as the very pinnacle of Jesus' teaching about the kingdom: "Being asked by the Pharisees when the kingdom of God was coming, he answered them, 'The kingdom of God is not coming with signs to be observed; nor will they say, "Lo, here it is!" or "There!" for behold, the kingdom of God is in the midst of you [plural]'" (17:20–21). Modern interpreters are divided as to whether the last preposition should be translated "in the midst of" (RSV) or "within" (NIV), since both are possible grammatically. However, given that Luke also records a version of the story in which Jesus linked the kingdom's advent to his exorcisms (see 11:19–20), and given Jesus' many statements about the outward, cosmic significance of the kingdom, it seems altogether unlikely that his words to the Pharisees are meant to restrict the residence of God's rule to the hearts of human beings. Nor do these words suggest that Jesus considered the "real" meaning of the kingdom to be psychological rather than social-political.[3] The kingdom envisioned by Jesus requires that God's will be done *on earth* in all its dimensions. "In the midst of" is probably the better translation.

On the other hand, Jesus clearly expects people to encounter the present kingdom consciously, as individuals (Mt. 13:44–46), and to "see" it with something other than everyday eyes (Lk. 17:20–21; Jn. 3:3).

This means that we may find it, or be found by it, in the course of our thoughts and prayers. So it follows that the inner life of each human being does play a crucial role in the kingdom's appearance. Otherwise, why does Jesus teach us to pray, "Thy kingdom come"?

We learn more about the mystery of the kingdom by looking at the verbs that typically connect its presence with our everyday life. Sometimes, Jesus says, the kingdom simply comes or comes near to us, which indicates that God is the moving force. The best possible response to such an unexpected advent of the kingdom is to "receive" it like children (Mk. 10:15), to rejoice over it like the person who stumbles on a treasure hidden in a field and then runs off to sell everything he owns to acquire that field (Mt. 13:44). On other occasions Jesus urges us to "seek" the kingdom as if we already had some notion of what we were looking for (Mt. 6:33; Lk. 12:31). Surely one feature of this seeking would be petitionary prayer. Finally, there is a sizable group of passages that describe people entering into the kingdom. Some of these refer to a completed state of blessedness, an enjoyment of the kingdom when it has been fully established (Mk. 9:47; Mt. 5:20; 7:21); but most passages in this category seem to allow for an entrance now, prior to death or the final victory of God's righteousness on earth.

The most endearing and instructive of these texts is the familiar story of Jesus blessing the children. Here is the complete narrative according to Mark:

> And they were bringing children to him, that he might touch them; and the disciples rebuked them. But when Jesus saw it he was indignant and said to them, "Let the children come to me, do not hinder them; for to such belongs the kingdom of God. Truly, I say to you, whoever does not receive the kingdom of God like a child shall not enter it." And he took them in his arms and blessed them, laying his hands upon them. (Mk. 10:13–16; parallels in Mt. 13:13–15; Lk. 18:15–17)

This is not simply a picture of Jesus' compassion toward needy youngsters. It is also an insight into how people of every age must enter the kingdom. Like children (who call God Abba), we are brought to Jesus by others, but we must then decide, when a moment of freedom is given, to approach him for a blessing. In this coming near to him we not only "receive" the kingdom, with his touch, but also enter into it.

Joel Marcus has put forward the quite plausible view that when Jesus spoke of entering the kingdom now, the image he had uppermost in mind was that of a festival procession, like the ancient Israelite enthronement ceremony depicted in Psalms 24 and 68. In this liturgical event God, "invisibly present over the ark," led the people of Israel through the main gates of the temple. That is, the worshipers join God as "he manifests his kingly power by invading the city and the temple."[4] There is evidence that in the first century similar processions were recalled or enacted at the Feast of Tabernacles (Sukkoth).[5] Such events could have made a profound impression upon the young Jesus. The point of Marcus's suggestion is that when we enter into the kingdom, as Jesus understands this, we are drawn by God into participation with some concrete, discernible epiphany of royal power from on high. Moreover, this entry is an act of worship.

Such an interpretation helps to make good sense of Jesus' response to the chief priests and elders who questioned his authority to drive money changers out of the temple: "Truly I say to you, the tax collectors and harlots are preceding you into the kingdom of heaven. For John came to you in the way of righteousness, and you did not believe him, but the tax collectors and the harlots did believe him; and even when you saw it, you did not afterward repent and believe him" (Mt. 21:31–32, my translation). Jesus did not say that his hearers would never get in, but he did insist that they, as religious officials who should naturally *lead* the festive procession, must now follow in the footsteps (by following the example) of people whom they regard as undeserving.

Marcus emphasizes that "entering the kingdom is not an autonomous human action that transfers the disciple into another world, but rather an incorporation . . . into God's powerful invasion of *this* world."[6] True, "autonomy" is not the right word, for we do not create entries into God's kingdom on our own. And yet when the kingdom comes near in divinely given opportunities for blessing and repentance, real decisions must be made.

Is it possible to isolate specific, everyday events that distinguish our entering into the kingdom? I think so. In a previous study of God's reign, I was surprised by the way one large group of metaphors functioned to describe it. I put my conclusion this way:

> The images of God's kingdom that predominate overwhelmingly
> in Jesus' teaching are those associated with the production of food

and drink or homelike refuge for God's creatures. Thus the kingdom is said to be like seed being sown (Mt. 13:3–9, 24–30), as well as seed growing (Mt. 13:8; Mk. 4:26–30) and yielding food (Mt. 13:8; Mk. 4:28–30) or shelter (Mt. 13:32); it is like grain being harvested (Mt. 13:30) or fish caught (Mt. 13:47–48); it resembles a wedding feast (Mt. 22:1–13). It is analogous to the way a vineyard owner negotiates with his hired laborers (Mt. 20:1–16).[7]

If there is one single metaphor for the kingdom that stands out from all the others, it is that of God's abundance, graciously offered to all in festive meals. If we combine this with the notion of a procession, what emerges is a kind of movable feast. Again and again in Jesus' ministry we have the distinct impression that both those who followed him and those who simply met him on the way were being invited to a great supper where fullness of life was the food and drink.[8] To become a guest at this banquet was to enter the kingdom, and one needed only to accept Jesus' invitation. But such a decision amounted to nothing less than repentance from everything (thought, feeling, or act) that hindered one from companionship with him. The cost was high for those who had different conceptions of God's rule. And it still is.

But many people did respond, especially the marginal people of Jesus' day (Mt. 11:16–19; Lk. 15:1–2). Among them there developed powerful works of mutual forgiveness and healing, a generous sharing of possessions, and a practical love for self, neighbor, and enemy. From this loose network of Jesus' itinerant followers and residential supporters living in households, the renewal community called church arose. Neither before nor after the resurrection did Jesus' followers identify *themselves* with the kingdom of God. They did not even claim to be steadily living "in the kingdom." Jesus had taught them that this completed state of righteousness was yet to come (Mt. 8:11; Mk. 14:25), and they understood him correctly. But they also remembered his words about the kingdom's presence among them, hidden for the most part. And they recalled his sayings about entering the kingdom now, if only imperfectly, through joining themselves to manifestations of God's redemptive love. Thus when they prayed, "Thy kingdom come," as Jesus had instructed them, they knew they were asking not only for the final establishment of God's rule on earth but also for everyday signs of it in their midst as sustenance for their life and work.

Praying at the Threshold

When we offer the Lord's Prayer today, we are united with the great expectations of those earliest believers. Like them, we may hope and believe that God will answer our petitions with real disclosures of royal power, and we may trust as we pray that God will also renew our hearts and wills so that we can enter freely into the kingdom coming. In short, we ask what every New Testament prayer asks, to be taken more deeply into the redeeming life of the Holy Trinity.

We address the Lord's Prayer to "Our Father in heaven." The God we worship is both the Abba of intimacy experienced by Jesus and the almighty Ruler of the Universe, whose cosmic reign of peace we desire. Jesus taught this prayer, which must mean that he had prayed the substance of it himself and that he gave it to his disciples as a summary of what he stood for. Moreover, because the risen Christ intercedes for us, we can be sure that he particularly enriches our efforts to pray what he teaches. In a very real sense, the Lord's Prayer is the first ever in Jesus' name, even though we do not explicitly speak his name when we offer it up.

And finally, the prayer Jesus taught us is also an instrument of the Holy Spirit. Paul may have been thinking of the Lord's Prayer when he wrote that our cries to our Abba arise from the Spirit's voice within us (Gal. 4:6; Rom. 8:15–16). Particularly imbued with this holy breath is our petition for the kingdom. Jesus' kingdom-centered ministry was shaped by the Spirit's guidance (Mk. 1:9–13; Lk. 4:14–21; Jn. 3:3–8), and he understood his healings to be Spirit-empowered manifestations of the kingdom. It makes perfect sense that the Go-Between God, who leads all our prayers, is most eager to inspire our requests for the kingdom.

Paul teaches us more about this prayerful cooperation. In referring to the presence of God's reign, he states, "For the kingdom of God is not food and drink but righteousness and peace and joy in the Holy Spirit" (Rom. 14:17). It would be easy to misunderstand this passage. The context indicates that Paul did not mean to separate the inbreaking of God's rule from community meals, but precisely the opposite. The problem in Rome he addressed had to do with disputes about purity in food and drink that were causing ruptures in table fellowship (14:1–15:7). Paul asserts that while the kingdom is not served by arguments over meal arrangements, it does regularly appear (as Jesus had taught) in banquetlike gatherings where one can "taste" God's righteousness, peace, and joy. God brings about this real presence through the power of the Holy Spirit (see also Rom. 5:1–12, where righteousness, joy, and peace are bound up with God's love, "poured into our hearts through the Holy Spirit"). Paul does not mention prayer for the kingdom as such, but if, as we must suspect, some of the divided meals in Rome were Eucharists, they were probably accompanied by such a petition, and maybe even the Lord's Prayer itself.[9]

Here we should pause for a moment in the light of this rich biblical language and reflect on our actual experience with the prayer that Jesus taught us. I suspect that even when we pray "Thy kingdom come" most intentionally, most of us do not think of ourselves as true insiders, residents of God's reign who know pretty well how to enact it on earth. At best, we are petitioners at the doorway of the kingdom, painfully conscious that we have not yet arrived at anything resembling a condition of righteousness, peace, and joy in the Holy Spirit. At most, we receive glimpses and foretastes of the feast.

But that is just the point, for our self-perception is nothing other than an accurate mirroring of the human situation as seen by Jesus and the New Testament writers. Indeed, Paul reminds us that even when we are led by the Spirit, "we do not know how to pray as we ought" (Rom. 8:26). When we pray "Thy kingdom come," we are not relying on our virtue or ingenuity, or even our understanding of what we ask for, but on the power of the Holy Spirit to help us welcome God's loving interventions. Precisely in the chief petition of the Lord's Prayer the Spirit leads us by renewing our hearts, guiding us into truth, and sanctifying what we offer. We do not stand alone at the doorway to the feast but in company with the Go-Between God. And somehow, through God's overflowing mercy, our prayer helps to bring the kingdom in, and us into the kingdom.

Charles Elliott writes that in the petition for God's kingdom "one is adding one's own soul-force to the cosmic struggle of the love of God against the powers of darkness." But we do this in the midst of a soul-refining process:

> Prayer for the Kingdom . . . begins with a psychic, spiritual opening to the poor [defined as "all who suffer from the sin of their fellow men"] which is likely to be dialectically related to an actual process of becoming acquainted with the poor. This inward opening to the poor is held in counterpoint to an inward opening

to God, to his infinite love and his infinite power of transformation. It is thus a simultaneous standing in the presence of the
poor and of God; a baring of the deepest parts of one's being to the
stuff of the Kingdom and the King.[10]

We shall have more to say about how prayer changes the lives of the
poor—and the poverty of our own hearts—through the abundance
brought near in God's reign. Here we need to stress Elliott's insight
that prayer for the kingdom effects a major shift in our stance before
God. Donald Bloesch describes this change quite pointedly: "To pray
for the coming of the kingdom means to pray not for social revolution (though this may come as a result) but for spiritual invasion. It
means to be willing to carry the cross, to suffer afflictions for the
sake of Christ."[11] In our prayer for God's reign both abundance and
the need for sacrifice become startlingly real. At the very least, all of
this suggests that both in public and in private we ought to pray the
Lord's Prayer more meditatively so that we can discern what God is
doing with us in these all-too-familiar words.

The Rainbow Prayer

The prayer that Jesus taught is among the shortest of the daily dis-
ciplines in the world's great religions. But to the eyes of Christian
faith it shimmers like the most precious of diamonds. When we pray
it, allowing ourselves to be centered in the kingdom petition, a prism
effect occurs. With light from the Spirit, other parts of the prayer fan
out into a rainbowlike display of what it means for us to participate
in the coming reign of God. C. S. Lewis wrote that he had gotten into
the habit of mentally "festooning" individual petitions of the Lord's
Prayer as he prayed them. Festooning means "to adorn with colorful
decorations," and Lewis used the term to describe his way of adding
"private overtones" to certain of the petitions.[12] I think we can all do
that. Both the prayer itself and the Spirit within us encourage our
imaginations to paint with the full palette of the kingdom. What can
we learn from the first-century meanings of the prayer that will help
to enrich and discipline this process?

Our Father . . . hallowed be thy name. Jesus taught his prayer to a
group of disciples, which means that even when we pray it as indi-

viduals, we must remember that we offer both our words and our festoonings from within the communion of saints. We join our voices not only with the worldwide church on earth but also with the hosts of heaven. Consequently the Lord's Prayer can never be only a private supplication; it is always, to some degree, a corporate intercession. We do it for one another.

To pray that God's name might be hallowed or sanctified would signify to a first-century Jew that God takes the initiative ("hallowed be" is a divine passive, with God as the primary actor) in manifesting kingly power, especially in gathering a community receptive to the reign of heaven.[13] On the other hand, this community must respond to God's outreach with active obedience, particularly to the first commandment. We sanctify the Name by seeking God's reign above all else (Mt. 6:33), by putting no person or power before the Holy One of Israel. Praying the invocation and first petition helps to bring us into a special place before God for the sake of the kingdom. The author of the Epistle to the Hebrews knew this when he wrote, "Let us then with confidence draw near to the throne of grace that we may receive mercy and find grace to help in time of need" (4:16).

Give us this day our daily bread. Here too there is a double mean-ing. Our constant dependence on God's good favor was strongly etched in Jesus' mind. He knew about God's daily gift of manna to the Israelites in their wilderness wanderings and was probably alluding to it when he said, "Do not be anxious about your life, what you shall eat or what you shall drink. . . . Look at the birds of the air: they neither sow nor reap nor gather into barns, and yet your heavenly Father feeds them" (Mt. 6:25).

But there is also evidence that when Jesus first taught the bread petition, he was thinking particularly about the great feast of the kingdom. The word *daily* in English versions of the Lord's Prayer comes from a very unusual term in Greek (Mt. 6:11; Lk. 11:3). No one knows for sure what *epiousios* means, but linguistically it seems closer to "supersubstantial" than to "daily." According to the church father Jerome, a Christian document from the second century, the Aramaic Gospel of the Nazarenes, understood Jesus' petition to mean "our bread for tomorrow" (*machar*). The Greek *epiousios* of our Gospels would then be an attempt to render this original Aramaic word. Thus Jesus probably had in mind the Great Tomorrow of our feasting in the kingdom (Mt. 8:11).[14] To ask that God's joyful abundance might come

49

to us "this day" (Mt. 6:11) or "every day" (Lk. 11:3) exactly parallels Jesus' other teachings about the kingdom. He proclaimed its arrival, in glimpses and foretastes, within the everyday gatherings of his disciples. And indeed, that is how Luke appears to understand the Lord's Prayer, for in his shorter (more original?) version, the bread petition follows immediately after the phrase "Thy kingdom come," as if to interpret it (11:2–3).

Forgive us our trespasses (or debts) as we forgive. The troublesome question arising from this petition has always been, Does God's forgiveness of our sins depend on our forgiving others? The best answer, I think, is contained in two of Jesus' parables about the kingdom. In Mt. 18:23–35 the servant of a king has run up a huge debt to his master. Because he cannot pay, he pleads for mercy, and the king responds magnanimously by writing off the entire debt. But then the servant meets a fellow servant, someone roughly equal to him in rank, who owes him a smaller sum of money. The man who has received mercy from the king shows no mercy to his colleague, "seizing him by the throat" and demanding full payment on the spot. We all know how this story ends, and the lesson is clear: We are quite capable of canceling out the forgiveness we receive from God by failing to forgive our neighbors.

In the second parable, that of the prodigal son (Luke 15:11–32), an errant man comes home to undeserved forgiveness and a great feast hosted by his father. The prodigal's elder brother is angry because he has served the father steadfastly all his life but has never received such a lavish outpouring of love. The father tries to reassure him ("Son, you are always with me, and all that is mine is yours"; 15:31), but the elder brother refuses to take part in the feasting. We do not know how the story ends. If we look at the sum of Jesus' teaching, I think we must conclude that he wants us to see ourselves as both the prodigal and the elder son. Both of them need to move toward reconciliation: the elder because he does not accept his brother's repentance and probably cannot feel his father's love until he does; the younger because he knows of his brother's hostility and is in a position to deal graciously with it by virtue of the abundance poured out on him.

The petition for forgiveness presupposes God's mercy toward us in the kingdom coming and exhorts us to act generously with our riches, even when we are but dimly aware of them. In some circles of the early church this petition was probably understood as a mandate for canceling financial debts within the community (Lk. 6:34–36; Acts 2:42–46), although we have no evidence that Jesus required such a practice among his first followers.

Lead us not into temptation. Luke's shorter version of the prayer ends with this petition, but the one we pray most frequently (based on Matthew) adds, "Deliver us from evil," or more accurately, "Save us from the evil one." In both versions of the prayer Jesus was thinking of an apocalyptic situation. The inbreaking of God's rule is the world's greatest hope, but it always provokes a violent reaction from Satan (Mt. 11:12; Mk. 1:23–25; 5:1–13). Perhaps Jesus recalled his own baptismal experience of receiving the Spirit, the preeminent sign of the kingdom, and then being led by that very Spirit into a time of testing by Satan (Mt. 3:13–4:1 and parallels). Does he mean by this petition that we may ask to escape such a radical confrontation with evil because he has done it for us? Or does he foresee that all of us will have to withstand demonic powers of deception? In any case, "Lead us not" is a form of semitic irony. Paul expressed the positive hope behind this request when he wrote: "God is faithful and . . . will not let you be tempted beyond your strength, but with the temptation will also provide a way of escape, that you may be able to endure it" (1 Cor. 10:13). The contemporary rendering of Jesus' words on temptation used in many of our churches today ("Save us from the time of trial") is a legitimate attempt to interpret this petition in the light of Paul's thinking.

In neither of its biblical versions does Jesus' prayer end with the phrase "For Thine is the kingdom and the power and the glory . . . " This doxology or short hymn of praise was probably added later by a Christian scribe. And we can understand why someone would feel the need for such an acclamation. The original rainbow prayer of the Lord is mostly composed of brightly tinted petitions, but it ends in the hues of the passion, in somber purples and indigos. Jesus teaches us to pray for the triumphant inbreaking of God's reign and then, with the last petition, reminds us that our very request puts us in mortal danger. Those to and through whom the kingdom appears become special targets of Satan's wrath. Like all prayers in Jesus' name, this one is answered, in part, with the command to take up our cross. We may well experience the deeper levels of the Lord's Prayer if we offer it up more frequently in the current Roman Catholic form, that is, without the doxology.

Does the kingdom really come through our praying? Here is a story to consider as we fashion our answer. It appears in a newsletter from Luther Place Memorial Church, a Christian community in Washington, D.C., that offers many forms of hospitality to people with desperate needs. This story concerns one of the residents at an emergency shelter whose throat had been slashed in an unprovoked attack just outside the church. Judi Goodenough, coordinator of the shelter, recalls what happened after she rushed to the side of the wounded man:

> The next few minutes seemed a lifetime. . . . Much of it is a blur, but some moments stand out. The stranger, a black man I'd never seen before, helping to lay Ronnie down and calm him. The anguish and the anger of the crowd surrounding us. . . . The fear of death. The stranger was calming me and the people around us. He knelt beside me, talking quietly about God's love and giving my heart strength. . . .
>
> He led us all in the Lord's Prayer in the moments while we waited for the ambulance to arrive, and I felt the Lord's presence with us on that bloody sidewalk. Medical help arrived. Ronnie was taken away [and eventually recovered]. . . . The stranger and I walked away and embraced, and as we held each other he whispered, "Just keep praying. Just keep prayer in your heart." He walked around the corner and was gone.[15]

Is this simply a bizarre incident, far removed from the quiet events of our mostly middle-class lives? Or is it a window into *the way things are* frequently, maybe even typically, just beneath the surface of our ordinariness? I think I know how Jesus would answer. I think he would talk to us about recognizing festal processions that do not look exactly festive and about joining them, with our prayers, at a moment's notice.

Whatever
You Ask for
in Prayer

EVERYWHERE THE NEW TESTAMENT WRITERS remind us that God's royal power is close at hand, entering into human life in diverse ways, but always where the need is greatest. Again and again the kingdom comes, and in some mysterious fashion our praying helps to bring it about. God's abundance has drawn near; it is there for us, for the asking. Nowhere does this promise find bolder expression than in a short discourse by Jesus on the efficacy of prayer. "Keep having faith in God," he urged his disciples. "Truly I tell you that all who say to this mountain, 'Be taken up and thrown into the sea' and do not doubt in their hearts but believe that what they speak is going to happen, it will take place for them. Because of this I tell you, with all things that you are praying and asking for, keep on believing that you have received them, and they will come to pass for you" (Mk. 11:22–24, literal translation; see also Mt. 21:21–22).

There is something outrageous about this promise. To be sure, there are escape clauses built in. If such a prayer is to bear fruit, the petitioner must have faith without doubting and even picture the thing requested as already granted. On the other hand, Jesus elsewhere told his disciples that the quantity of faith required for this is no more than a grain of mustard seed (Lk. 17:5), so his accent must surely lie on the wondrous power of prayer and (by implication) our self-depriving failure to make full use of it. James made a similar point when he wrote, "You have not because you ask not" (4:2).

Perhaps we shall never achieve a prayer without doubt, but the words of Jesus and James encourage us to do what we can, to suspend our disbelief, trusting that every sincere petition will gain its reward from the Abba who sees in secret (Mt. 6:6). According to Jesus, not one of us who asks or seeks or knocks (Mt. 7:7–8; Lk. 11:9–10) will find our efforts ignored or unacknowledged by the Most High. How does this happen?

Receiving Our Answer from God

One of the least-heralded truths among people of faith is that when they pray regularly and repeatedly for something to happen, it often does. This is particularly so when we intercede for the physical and spiritual welfare of others. Sharyn Dowd reminds us that in the whole of Mark's Gospel, where Jesus' most radical words on prayer occur, "there are no stories in which people who come to Jesus for help are refused." Indeed, "the miracle stories appear to have the function of encouraging prayer for healing and exorcism."[1] Dowd puts it well when she concludes that in Mk. 11:22–24 "the praying community is exhorted to hold on to its worldview in which everything is possible for God and not to give in to the doubts that challenge that worldview from every side. When what they ask is not given immediately they are to trust that their prayers are answered on the first request and continue to pray."[2] We are not so different from the wavering members of that early Roman church to which Mark wrote. Tremendous power for good is available to us if only we persist in bringing our requests to God.

"Keep having faith in God," Jesus says. The first and *always granted answer* to our petitions is a deepened relationship with our Abba, from whom comes "every good endowment and every perfect gift" (Jas. 1:16). To his disciples Jesus declares, "If you . . . know how to give good gifts to your children, how much more will the heavenly Father give the Holy Spirit to those who ask him!" (Lk. 11:13). More than likely, Jesus does not mean to say that the Spirit comes only when we ask specifically for it, but rather that the Spirit is always granted, whatever else we ask for (see Acts 4:24–31; Rom. 8:26–27). Thus, every time we petition God for some *thing*, God's own Self comes closer or is rekindled within us. Paul Minear may well be right in holding that the chief "reward" God grants us for approaching the throne of grace is a renewed sense of the divine presence, specifically as the Abba who loves everyone compassionately and thus empowers us, as children of God, to love even our enemies and pray for them (Mt. 6:5–6 in the light of 5:43–45).[3] At certain moments our very act of praying becomes its own best answer: "When we cry 'Abba! Father!' it is God's own Spirit bearing witness with our spirit that we are children of God" (Rom. 8:15–16, my translation).

As believers, we do not receive answers to our prayers from some vague, impersonal force but from the living God of Israel, who raised up Jesus and sent the Holy Spirit. Consequently God never bestows generic, mass-produced answers but always those uniquely suited to each one of us, and to our praying communities. Part of what Jesus means by his reference to the Father "who sees in secret" (Mt. 6:6) is that God shapes the answers to our prayers according to the deepest desires of our hearts. Indeed, it can happen that what we pray for, "not doubting in our hearts," is something we are not fully aware of. For God knows our inmost stirrings far better than we do and honors them (Rom. 8:26–27; 1 Cor. 2:9–10)

Jesus expressed a similar conviction in his parable of the importuning widow. There he assured his followers that unlike the indifferent judge, who responds to the widow's persistent cries only with great reluctance, God will speedily "vindicate his elect, who cry to him night and day" (Lk. 18:7–8). The word *vindicate* means to "bring justice," so this parable clearly urges us to pray that social and political wrongs may be set right. But in its Lukan context vindication refers particularly to a release from the shameful deprivation being inflicted by the widow's adversary in public court proceedings.[4] This is the worst injustice: to be demeaned by other people or systems of power or by hostile voices within our own psyches. From such bondage, Jesus promises, God will always and speedily release us. Indeed, it will happen even as we pray, which is why we must continue in conversation with God night and day. Then other results will follow. It should not surprise us to learn that a strong case can be made from history that those who are freed from shame in their hearts turn out to be the most effective social-political reformers.

"Whatever you ask for in prayer . . . " Sometimes the answer we most consciously and earnestly seek comes only gradually, over a long period of time. On the other hand, it may come suddenly after a time of trial when we have almost given up hope. We can understand why Jesus virtually equates faith with persistence. Again, it is not so much the quantity of faith that matters; a grain of mustard seed will do if we exercise it boldly in moments of great need. Mark's story of the father who sought healing for his epileptic son furnishes a poignant commentary on the daring of faith in prayer. The man had brought his son to Jesus' disciples, but they could not heal him. Then Jesus himself came on the scene, questioning the father about the evil spirit that was afflicting his boy: "And Jesus asked . . . 'How long has he had this?' And he said, 'From childhood. And it has often cast him into the fire and into the water, to destroy him; but if you can do anything, have pity on us and help us.' And Jesus said to him, 'If you can! All things are possible to him who believes.' Immediately the father of the child cried out and said, 'I believe; help my unbelief!'" (Mk. 9:21–24). At this very moment Jesus acted to cast out the spirit and cure the boy. Clearly the father's faith was not adequate to make all things possible. He knew that he doubted in his heart; but then he dared to take even this doubt into his petition for healing. And Jesus responded. He added his own faith-filled prayer to the father's doubt and accomplished the healing.[5]

Sometimes when we pray, the first order of business must be that of asking God to heal our unbelief. At such moments one thing we can be absolutely sure of is that Jesus and the Holy Spirit are praying with us for exactly this result.

But we may feel a great deal of tension in such experiences. Donald Bloesch is right to emphasize that petitionary prayer especially often takes the form of a struggle.[6] Quite frequently we must labor to overcome a troublesome inertia that discourages us from praying. And then, once we have begun, we must contend against strong voices within us that question our integrity or God's existence, or both. Anyone who has attempted to pray on a regular basis knows how diabolically creative the forces of unbelief can be. On occasion, we have to struggle against nothing less than God's (apparent) reluctance to grant our most urgent petitions. The Syrophoenician woman had to argue with Jesus in order to gain healing for her daughter (Mk. 7:26–39), and the Psalms are full of protests that God is not living up to the covenant promises made with Israel. In more recent times we can point to Luther's candid description of his combat with God for the healing of his friend Melanchthon: "This time I besought the Almighty with great vigor. I attacked him with his own weapons, quoting from Scripture all the promises I could remember, that prayers should be granted, and said that he must grant my prayer, if I was henceforth to put faith in his promises."[7] These straightforward sentiments may well embarrass us. Or they may strike us as petulant and mercenary. Yet similar passages can be found in the writings of Saints Teresa of Avila and Catherine of Siena, who are acknowledged by Roman Catholics as Doctors of the Church. Perhaps God is not overly concerned about the distinction between childlike and childish when it comes to praying. Perhaps our status as God's daughters and sons allows us to offer up *absolutely everything* to our Abba in prayer.

Persistence, struggle, boldness—Scripture and tradition alike witness to these three as foundational elements in the prayer of faith. Sometimes our petitions will ascend to God with the quiet confidence that they have already been answered. But more often, the opposite holds true. It has been said that those who find it easy to obtain just the answers they want from God should be careful about congratulating themselves on their spiritual maturity. And to this we must add the vexing problem of a clear divine no to the petitions we offer. Such answers come to people who appear to suffer from no deficiency of faith. Perhaps this was true of Paul when he prayed diligently for the healing of his "thorn in the flesh" (probably a physical ailment that curtailed his apostolic work) but was told quite explicitly by the risen Christ, "My grace is sufficient for you, for my power is made perfect in weakness" (2 Cor. 12:9). And of course we have the disturbing example of our Lord himself, the quality of whose faith is beyond question. Not only did Jesus acknowledge that certain requests from his disciples were beyond his power to grant or receive through prayer (Mk. 10:40); he also had to contend with his Abba on the very night of his arrest in a soul-wrenching effort to change the divine will. For both Paul and Jesus, the answer was no. And that will happen to us as well.

How can we reconcile such an answer with Jesus' buoyant confidence that God will move mountains to grant what we ask for in prayer? One possible explanation, hinted at above, is that our conscious desires are not always single-minded. The impediment is not so much a lack of faith as a request made in conflict with ourselves (Jas. 1:7). Part of us, either the true or the false self, does not actually want what we are asking for; and God honors this duplicity by refusing to grant our petition until we can be taught what we truly desire by the Holy Spirit (Rom. 8:26). Yet this is only one approach to an almost impenetrable mystery, and it does not really do justice to Jesus' prayer in Gethsemane. We need to explore other possibilities.

57

Conditional Answers—and the Cross

Jesus' saying on petitionary prayer in Mk. 11:22–24 has been transmitted somewhat differently by other New Testament writers. The chief variations have to do with conditions that may be attached to our praying. Matthew pretty much repeats the Markan view ("If you have faith and never doubt . . . whatever you ask in prayer, you will receive it if you have faith"; 21:21–22). But John's Gospel contains words by Jesus on the efficacy of prayer in which the focus shifts significantly:

> Whatever you ask in my name, I will do it, that the Father may be glorified in the Son; if you ask anything in my name, I will do it. If you love me, you will keep my commandments. And I will pray the Father, and he will give you another Counselor . . . even the Spirit of truth [14:13–16]. If you abide in me, and my words abide in you, ask whatever you will, and it shall be done for you [15:7]. Truly, truly, I say to you, if you ask anything of the Father, he will give it to you in my name [16:23].

And the author of 1 John adds, "We receive from [God] whatever we ask, because we keep his commandments and do what pleases him. . . . And this is the confidence which we have in [the Son of God], that if we ask anything according to his will he hears us. And if we know that he hears us . . . , we know that we have obtained the requests made of him" (3:22; 5:14–15). In these Johannine passages the basic promise still stands. We are to expect magnificent things from our prayer requests, whatever they are. But now we see a new accent on praying to Jesus himself, or in Jesus' name to the Father. Moreover, the effectiveness of our praying is said to depend not on faith alone but on abiding in Jesus, making our requests according to his will, or rendering obedience to him and God. The change in emphasis is not radical, but we are forcefully reminded that conformation to the personhood of Jesus is vital to the granting of our requests. Jesus the teacher and priest once again emerges as the ruling figure in our prayer life. To put this a little differently, we might say that the pronoun in "whatever you ask" now includes Jesus, praying alongside us or within us. As we formulate our petitions, we are no longer strictly autonomous individuals. If we were, we could not really be praying in the New Testament sense of the term.

Still another way of reflecting on this truth is to recall Paul's teaching that the Holy Spirit (who is the Spirit of Christ) helps us and intercedes for us because "we do not know how to pray as we ought" (Rom. 8:26). It is a mark of maturity in believers to hold their own petitions up to the wisdom of the Spirit even as they persist in offering them (see Jas. 1:5). And sometimes the Spirit will tell us in no uncertain terms just to stop, just to "let go and let God." The Spirit knows better than we do how to express our inmost hopes and fears to the Searcher of Hearts.

Petitionary prayer that seems not to be yielding the results we desire may also become an occasion for the Spirit's sanctifying work: "Through both Scripture and prayer the Holy Spirit reveals to us *our own hearts*. This is critical to the life of holiness. Often one struggles with the same faults and weaknesses, commits the same sins again. . . . The way out is to turn to the Lord in prayer and ask for the Holy Spirit to reveal the nature of the difficulty. Perhaps its hidden roots lie buried in our unconscious and must be revealed through the operation of a spiritual gift."[8] One such problem, recognized quite early in the life of the church, is a breakdown in mutual forgiveness. Sharyn Dowd has noticed that Jesus' instructions on petitionary prayer in Mark are followed immediately by his saying: "And whenever you stand praying, forgive, if you have anything against any one; so that your Father who is in heaven may forgive you your trespasses" (11:25; see also Jas. 5:16).[9] In Mt. 5:23 Jesus turns this teaching around: "So if you are offering your gift at the altar [as an act of prayer], and there remember that your brother or sister has something against you, leave your gift there before the altar and go; first be reconciled with that person, and then come and offer your gift" (my translation). We should not overstate the degree to which our failures at forgiveness count against our prayers, as if some mathematical formula were operative. The fact is that God's grace constantly triumphs over our sin. Otherwise, none of our prayers would "get through." Still, it is clear that for Jesus the quality of our relationships with other people can become a major factor in the efficacy of our prayers.[10]

But now we must return to the apparent contradiction between Jesus' bold claims for the power of prayer and his inability to obtain what he asked for in Gethsemane. "Abba, Father," he cried, "all things are possible to thee; remove this cup from me; yet not what I will, but what thou wilt" (Mk. 14:36). We know of course that the cup of the crucifixion was not removed from him. Are we to think then that his request was double-minded, that from the beginning of his prayer he was not quite serious about wanting to escape this awful suffering but had already submitted to God's will for his death? Perhaps, but this view does not fit with his conviction that *all things* are possible for God (see also Mk. 9:23; 10:27), even redemption without a cross. Surely it is better to conclude that Jesus learned something new in Gethsemane about the goodness of God's will, terrible as it was (Heb. 5:7–8). Precisely in his prayer that his Abba might save him, something more was revealed to him about the role he was to play in God's glorious redemption of the world; and he chose it anew. He freely let go of his petition and freely took up his cross.

This confluence of glory, cross, and redemption occurs repeatedly in the pages of the New Testament (see especially Mark 8–10; John 17; Phil. 2:5–11; 2 Corinthians 3–5; 1 Peter 5), but nowhere more emphatically than in the letter to the Romans. Here again are Paul's magisterial words on the Abba experience and the vocation of suffering that follows from it:

> When we cry "Abba! Father!" it is God's own Spirit bearing witness with our spirit that we are children of God, and if children, then heirs, heirs of God and fellow heirs with Christ, provided we suffer with him in order that we may also be glorified with him. I consider that the sufferings of this present time are not worth comparing with the glory that is to be revealed to us. For the creation waits with eager longing for the revealing of the sons and daughters of God; for the creation was subjected to futility, not of its own will but by the will of him who subjected it in hope; because the creation itself will be set free from its bondage to decay and obtain the liberty of the glory of the children of God. We know that the whole creation has been groaning in travail together until now; and not only the creation, but we ourselves, who have first fruits of the Spirit, groan inwardly as we wait for adoption, that is, the redemption of our bodies. . . . Likewise the Spirit helps us in our weakness, for we do not know how to pray as we ought, but that very Spirit intercedes for us with sighs too deep for words. (8:15–26, my translation)

This is a complex passage, but its overall thrust with regard to our prayer life is clear enough. To call God Abba, as Jesus did, to be led by the Spirit in prayer, means to share in the sufferings of Christ for the sake of the world's healing and ultimate glorification.

What this means is that God regularly answers our petitions not only with a yes or a no or a wait but also with a call to take up our cross. This cross might signify our personal suffering, understood anew in the light of God's cosmic plan. But it might also denote a specific ministry to alleviate the suffering of others. To be called to the cross is not a judgment on our sins but an invitation to share more deeply in the divine mystery of redemption. Responding to God's call may cause us simply to drop our original petitions because they have become irrelevant. Or perhaps we shall continue to offer up those requests, but now within our larger vocation as God's co-workers (2 Cor. 5:18–6:1). The energy for our obedience comes from a vision, or at least a glimpse, of God's glory (1 Cor. 2:6–16; 2 Cor. 3:18–5:5). This is granted not so much to take away our suffering as to show us "in a mirror, dimly" how it will all count somehow in the final restoration of God's wonderful world.[11]

Can cancer and AIDS and earthquake and famine really count for good in God's plan? It seems blasphemous to answer in the affirmative. But the Christian gospel dares to speak that answer, while at the same time insisting that our appropriation of it will depend on learning to join our sufferings to the cross of Christ, especially in the school of prayer and compassionate service.

More Than We Ask or Think

Jesus urges us to ask God in faith for whatever we want, expecting that it will be granted to us. This is something close to an axiom in his teachings. But then we are told, by Jesus and others, that there may be factors in us or in God, or in both, that prevent us from getting exactly what we ask for. This teaching certainly meshes with our experience. But does it mean that we must always be ready to accept less than the object of our petitions? There is a strong word to the contrary from our New Testament authors on just this issue. It is most clearly stated in Ephesians, where Paul (or one of his trusted disciples)[12] concluded a discourse on prayer with this stirring doxology: "Now to [God] who by the power at work within us is able to do far more abundantly than all that we ask or think, to him be glory in the church and in Christ Jesus to all generations, for ever and ever. Amen" (3:20–21). The apostolic author in no way plays down the importance of our asking (see 6:18, where he urges us to "pray at all times in the Spirit, with prayer and supplication"); but at the same time he assures us that something much greater than our petitions takes over, even as we begin to pray. The "power at work within us" is the Holy Spirit, renewing, guiding, and sanctifying our petitions. And here again is the now-familiar word "abundance," this time in the exaggerated Greek form *hyperekperissou,* which means something like "infinitely beyond everything imaginable." In other words, the hopes and dreams that we meld into our petitions are taken up into God's plan and magnified into something far better, for us and for the world, than we can possibly comprehend.

This means that sometimes we may not get just what we consciously ask for *because it is not good enough.* Or, to put it another way, the no or wait that we receive from God turns out to be part of an immeasurably larger yes. Thus the same Paul who has previously experienced a negative answer to his prayers for personal healing (2 Cor. 12:9) can tell the Corinthians that "in [Christ] it is always Yes. For all the promises of God find their Yes in him. That is why we utter the Amen through him to the glory of God" (2 Cor. 1:19–20). And to the Romans Paul wrote, "[The God] who did not spare his own Son but gave him up for us all, will he not also graciously bestow upon us all things with him?" (8:32). Not *some* things, not just the things we ask for, but *all things* (see also 1 Cor. 3:21–23). To be in Christ is to live in a new creation (2 Cor. 5:17) where our petitions are being constantly reformed by the Spirit to help us receive fullness of life. With Christ pleasant things and fearsome things alike take on the quality of answers to prayer. It is in prayer that we may expect the Spirit to "sanctify to us our deepest distress."[13]

Of course this does not happen easily, with a steady and predictable unfolding of confidence on our part. Always we stand next to the father of the epileptic boy, crying, "Help my unbelief!" (Mk. 9:24). But this prayer too is answered "far more abundantly than all that we ask or think." There are experiential breakthroughs into the grandeur of God's redemptive love; there are real advents of the kingdom. Paul describes how it feels for the love of God to be "poured out in our hearts through the Holy Spirit" (Rom. 5:5). And the author of Ephesians speaks from deep personal knowledge when he prays on behalf of his readers that "according to the riches of [God's] glory he may grant you to be strengthened with might through his Spirit in the inner self . . . that you, being rooted and grounded in love, may have power to comprehend with all the saints what is the breadth and length and height and depth, and to know the love of Christ which surpasses knowledge, that you may be filled with all the fullness of God" (3:16–19, adapted from the RSV). Still, as the rest of Ephesians makes clear, these unitive experiences seldom come without preparation, without the receptivity generated by the faithful saying of our daily prayers (5:19–20; 6:18).

There are at least three ways in which God can be said to answer our petitions with more than we ask or think. First, on some occasions we may receive exactly what we ask for, *plus* the heartfelt knowledge that we have received it even as we pray (Mk. 11:24). Hanina ben Dosa, a rabbinic healer who lived about the same time as Paul, was reputed to have said, with regard to his petitions, "This is how I am favored. If a prayer is fluent in my mouth, I know that he [the sick man] is favored; if not I know that it [the disease] is fatal."[14] Many Christians can attest to a similar phenomenon in their petitions. C. S. Lewis held to the view that such prayer "occurs only when the one who prays does so as God's fellow-worker, the companion or (dare we say?) the colleague of God who is so united with Him at certain moments that something of the divine foreknowledge enters his mind."[15] Lewis seems to have considered this prayer of faith beyond the reach of ordinary Christians and therefore not to be sought after. On the one hand, we can acknowledge the wisdom of such a humble approach. But Paul thought that every believer should consider him- or herself a co-worker of God (2 Cor. 6:1). And as far as I can tell, Jesus' encouragement to "believe that you have received it, and it will be yours" (Mk. 11:24) was intended for all his disciples. Andrew Murray probably comes closer to the boldness and blessing inherent in this saying when he exclaims: "What a promise! . . . In every possible way we seek to limit it to what we think is safe or probable. We don't allow it to come in just as He gave it to us with its quickening power and energy. If we would allow it, that promise would enlarge our hearts to receive all of what His love and power are really ready to do for us."[16] In the school of prayer this course on miracles is open to all believers.

Second, we may receive superabundant answers to our prayers by paying close attention to those petitions that seem to call forth not a yes or a no from God but a less definite response, on the order of "Wait and keep praying." Frequently messages from God are given along with such petitions, other wishes and goals to instruct us as we persist in our requests. Ethel Barrett tells of a man who prayed from childhood onward that God would remove the serious speech defect that afflicted him. For many years Steve Paxon did not receive a positive answer, but he continued to ask for healing. At the same time, he learned basic communications skills, became a successful businessman, and took part in several public ministries of the church. Finally, in the midst of this active life, his constant prayer was answered, and he ceased stammering. Later on he became well known in evangelical circles as a missionary and, of all things, a popular speaker.

We cannot know the inner dynamics of Steve Paxon's faith. We cannot be sure how his conviction was formed that God wanted him to step boldly into the public arena, speech defect and all. In any event nothing was wasted. As Barrett puts it, "The long years of waiting had tested his mettle, rubbed off the sharp edges of his personality, taught him patience, so that when the answer came he was ready for it."[17] There are many of us who need to learn this patience so that we can be ready for the answers to our prayers. And we do learn it insofar as we allow ourselves to receive the good gifts and challenges that God bestows on us in the course of our petitioning.

The life of the poet and hymn writer Charlotte Elliott (1789–1871) shows us a third way in which God answers our petitions with more than we ask or think. For many years Elliott suffered from a variety of illnesses that left her a semi-invalid. As the daughter and sister of clergymen, she prayed dutifully for a full recovery; and sometimes it appeared that physical healing had indeed been granted. In her forty-second year, however, she experienced a particularly severe relapse. Weighed down by depression, she became convinced that her life was utterly useless. We do not know exactly what she prayed for during this period of despair, but she later reported to her sister that at one particularly low moment she was able to recall a consoling sentence spoken to her years earlier by a family friend. The words were: "Come to Christ just as you are, Charlotte." Immediately she reached for a pencil and wrote this prayer, which was at the same time an answer to prayer, and a blessing to thousands of future believers:

> Just as I am, without one plea,
> but that thy blood was shed for me,

and that thou bidd'st me come to thee,
O Lamb of God, I come, I come.

Just as I am, though tossed about,
with many a conflict, many a doubt;
fightings and fears within, without,
O Lamb of God, I come.[18]

Charlotte Elliott did not know that she had composed a Christian classic. She knew only that something beyond her petitions had been granted.

The word that keeps shining through virtually all of the scriptural teachings on petitionary prayer and their outworking in the lives of believers is *abundance.* It is probably true to say that we never get exactly what we ask for in prayer. Instead we receive the thing desired (or something better), along with a new form of God's presence. And that presence, in turn, draws us more completely into the divine work of redemption. This is beautifully expressed by the eighteenth-century Jewish teacher and founder of the Hasidic movement who was known as the Baal Shem Tov ("Master of the Good Name"). He wrote: "God's abundance fills the world at all times . . . and it always seeks a channel through which it may descend unto [humans]. If our words of prayer . . . are concentrated upon God, they unite with His abundance and form the channel through which it descends upon the world."[19] Jesus was getting at the same thing when he taught us to gather all our petitions into one primal request for God's fullness on earth: "Thy kingdom come!"

The Heartbeat of Praise and Thanksgiving

A TALLY OF PASSAGES in the New Testament that describe or encourage the praising of God and Christ yields a number well over two hundred. When we consider that the New Testament is rather a small book and contains no liturgical manual like the Old Testament Psalter, this number looms quite large. Furthermore, the words used for acts of praise turn out to be extraordinary in their variety. In addition to the verb "praise" itself (*aineo* in Greek), the following expressions occur: bless, thank, worship, glorify, fall on one's face, kneel, honor, magnify, extol, rejoice in, confess, acknowledge, sing hymns and psalms to, offer gifts or sacrifices, boast in, speak in tongues, invoke, present or yield oneself to, be devoted to, live to, declare the mighty works of, and sanctify the Name. Special words of acclamation like Hosannah, Hallelujah, and Amen are found throughout the New Testament, while the Revelation of John in particular abounds with outbursts of praise like "Holy, Holy, Holy," "Worthy art thou," and "We give thanks to thee, Lord God Almighty." Moreover, scholars have identified hymnlike poems and doxologies in the Gospels and several of the epistles (Lk. 1:46–55, 68–79; 2:29–32; Jn. 1:1–18; Rom. 11:33–36; Phil. 2:5–11; Col. 1:15–20; 1 Tim. 3:16). The consensus is that these are not simply literary pieces but were actually used in the worship of the earliest church.

It is also worth noting that New Testament praise can take the form of deeds as well as words and songs. Here are a few examples: "Welcome one another, therefore, as Christ has welcomed you, to the glory of God" (Rom. 15:7). "So, whether you eat or drink, or whatever you do, do all to the glory of God" (1 Cor. 10:31). "Do you not know that your body is a temple of the Holy Spirit? . . . So glorify God in your body" (1 Cor. 6:19–20). "Do not neglect to do good and share what you have, for such sacrifices are pleasing to God" (Heb. 13:16).

How shall we account for this great outpouring of praise language? Perhaps the best answer is to recall that the New Testament grew out of something it calls the gospel, the good news of what God did and does through Jesus. The first believers seem to have spent a great deal of time thanking God for the renewal of their lives in Christ and passing this joy on to others in the form of gospel proclamation (see Acts 2:1–47, which begins and ends with praise) or reflection (Rom. 1:8–17). In fact, the New Testament functions as a kind of guidebook for eucharistic (thankful) living.[1] It reflects the conviction of the earliest believers that whatever their communities said and did was to be offered up in gratitude for the saving guidance of the Holy Spirit, an experience they traced directly to God's raising of Jesus from the dead (Acts 2:32–33). In this vein, the author of Ephesians urges his readers to "be filled with the Spirit, addressing one another with psalms and hymns and spiritual songs, singing and making melody to the Lord with all your heart, always and for everything [or on behalf of all people] giving thanks in the name of our Lord Jesus Christ to God the Father" (5:18–20). If we can talk of something like a heartbeat within the New Testament, a pulsating center that pumps life to the whole body, it is properly named by the words *praise* and *thanksgiving*.

Praise is the comprehensive term for all the words and music and bodily motions we use in ascribing ultimate worth to God, simply because of who God is. Thanksgiving is a type of praise. It means spelling out the details of God's redemptive work in our lives and expressing our gratitude for them. In the Judaism of the first century, especially in what later emerged as rabbinic Judaism, the most prominent word for the praise of God seems to have been "blessing" (*berakah* in Hebrew, *eulogia* in Greek). Usually we think of God blessing us. But it is also quite appropriate to bless God in return, to reflect divine favor back to the Creator by sanctifying the Name (as in "Bless the Lord, O my soul; and all that is within me bless his holy name"; Ps. 103:1).

The New Testament too contains many references to the blessing of God by humans (e.g., Mt. 14:19; 26:26 and parallels; Lk. 1:68; Rom. 1:25; 9:5; 2 Cor. 1:3; 11:31), but it is the language of thanksgiving that predominates in our canonical Gospels and epistles. One reason for this distinctive feature of New Testament praising emerges from the very structure of the word *eucharistia*.[2] It is constructed from the Greek *charis*, meaning "grace," and the prefix *eu*, which means "good" or "well." Thus we might think of *eucharistia* and the verb *eucharisteo* as a "speaking well of grace." Because the New Testament believers felt God's grace so intensely in the forgiveness, healing, and strength of purpose that God had granted them, they delighted in it among themselves and offered up their words and songs about it as *eucharistia*. We can see this wordplay actually happening in 2 Corinthians 8 and 9, where Paul begins by extolling the *charis* God has bestowed on the Macedonian churches and ends with a prophetic description of the Jerusalem church, overflowing with *eucharistia* to God (see esp. 8:1 and 9:12–15). It is no exaggeration to claim that this wondrous spiral of grace descending and thanks ascending forms the very axis of Christian faith.

Pray Constantly, with Thanksgiving

That is why several New Testament writers can exhort us to do something that seems quite impossible for ordinary people immersed in busy lives, that is, pray constantly. If grace truly abounds, then thanksgiving, in the New Testament view of things, becomes a natural inclination toward offering ourselves to God. Here are some passages that will help us explore the rich connections between thanksgiving and continual prayer:

> Rejoice in the Lord always. . . . Have no anxiety about anything, but in everything by supplication with thanksgiving let your requests be made known to God. And the peace of God, which passes all understanding, will keep your hearts and minds in Christ Jesus [Phil. 4:4–7]. Live in [Christ], having been rooted in him, constantly built up and confirmed by faith, abounding in thanksgiving [Col. 2:6–7]. And whatever you do, in word or deed,

do everything in the name of the Lord Jesus, giving thanks to God the Father through him [Col. 3:17]. Rejoice at all times. Pray unceasingly. Give thanks in every situation, for this is God's will in Christ Jesus for you [1 Thess. 5:16–18]. Through [Christ] then let us continually offer up a sacrifice of praise to God [Heb. 13:15]. In your hearts be constant in sanctifying Christ as Lord [1 Pet. 3:15; in some cases my own translations differ slightly from the RSV].

One lesson to be learned from these passages is that thanksgiving is more than a pleasant feeling, spontaneously and effortlessly expressed in word or song. Clearly we should not exclude this kind of exuberance (and most of us have a great deal to learn about it from the black and pentecostal churches). But since thanksgiving is commanded, it must reside more in the realm of obedience and discipline than in the emotions as such. We might say that thanksgiving lives just beneath the ordinary awareness of believers but is always ready, with the Spirit's urging and our cooperation, to rush forth into sound. For maturing Christians, praise and thanksgiving are a kind of foundation for their everyday perception and decision making, like the *cantus firmus* of a chorale prelude or a mighty fugue.

Paul says that we are to rejoice in the Lord always and give thanks in every situation. Furthermore, whatever we *do* is to be accompanied by thanksgiving. If this counsel is anything more than pure exaggeration, an element of choice is involved. We must *decide* to offer up our gratitude. Yet our conscious resolution alone, distracted by the many thoughts and events of the day, will not suffice to accomplish this. Precisely in giving thanks we do not know how to pray as we ought but must rely on the Spirit's aid (Rom. 8:26). Still, the constant offering of gratitude is a goal toward which our life of prayer can move, even as we quite properly focus on our daily responsibilities.

In recent years I have become acquainted with a busy young woman, an attorney and general counsel for a large corporation. And I have learned to respect her faith. Once I asked her if she could describe her prayer life for me. She seemed bemused by the question and at first answered that she didn't pray all that much. But then she corrected herself and said, "Well, maybe I do pray rather often, though not always in words. I guess I would call it adoration." This second-thought response makes a great deal of sense to me.

How can we walk more confidently in the path of thanksgiving? In her article "Marathons, Daily Races, and Thanksgiving," Margaret

Wold maintains that it is "not the big crises that devastate our faith in the reality of God. It's the wearisome progression of days and nights full of cares and pressures."[3] As an antidote to this constant chipping away at our trust, Wold recommends the repeated use of many short prayers. Most of her examples have to do with petitionary prayer, but toward the end of her essay she moves toward what we have called the heartbeat of praise and thanksgiving. I think we can all seek and find many occasions during the course of an average day when we can honestly say, "Thanks be to God" or "Praise the Lord" or whatever seems right to us to verbalize our gratitude. This practice may seem awkward at first, but if we continue with it the number of occasions is likely to grow.

To be sure, concerns for "undivided devotion to the Lord" (1 Cor. 7:35) can degenerate into an obsessive-compulsive behavior in which words of praise become magic charms, necessary to maintain our mental balance. For most of us, however, this is not a real danger; and if it becomes so, a spiritual director or good friend can help us to let go of it. From a New Testament point of view, the more serious pathology consists in not giving thanks at all, or only rarely.

"Give thanks in every situation" (1 Thess. 5:18). This discipline is harder, for even when we feel anxious or depressed or angry we need to trust that the Spirit is working within us to help us acknowledge God's redeeming presence. Even in our afflictions we must listen for the still, small voice that tells us, "Right now is a good time to give thanks, for the grace of Jesus Christ is restoring you, and it will accomplish far more than you ask or think."

Some writers on prayer hold that praise and thanksgiving ought to be offered not only *in* every situation but *for* every situation.[4] As far as I can tell, the only New Testament support for this view occurs in Eph. 5:20, where readers are urged to give thanks "always and for everything." But this phrase could also be translated "on behalf of everyone," so it may refer to an intercessory type of thanksgiving like the one Paul offers in Phil. 1:3–11. Even if we adopt the standard translation, we should probably understand it in the light of 1 Thess. 5:18, so that it comes to mean something like "We give thanks to you, O God, even for this terrible time, but only because we trust that you are in it, working for the good of us all and sanctifying to us our deepest distress." God asks for the sacrifice of praise and thanksgiving, but not for the sacrifice of our honesty.

For God's Sake, and the Kingdom

Jesus tells a Samaritan woman, "The hour is coming, and now is, when the true worshipers will worship the Father in spirit and truth, for such the Father seeks to worship him" (Jn. 4:23). This pronouncement echoes Ps. 27:8, where the writer confesses, "To you, O my heart, [God] has said, 'Seek my face'" (NIV alternative translation). We do not put it too strongly when we say that God longs for our full attention, embodied in words and songs of praise. We praise because God desires us to praise, and so we come to share in the very joy of heaven. The young Scottish university student in the film *Chariots of Fire* must have felt this when he said of God: "It pleasures Him that I run like the wind."

But the praise of God involves something more than our good feelings. In maturing believers it always progresses to adoration. "Gratitude exclaims, very properly, 'How good of God to give me this.' Adoration says, 'What must be the quality of that Being whose far-off and momentary coruscations are like this!' One's mind runs back up the sunbeam to the sun."[5] God wants this reflective admiration, and those who love God will be constrained by love to offer it, to "sing psalms and hymns and spiritual songs with thankfulness in [their] hearts to God" (Col. 3:16). This rule applies even to times of trial. Thus we learn from Acts 16:25 that the imprisoned Paul and Silas, still bleeding from cruel blows at the hands of Roman officials, sing praises to God with midnight hymns. But whatever our circumstances, we can be sure that we are never alone in our praying. Jesus intercedes for us and even leads our praises (Rom. 15:7–11; Heb. 2:12). He stirs up the Holy Spirit within us to fashion our words and melodies. Here too we pray through him, or in his name (Col. 3:17; Eph. 5:20; 1 Thess. 5:18).

There is still another way to appreciate the huge importance of our praise and thanksgiving from God's point of view. The psalmist writes: "Yet thou art holy, enthroned on the praises of Israel" (22:3). Does this passage actually mean that God's holiness and royalty are dependent on the acclaim of human beings? Such a thought seems heretical, for God surely rules the universe apart from anything we do. Nevertheless, there has always been a stream of thought in ancient Israel, in Judaism, and in the early church which holds that for God to be God in a fully satisfying way, all creation must acknowledge the divine goodness and sovereignty. This is part of what it means to glorify God. Glory is a quality of God's being, but it is also something we Christians perceive in God through Christ (2 Cor. 3:18; 4:6) and then return to our Abba with praise.

Often we find passages in the Old and New Testaments that may be called doxologies (from the Greek word *doxa*), that is, ascriptions of glory to God from humans. One of the chief songs in our eucharistic liturgy has been named the Gloria. It derives from a number of biblical texts but especially from Luke's account of the angels' song at Jesus' birth ("Glory to God in the highest," Lk. 2:14). A similar picture comes from Paul's letter to the Philippians, where the apostle quotes from an early Christian hymn that ends with these words: "Therefore God has highly exalted him [Jesus] and bestowed on him the name which is above every name, that at the name of Jesus every knee should bow, in heaven and on earth and under the earth, and every tongue confess that Jesus Christ is Lord, to the glory of God the Father" (2:9–11). Paul and his readers were quite aware that this cosmic acknowledgment had not yet happened. But they offered up their hymn to anticipate the fullness of that which was already dawning.

In fact some New Testament believers appear to hold the view that they can hasten the divine triumph by magnifying God's glory in their praise, especially when they render it in the name of Jesus. Thus Paul writes that we are to "utter the Amen through [Christ], to the glory of God" (2 Cor. 1:20), and this probably refers to a real liturgical practice. When Christians say "Amen!" they visualize the life and work of Jesus[6]—he himself is honored as "the Amen" in Rev. 3:14—and offer them up to God in a way that somehow enhances the divine stature. Paul understands his whole ministry to be moving toward one goal: "that as grace extends to more and more people it may increase thanksgiving [for our share in Christ's resurrection] to the glory of God" (2 Cor. 4:15; see also 1:11 and 9:11–15). For the New Testament writers, praise is no side issue. Those graced by the Holy Spirit to confess Jesus as Lord must be especially zealous in speaking and singing their thanks to God *for the very sake of God's Personhood.*[7]

But this Personhood can never be separated from the destiny of creation. God's consummate will is to share divine glory with everything that exists. In both first-century Judaism and the church, the redeeming of the world meant first of all its complete participation, as at the beginning, in the glory of God (Rom. 5:2; 8:17–30). During the period when our New Testament came into being, many Jews and Gentiles tended to think of this heavenly *doxa* as a kind of luminous substance, far more real than what we now call the material order. The latter changes or decays; the former does not. In the interim time before Christ's return to judge the nations, God grants visions of this final glory, allows us to touch and sense it in our hearts (2 Cor. 3:18; 4:6; 4:17–5:5). But at the same time we are enjoined to return it, with thanksgiving, so that the plan of God can move forward (2 Cor. 4:15). We have learned that when we pray, "Thy kingdom come," our petition has an actual effect on God's working out of the world's salvation. In the same way our praise and thanksgiving contribute tangibly to the healing of the cosmos.

Daniel Hardy and David Ford conclude that "praise . . . is best seen as part of an ecology of blessing." What they mean is that while the whole world renders homage to God in and of itself, even in its present "bondage to decay" (Rom. 8:21), we humans are uniquely gifted as the poets and priests of creation. We are called to articulate the worship it offers, along with our own, in fresh new ways, thus becoming what George Herbert called "secretaries of [God's] praise."[8] The Judeo-Christian tradition as a whole teaches that every human being is a special herald of God's presence in his or her own corner of the universe. Yet some, like Herbert, stand out as exemplars of praise, schoolmasters of worship for the rest of humanity.[9] Johann Sebastian Bach was also one of these. His biographers tell us that he always inscribed the words "Soli Deo Gloria" (to God alone be the glory) on his working manuscripts, even on the scores we now call secular. Those who know Bach's life and music well agree that for him these words were no pious convention but a real prayer that the notes he inked would rise as a melody to the Lord.[10]

In the New Testament praise of God on behalf of the world is always mediated through Jesus, who is confessed as "the image of the invisible God, the firstborn of all creation; for in him all things are created, in heaven and on earth, visible and invisible, whether thrones or dominions or principalities or authorities. . . . He is before all things, and in him all things hold together. . . . For in him all the fullness of God was pleased to dwell, and through him to reconcile to himself all things, whether on earth or in heaven, making peace by the blood of his cross" (Col. 1:15–20). In this hymn the early church sang forth its praise, not only for the wonders of creation (which it had come to understand christologically) but also for the costly reconciliation of all things to God won by Jesus' death. These two are now inseparable. By honoring the creative-redemptive work of Christ with their voices, believers are drawn into it more deeply.[11] It is hardly accidental that when the Risen One pours out "the promise of the Father" on his disciples at Pentecost, their very first Spirit-filled act is to proclaim God's works in ecstatic tongues of praise (Acts 2:1–11). And this praise is met with a receptiveness on the part of many onlookers that prompts the church's first missionary effort (2:12–42).

For Our Own Sake

We have referred to praise and thanksgiving as a heartbeat because they throb at the very center of our Christian faith. But we have also said that praise and thanksgiving are a discipline. A decision is required before words and songs can burst forth. Sometimes this is a natural decision, made without effort because of our overflowing gratitude for a special work of God in our lives. At other times we must struggle to praise God because we feel dry or deprived. Yet even then, when we are able to overcome our resistance, we can begin to taste joy. For a significant number of Christians this happens when they give themselves over to the Spirit's urging and pray to God in tongues. More than any other form of devotion, praise and thanksgiving engage our whole physical being. Music, poetry, dance, and just plain loud noise are the basic stuff of praise. God commands such offerings not only because they are needed for the divine plan but also because God knows that we will take pleasure in their benefits. "The duty exists for the delight."[12]

The New Testament has a good deal to tell us about the felt benefits of praise and thanksgiving. Together they may be thought of as a training course in righteousness. Through praise we learn virtue, and we discover, in ever-richer patterns, God's regenerating love for us. Thus the author of Acts tells us that when Paul, en route to Rome as a prisoner, encountered some bold Christian friends who had journeyed out from the capital to welcome him, "he thanked God and took courage" (28:16). The very sight of these believers was probably enough to lift Paul's spirits, but by voicing his gratitude to God he also found new bravery. Earlier, in writing to the Romans, he himself had cited the example of Abraham, "who grew strong in his faith as he gave glory to God" (4:20). And some verses later the apostle urged his readers to present their bodies to God as a living sacrifice, to "be transformed by the renewal of your mind, that you may prove [i.e., test out in experience] what is the will of God, what is good and acceptable and perfect" (12:1–2). According to the logic of this text, thankful self-offering results in a heightened ability to discern and embrace God's purposes.

Other acts of worship are equally productive. Paul writes to the Corinthians, "The cup of blessing which we bless, is it not a participation [*koinonia*] in the blood of Christ?" (1 Cor. 10:16). Here the reference is to Holy Communion, and the major point is made in the little clause "which we bless." Obviously the saving force of Christ's blood is not dependent on human words. But Paul is telling his readers that when they speak actual blessings over the cup at the Supper of the Lord, they are joined together with Christ's offering at a new level. More than ever, they belong exclusively to the Lord (see 10:18–22).

Praise is also the trainer of our affections. When Paul urges the Philippians to "have no anxiety about anything, but in everything by prayer and supplication with thanksgiving let your requests be made known to God" (4:6), he is not making an impossible demand, on the order of "Stop being bothered." Rather, he exhorts his readers from a personal knowledge of what thanksgiving produces: "And the peace of God, which passes understanding, will keep your hearts and minds in Christ Jesus" (4:7). Prayer with thanksgiving gives us access to a profound well-being so that we no longer have to suffer domination by our troubled psyches. How different this is from the shallow comfort served up in our mass media: "Don't worry, be happy." From a quite practical point of view, the only medicine for inner turmoil is true worship. Thus the author of 1 Peter, addressing Christians who are about to undergo persecution, offers this counsel: "Have no fear of them, nor be troubled, but in your hearts reverence Christ as Lord. Always be prepared to make a defense [*apologia*] to anyone who calls you to account for the hope that is in you, yet do it with gentleness and reverence" (3:14–16). We need to be clear about the cause-effect sequence presupposed in this passage. As in Philippians, worship is understood to offer release from the oppressive power of negative emotions. The ability to "have no fear," to "be prepared," and to make our faith statements "with gentleness and reverence" stems from a constant devotion to Christ in our heart.

It is easy to criticize the impression given by Merlin Carothers that praising God relieves practically every affliction known to humanity.[13] Yet the New Testament passages we have just cited show that there is something authentic in his position. Carothers rightly states that "praising God is something more than a change in our . . . attitude. There is no power in our words of praise as such. There is no power in our attitude. . . . All the power in the situation comes from God."[14] Precisely this is what we need to rediscover. Not our words or the quality of our inner devotion, but God, acting through our praise, accomplishes far more than we can ask or imagine.

Praise is paradoxical. We learn it, but we also learn from it, especially during corporate worship. In Eph. 5:19 we are urged to address one another in psalms and hymns and spiritual songs. Our melodies are directed chiefly to God (v. 19b), but at the same time they teach and build up our brother and sister worshipers. This is how we are to understand Paul's advice to the Corinthians regarding the public use of glossolalia: "If I pray in a tongue, my spirit prays, but my mind is unfruitful. What am I to do? . . . I will sing with the spirit and I will sing with the mind also. Otherwise if you bless [God] with the spirit, how can anyone in the position of an outsider[15] say the 'Amen' to your thanksgiving when he or she does not know what you are saying? For you may give thanks well enough, but the other person is not built up" (1 Cor. 14:14–16, my translation). Paul endorses praising God in tongues (14:4, 13), but he also wishes to maximize the power of praise for nurture. Joining in the "Amen" means that we affirm what the giver of thanks has just said or sung. We connect with it and are ourselves lifted up to God. The black churches in America know this truth. The frequent outbursts from worshipers of "Praise the Lord" or "Amen" or "Thank you, Jesus" are personal (and quite biblical) ways of appropriating the grace of God that has been manifested in sermons and prayers.

We have already mentioned the enhanced discernment of God's will that derives from our self-offerings to our Abba (Rom. 12:1–2). We shall have more to say about this in a subsequent chapter on prayer in the church's worship. Here it is important to highlight another benefit of such praise, namely, a deeper plunge into the vast oceans of God's mercy. Before Paul asks his readers to present their bodies as living sacrifices, he takes them through a complex meditation on God's mysterious dealings with the church and Israel (Rom. 9:1–11:32). Then, at the end of this, he leads them—for we must assume that the apostle's letter was read out loud during a period of corporate worship—in a magnificent doxology: "O the depth of the riches and wisdom and knowledge of God! How unsearchable are his judgments and how inscrutable his ways! For who has known the mind of the Lord, or who has been his counselor? . . . For from him and through him and to him are all things. To him be glory for ever. Amen" (11:33–36). Only at the conclusion of this hymn does Paul issue his appeal for the offering of our bodies (12:1).

What happens in this section of Romans is an exponential progression of praise. We begin to see something of God's mercy and stand in awe of it (11:25–32). We offer up a doxology in thanksgiving (11:33–36). Then we are drawn by these words into a more complete self-offering (12:1–2) during which our minds are directed toward finding our own personal place in God's gracious work (12:3–8). And this results in new behavior, formed by praise: "Let love be genuine; . . . outdo one another in showing honor. . . . Be aglow with the Spirit. . . . Rejoice in your hope. . . . Bless those who persecute you. . . . Overcome evil with good" (12:9–21). The entire process becomes an interplay between the wideness of God's mercy and our response to it. Hardy and Ford put it beautifully when they write: "[Praise] is the life of faith, basic Christian existence, and it springs from our recognition, respect, and honoring being focused through Jesus Christ and being allowed to transform our network of relationships. Our whole life is continually thrown into the air in praise in the trust that it will be caught, blessed and returned renewed."[16] To live out that metaphor of throwing our lives into the air, even for a day, would be to experience richness beyond measure.

The language of cognition helps us express this reciprocity in yet another way. By choosing to entitle their book *Praising and Knowing God*, Hardy and Ford have caught hold of something absolutely essential to the Judeo-Christian understanding of praise. What we come to discover, finally, through our glorification of God in word and song, is the astonishing force of God's intimacy. It was the habit of praise that inspired the psalmist to exclaim: "O Lord, thou has searched me and known me. . . . Even before a word is on my tongue, lo, O Lord, thou knowest it altogether. . . . Such knowledge is too wonderful for me; it is high. I cannot attain it" (Ps. 139:1–6). We might well recoil in terror from this discovery, for it means that God intrudes upon our every thought and feeling, indeed, anticipates them before they occur. But what if this God is also our Abba, who searches us in love for the sake of our healing and the growth of our freedom? It was just such a revelation, given through Christ and the Spirit, that enabled Paul to conclude: "if one loves God, then it follows that this person is known by God. . . . For we see at present through a looking glass, indirectly, but then [at the end of time] we shall see face to face. Now I know in part; but then I shall know, even as I am fully known" (1 Cor. 8:3; 13:12, my translation). It goes without saying that we can apprehend the searching love of God only imperfectly, as the "eyes of our heart" are opened to Christ (Eph. 1:8; 2 Cor. 4:6). But we can grasp enough of it to praise and thank God. And in these acts of glorification we get some real sense of knowing as we are known. Praise is the doorway to blessed assurance. "When we cry, 'Abba! Father!' it is God's own Spirit bearing witness with our spirit that we are children of God" (Rom. 8:15–16, my translation).

There is one more facet of New Testament praise and thanksgiving that we dare not ignore, though it may seem extremely odd and even shocking to some readers. I have in mind the early church's practice of joining its voice with the hosts of heaven to laud and honor God. We catch a glimpse of this in an extraordinary passage from Hebrews. Addressing his readers as a congregation and referring (I believe) to their regular corporate worship, the author states: "You have come to Mount Zion and to the city of the living God, the heavenly Jerusalem, and to innumerable angels in festal gathering, and to the assembly of the firstborn who are enrolled in heaven, and to a judge who is God of all, and to the spirits of just people made perfect, and to Jesus, the mediator of a new covenant" (12:22–24). Does this passage really describe the church's praise now? Almost certainly it does. The Greek word translated "you have come" (*proserchomai*) occurs earlier in Hebrews in a section on petitionary prayer. Having reminded his readers that they are aided by none other than Jesus himself in his role as great high priest, the author concludes: "Let us then with confidence draw near [*proserchomai*] to the throne of grace, that we may receive mercy and find grace to help in time of need" (4:16). Thus prayer means approaching a special "place" within God's presence. Mount Zion stands for that part of the heavenly sanctuary where music and praise are offered to God,[17] hence the "innumerable angels in festal gathering."

But the writer to the Hebrews is not alone in highlighting this conjunction of heavenly and earthly worship. The synoptic evangelists portray it in the words of the crowd that welcomes Jesus to

Jerusalem: "Hosanna in the highest," they cry (Mt. 21:9; Mk. 11:10). "Peace in heaven and glory in the highest" (Lk. 19:38). According to John, Jesus is both on earth and in heaven when he intones his high-priestly prayer (chapter 17.) Paul presupposes a joining in heavenly worship when he orders women in the Corinthian church to pray and prophesy with their heads covered "because of the angels" (1 Cor. 11:10). And the author of Ephesians refers to the church's mission with Christ "in the heavenly places" (2:6; 3:10), while noting that congregational life on earth is sustained by praise and thanksgiving in Christ's name (5:19–20). Finally, large portions of John's Revelation depict scenes from the heavenly temple, where angels, beasts, elders, and a huge multitude of believers (some of whom appear to be still alive on earth) engage in singing hymns of praise to God or Christ (4:8–11; 5:8–10; 6:9–10; 11:16–18; 15:3–4; 16:5–7; 19:1–8). John reports that he was already "in the Spirit on the Lord's day" (1:10) when visions of the exalted Christ first came to him. And toward the end of his mystical journey he is commanded by an angel to join in the heavenly worship (19:10; 22:8).

For centuries the Greek and Russian Orthodox churches, along with several other branches of Eastern Christianity, have simply assumed, on the basis of these passages and a rich fund of worship experience, that they are offering up their praise and thanksgiving together with the heavenly hosts. Indeed, they usually refer to their order of worship as Divine Liturgy. A remnant of this tradition appears in some Western services of the Lord's Supper when the celebrant proclaims, "Therefore we praise you, joining our voices with Angels and Archangels and with all the company of heaven, who forever sing this hymn to proclaim the glory of your Name." To which the people respond: "Holy, holy, holy Lord, God of power and might, heaven and earth are full of your glory. Hosanna in the highest."[18]

What if it is all true? What if our praising matters so much to God that it draws us up into the worship of the heavenly court? If this *is* the case, some of us will have to rethink our position on angels, or on heaven itself for that matter. And here again we may also recall Jesus' imaging of God's kingdom as a festal procession that can be joined as we pray the Lord's Prayer. Praise and thanksgiving would be yet another entry into that movable feast where heaven and earth are found to intersect.

These are challenging thoughts. They call us to nothing less than a re-visioning of how our universe works. And so does this story, based on the personal testimony of an elderly woman who had suffered for years from severe arthritis. She had just dropped a tray of kitchen utensils because her twisted fingers could no longer respond to her mental commands. In frustration she began to cry. But then she remembered, dimly, that she had made a promise to praise God, no matter what. With all the will she could muster she spoke a few words of thanks for God's working in her life, and even for this moment, which seemed so pathetic. "In a flash she became aware of other beings in the kitchen. . . . She had been alone—yet now she sensed others present. Startled, she realized she was surrounded by angels. [They] were laughing and rejoicing, and she knew their joy was for her."[19] After a short time her acute sense of the festal gathering faded, and the heavenly host moved on, as it were. Readers will have to judge for themselves whether this story resonates with anything in their own experience. My own consciousness of communion with angels has been minimal, but I know stable, intelligent people who would nod and smile knowingly at this woman's testimony.

It may be that petition and intercession will always come easier to us than praise and thanksgiving. But the New Testament does not allow us to rest content with this state of affairs. If anything, the opposite is true. The profusion of praise language in our apostolic writings stands as a constant remainder that words and hymns to the glory of God must occupy a certain primacy in our life of prayer. Without them something quintessential is lost from our faith. With them the gospel begins to be embodied. Praise and thanksgiving in Jesus' name require an extra measure of boldness on our part in this era of great confusion about Christian worship. But the command is clear, the promise is sure, and the blessings are many. I suspect that for many of us today the Holy Spirit's word on this matter will turn out to be a slightly impatient "Just do it!"

Our
High Calling
to Pray
for Neighbors

IF PRAISE AND THANKSGIVING are the heartbeat of Christ's Body, the pulsating center of its common life, then we may think of intercessory prayer as oxygen-rich blood, rushing through the aorta and into each tiny artery. As we pray for one another, the Spirit breathes through our petitions and fills the whole church with new life.

But not only the church benefits from intercession. When the members of Christ's Body hold up their neighbors to God's loving gaze, every corner of the world receives a blessing. More than any other form of prayer, I believe, intercession leaps over the fences we humans tend to build between sacred and secular, insiders and outsiders. Yet paradoxically, it cannot do this, in the New Testament view of things, without being grounded in Christ's ministry of intercession. What can we learn about this mighty work that will help us fulfill our own high calling to pray for neighbors?

Sharing Jesus' Priesthood

Intercession comes from the Latin word *intercessio*, which denotes an act of mediation, or going between. We have already looked at the Spirit's activity in our prayers as "Go-Between God" (see chapter 3), so it comes as no surprise when Paul reminds his Roman readers that the Spirit intercedes for them "with sighs too deep for words . . . according to the will of God" (Rom. 8:26–27). The Spirit dwells inside us but also discourses constantly with the Ruler of the Universe on our behalf.

In this same chapter of Romans Paul also names Jesus as our intercessor at God's "right hand" (8:34). Does Paul think that there are two distinct intercessors and one (somewhat detached) recipient of intercessions? Such an image proves inadequate because we know that God's very Self initiates the process of intercession by sending us the Holy Spirit (Lk. 11:13; Acts 1:4; 2:33) or rekindling it in our hearts (Acts 4:29–32). Thus our Abba is no passive monarch but an active Giver. Moreover, we know that the Holy Spirit is experienced not as an impersonal force but as God present to us with the face of Jesus (2 Cor. 3:18; 4:6). "God has sent the Spirit of his Son into our hearts, crying 'Abba! Father!'" (Gal. 4:6). This means that the whole Trinity works simultaneously in our prayers. "Abba" is a cry we utter, but we must also say that Jesus speaks the word through us at God's bidding. Exactly how this labor of love divides itself among the Persons of the Trinity we are not given to know. But one thing is clear. Of the Three, only Jesus is named and visualized by the New Testament authors as our great High Priest. Almost certainly this title results from a grateful celebration of Jesus' real humanity: "For we have not a high priest who is unable to sympathize with our weaknesses, but one who in every respect has been tempted as we are, yet without sin" (Heb. 4:15). It is this (still human) priest who prays at the heavenly throne on our behalf.

But there may be readers who find the very notion of a divine intercession difficult. Why, some will ask, is prayer by a heavenly figure deemed necessary? Can't we humans, who are created in God's image, go directly to the throne of grace with our requests? Here we enter into the deep mysteries of redemption as Jesus and the New Testament writers perceived it. Redemption is both completed, by Jesus' cross and resurrection, and ongoing. This means that for our prayers to work their effect in God's plan they must be taken up into the cosmic ministry of God's appointed Viceroy, *Kyrios Iesous*.[1] His sacrifice for sin continues in his prayer as our "advocate with the Father" (1 Jn. 2:1–2). He continues to suffer with his people (Acts 9:4–5; 2 Cor. 4:10), struggling alongside us between the ages, until the final glorification (Rom. 8:17–21, 34–39). And he intervenes in the church's life so that we may not be severed from the love of God by the hostile forces of this present world order (Rom. 8:38–39; 1 Cor. 11:32).

If we are already rescued from evil through receiving Christ by faith, we are also *being* saved through him in the midst of danger. According to the author of Hebrews, Christ "is able . . . to save completely those who approach God through him, since he lives always, to intercede on their behalf" (7:25).[2] A hymn by Martin Luther helps us to imagine this from Christ's point of view. Addressing each one of us, the Lord says:

> "Stay close to me,
> I am your rock and castle.
> Your ransom I myself will be;
> For you I strive and wrestle;
> For I am yours and you are mine,
> That where I am you may remain.
> The foe shall not divide us."[3]

Christ's intercession for us is a costly labor; and as we shall see, joining in his prayer for others also exacts a great price. Our ministry of intercession is one way in which we "work out" our salvation (Phil. 2:12–13). In prayer we "bear one another's burdens and so fulfill the law of Christ" (Gal. 6:2). This is a calling quite properly termed "high."

In fact, though, we do not really have a choice about our identity as priests within Christ's heavenly prayer. We are united with him in his work simply by virtue of our faith. We see this in the following words of intercession by Jesus: "I do not pray for these [disciples] only, but also for those who believe in me through their word, that they may all be one, even as thou, Father, art in me, and I in thee, that they also may be in us, so that the world may believe that thou hast sent me" (Jn. 17:20–21). Some interpreters hold that Jesus is speaking here of a mystical union between believers and the Godhead already here on earth, an experience of bliss that will shock the world into a recognition of Jesus' true identity. Others think that Jesus refers to an everyday community life where God's presence is so evident in the love of believers for one another that many will be attracted to the church. Perhaps these positions are not mutually exclusive,[4] but what needs to be added to both of them is the simple observation that, first and foremost, our unity with Christ and God means incorporation into the unique prayer relationship that exists between these two. Andrew Murray expresses this well in a personal petition to Christ: "And, O my Lord, let me know, just as you promised your disciples, that you are in the Father, I am in you, and you are in me. Let the uniting power of the Holy Spirit make my whole life an abiding in you and in your intercession. May my prayer be its echo, so that the Father hears me in you and you in me."[5] In other words, Jesus' heavenly work of intercession is fundamentally devoted to the forming and strengthening of our priestly vocation (see Jn. 17:11–19, 24).

We are to become "a holy temple in the Lord" (Eph. 2:21), "a holy priesthood, to offer spiritual sacrifices acceptable to God through Jesus Christ" (1 Pet. 2:5). "Through him [we are to] offer up a sacrifice of praise to God" (Heb. 13:15). And we are to pray for all those in special need, including our enemies (Mt. 5:44), just as Jesus did (Lk. 23:34). He is the foremost model of prayer for us, but he is also the priest who sustains our prayer. Thus we become his partners in priesthood, making our own real contributions to his heavenly intercession. Murray probably overstates the case when he asserts that "he cannot do it without us,"[6] but not by much. At the very least we must agree that "creation seems to be delegation through and through. [God] will do nothing simply of Himself which can be done by creatures."[7]

To pray in the name of Jesus means to step forward boldly, to claim our fair share in the ongoing redemption of the world. The Quaker philosopher Douglas Steere defines this vocation nicely as "our communion with God for others" and stresses that because we pray in the compassionate Spirit of Christ, our intercession can never be understood as coercive. True intercession cannot manipulate. Rather, "the effect of our prayers . . . would be at most to lower the threshold in the person prayed for and to make the besieging love of God . . . slightly more visible and more inviting. . . . We touch another's soul in the being of God, and [our prayer] can be used by God to affect the life of the other."[8] In this manner Jesus prays for us and for all people. During his ministry on earth he respected the freedom of others to decide against him, even as he interceded on their behalf.

One of the most poignant references to prayer in the entire New Testament occurs in Luke's version of the Lord's Supper, where Jesus tells the uncomprehending Peter, "Simon, Simon, behold, Satan demanded to have you, that he might sift you like wheat, but I have prayed for you that your faith may not fail" (Lk. 22:32). Did Jesus know as he spoke that Peter's faith *would* fail, or at least fall, in the imminent denial of his master? Probably (see 22:34). In any case, we the readers know that Jesus' request will be granted only through the pascal trauma of cross and resurrection, with much anguish for all. It may do us good to visualize Jesus praying for us in the dire straits that we have yet to pass through.

Which Neighbors?

According to Luke, a lawyer once asked Jesus, "And who is my neighbor?" We have come to know the response to this question as the parable of the good Samaritan (10:29–37). Presumably the lawyer wanted to know which of the many people who might qualify as his neighbor he ought to love as himself, that is, with special care and intensity (see 10:25–28). Technically speaking, the word "neighbor" (*plēsion* in Greek) simply means the one who is closest to us, either geographically or emotionally. Though we are told that the lawyer was trying to test Jesus (10:25), we should not dismiss his question as altogether cynical. Indeed, it carries great meaning for all who want to share in the priesthood of Jesus. If we are to pray for others with a serious intent, which members of the world's population are we to raise up before God? Not even the great saints can pray for everyone, equally, at all times.

Fortunately the New Testament offers us a wealth of guidance on this matter. In a few places we find general admonitions to pray for "all the saints" (Eph. 6:18) or "for all people," especially those in positions of authority (1 Tim. 2:1–2). Jesus himself prayed that the whole world might come to know his true identity through the love of God which had inspired his mission (Jn. 17:21–23). But typically, New Testament believers were instructed to pray for particular individuals or groups of people with special needs. Today, our neighbors will often be revealed to us by the news media as people requiring a special measure of forgiveness and healing. (See chapter 8.)

But even when healing and forgiveness are not the paramount concerns, specific individuals and groups will rise to the surface of our intercessory consciousness. Quite naturally we shall call to mind our personal circles of family, friends, work associates, and those for whom we have special responsibilities. Jesus offered most of his high priestly prayer in John 17 on behalf of his disciples and those who would come to believe in him through their word. Indeed, we must suspect that a great deal of Jesus' private prayer time was devoted to intercession for his followers (e.g., Lk. 6:12–13; 10:21–23; 22:32). Paul prayed regularly for his brother and sister Jews who could not accept Jesus as Messiah (Rom. 9:1–5; 10:1) and for the congregations he had founded (1 Cor. 1:4–9; Phil. 1:3–11; 1 Thess. 2:1–3; 2 Thess. 1:11–12) or hoped to visit (Rom. 1:8–10; Col. 1:9). The apostle's short personal letter to Philemon shows that he also interceded for an individual whom he knew and valued as a partner in the gospel (4–7, 17; see also 2 Tim. 1:3, 16–18). Like the rest of us, Paul obviously enjoyed some intercessory prayers more than others. He took special delight in prayer for his favorite congregation, the church at Philippi (Phil. 1:3–11). Nowhere do the New Testament writings suggest that we need to suppress our natural feelings (positive or negative) in our prayers for our neighbors.

And this leads us into the difficult matter of praying for enemies, which is no side issue in the New Testament but a central teaching of Jesus and the apostolic writers (see Mt. 5:44; Lk. 6:28; 23:34; Acts 7:59; 9:10–18; Rom. 12:14; 1 Pet. 3:9). In only two of these citations (Lk. 23:34; Acts 7:59) is the enemy's forgiveness by God stated as the object of intercession. But what else are we to say on behalf of those who trouble us? We are to bless them (Lk. 6:28; Rom. 12:14; 1 Pet. 3:9), which probably means to pronounce God's grace on them, trusting that it will enrich their lives for the benefit of all. Or perhaps blessing sometimes means just holding them up to God with a good will so that we can begin to see them as real human beings, real sisters and brothers with great needs like our own. I wonder if the "good" Samaritan was not practicing this kind of prayer at some level of his being when he came upon a Jewish "enemy," lying half dead on the road to Jericho.

During the 1980s, when the United States and the Soviet Union were rattling missiles at each other in righteous anger and the threat of nuclear war seemed all too real, I once suggested in a sermon that each of us should get to know the name of a Russian general and begin to pray for him in whatever words came to us. This admonition burst out quite spontaneously and surprised me as much as it did the congregation (for I am not by nature a dove). I now think that it evolved, with the Spirit's guidance, from my first personal encounter ever with a Russian Communist, which had occurred just a few weeks earlier at a church-sponsored forum on international relations.

Andrei was a diplomat at the UN, and what I thought I saw in him was a great love for his country coupled with a sadness about having constantly to struggle with the U.S. government. Was this merely effective propaganda on his part? Perhaps. But maybe it is really true that the Spirit leads us in prayer, especially when it comes to intercession for those whom we believe to be our enemies.

These days, I suspect, our more difficult task will be to offer up regular prayer for leaders of the world's most oppressive regimes. But most difficult of all is faithful intercession for those members of our personal circles who are causing us daily trouble. Most likely these are just the people Jesus refers to when he asks us to "bless those who curse you, pray for those who abuse you" (Lk. 6:28).

Others for whom we need to pray are neither friends nor enemies but people we know who live in constant deprivation, whether physical or spiritual. Today many of these would be individuals or groups whose basic rights and privileges are severely curtailed by their own societies. In Jesus' time such people included the children whom he blessed (Mt. 19:13–15) and the tax collectors and sinners whose friend he became (Mt. 11:19). By analogy, we as disciples are expected to exercise an odd sort of perception (apparently preconscious and formed by prayer) that enables us to recognize our master in the "least" of his suffering brothers or sisters, and come to their aid (Mt. 25:31–46).

But here a vexing question arises for modern Christians. How are we to focus our prayer energies on the needy people we know when there are simply too many of them for us to envision or name? We cannot pray intensively for all of them. There is no easy resolution to this difficulty; but I am convinced that when we pray in the words of the African hymn "Jesu, Jesu, fill us with your love, teach us how to serve the neighbors we have from you,"[9] directions will be given. Thus evangelical Christians often speak of a "prayer burden," a vocation to intercede for specific individuals or groups that seems uniquely crafted for them by God (see 2 Cor. 8:16).

My friend, the Reverend Valarie Whitcomb, is associate rector of All Saints Episcopal Church in Woodbridge, Virginia, not far from Washington, D.C. One day she tuned into a TV newscast and was confronted with a disturbing report on the likelihood, once again, of mass starvation in Ethiopia. This, the commentator predicted, would result from stepped-up military action in the ongoing civil war between the Marxist government in Addis Ababa and the Eritrean People's Liberation Front. Like the rest of us, Valarie had seen all too many video clips of children dying horribly from malnutrition. But this time, she said, she felt powerfully drawn to them and convinced that God could avert the impending tragedy. She began to weep with tears that seemed not to be her own. She spoke of the experience to her senior colleague, the Reverend John Guernsey, and together, with prayer and reflection, they concluded that an already scheduled course on the practice of intercession was meant to be shaped around the Ethiopian crisis. All during Lent in 1990 a large group of church members gathered to learn about the needs of Ethiopians on both sides of the conflict and to pray for them. Most of all, these Christians prayed—every Friday for five hours—that people would be fed. I learned of this concentrated effort in April. Some two months later I chanced upon an article in the *New York Times* entitled "Millions Are Fed as War Rages: With Luck and Ingenuity Ethiopian Aid Gets Through."[10] The story concerned an unusual series of breakdowns in the government bureaucracy that had enabled international church agencies to deliver huge amounts of food to remote, rural areas. Luck and ingenuity? Yes, and very likely something more. Of course one can never prove sequences of cause and effect when it comes to prayer, but here the coincidences are arresting. At the very least, this configuration of events should encourage us to become more intentional about translating our "holy desires and good counsels" into the "just works" of disciplined prayer for others.

Whether or not we receive clear guidance from the Spirit about which individuals or groups we should pray for, the New Testament reminds us of some whom we dare not forget. For example, those charged with the public proclamation of the gospel (not necessarily the ordained) should be near the top of our prayer lists (Lk. 22:31–32; Jn. 17:9–19; Acts 12:5; 13:3; Heb. 13:18). Paul was not shy about asking for the prayers of his readers (Rom. 15:30; 2 Cor. 1:11; Phil. 1:19; Phlm. 22), above all when he felt threatened by some danger or was suffering imprisonment (see also Col. 4:3; Eph. 6:18). Likewise, all New Testament believers were bidden to pray for the corporate life of their worshiping communities, and for individuals within them (Acts 4:29–31; 1 Cor. 11:29; 14:12–13; Gal. 6:2; Jas. 5:13–16). And finally, the earliest congregations were to intercede for their counterparts in other cities and provinces of the empire so that their sharing in Christ's Body would grow to maturity (Rom. 15:25–32; 2 Cor.

9:11–15). Happily, this kind of prayer relationship is being recovered as congregations in North America increasingly enter into close personal connections with individual churches abroad. Several churches I know have covenanted with parishes in Eastern Europe or Latin America for the sake of mutual ministry.

Which neighbors? This question can never be answered in an absolute sense, for new neighbors are always being revealed. Yet the written word and the Holy Spirit will teach us at any given time where we are to concentrate our efforts. We need not worry about where to begin our intercessions. If we are open, God will lead us into the "extended season of prayer" for particular people who are right for us.[11]

What Shall We Ask for Them?

The next issue becomes that of formulating our petitions on behalf of these neighbors. Apart from requests for healing and forgiveness, is there any clear indication of what Jesus and the first disciples wish us most especially to say? In fact there is. We may begin to spell it out by looking at the way New Testament intercessions typically unfold. On several occasions the process commences with thanksgiving on the part of the intercessor. Here are a few examples from the epistles:

> We give thanks to God always for you all, constantly mentioning you in our prayers, remembering before our God and Father your work of faith and labor of love [1 Thess. 1:2–3]. I thank my God in every remembrance of you, always in every prayer of mine for you all making my prayer with joy [Phil. 1:3]. I thank my God always when I remember you in my prayers, because I hear of your love and of the faith which you have toward the Lord Jesus and all the saints [Phlm. 4–5]. We always thank God . . . when we pray for you because we have heard of your faith in Christ Jesus [Col. 1:3–4; see also Eph. 1:15–16 and Jesus' intercessory thanksgiving for his seventy disciples in Lk. 10:21–22].

To be sure, these are all prayers for believers, who are dear to the heart of the writer. We have no examples in the New Testament of thanks offered in connection with enemies or others for whom we do not feel genuinely grateful. (In Paul's Epistle to the Galatians, where he expresses consternation over the behavior of his readers, the language of thanksgiving is omitted altogether.)[12] But when it does occur, the giving of thanks can lead naturally to prayers of intercession, and this seems to be the most frequent pattern. As we noted in the previous chapter, thanksgiving often functions as a way of learning God's will more clearly, both for ourselves and for others (see 1 Thess. 5:16–18; Phil. 4:6; Rom. 12:1–13).

What do the apostolic writers ask on behalf of their congregations when they begin with thanksgiving? Essentially two things: a greater personal knowledge of God's gracious will (Eph. 1:16–19; 3:17–19; Phil. 1:9–10; Col. 1:9; 4:12; Phlm. 6) and a growth in love and good works toward others (Phil. 1:9–11; Col. 1:10–11; 4:12; 1 Thess. 3:12–13; 2 Thess. 1:11; 2:17; Phlm. 6). These add up to what we have traditionally called sanctification. Moreover, the word *remember*, which occurs in three of the thanksgiving formulas just cited, suggests that Paul literally envisioned the people he prayed for by name or face, and probably imagined them moving forward in God's plan even as he prayed. This is a promising model for us all. When we intercede for the progress in faith of those who are especially close to us, it is fitting to "see" them, thankfully, in God's presence, and then to wait for more specific directives from the Spirit as to the shaping of our prayers on their behalf. On some occasions intercessory prayer in tongues may occur.[13] What people *ask* us to pray for should obviously be honored and included in this whole process, but under the Spirit's guidance it may not always turn out to be central in our petitions.

If intercessory requests for sanctification turn out to be frequent, so also must prayers for the coming of the Sanctifier. Jesus spoke from heaven so that Saul of Tarsus might receive the Holy Spirit. This happened through the human agency of the frightened disciple Ananias, who laid his hands on the blinded persecutor in obedience to the command of his great High Priest (Acts 9:10–19). In other cases, apostles placed their hands on believers and prayed for them to receive the Spirit (Acts 8:15; 19:6). Writing to the Romans, Paul twice indicated that he was interceding on behalf of his readers for a fuller measure of the Spirit: "I thank my God for all of you, . . . asking that somehow by God's will I may now at last succeed in coming to you . . . that I may impart to you some spiritual gift to strengthen you, that is, that we may be mutually strengthened by each other's faith, both yours and mine" (1:8–12). "May the God of hope fill you with all joy and peace in believing, so that by the power of the Holy Spirit you may abound in hope" (15:13).

Two observations need to be made here. First, as we can see in these and a number of the other passages cited above, intercessory requests frequently have as their aim an increased openness on the part of those prayed for to God's abundance (in the forms of knowledge, faith, love, hope, the Holy Spirit, etc.). This tendency fits with Jesus' vision of the kingdom as a great feast, and with his instruction to pray for its coming. In fact we may consider it an axiom of intercession that we should always seek for others those particular blessings from God that are revealed in the life and ministry of Jesus. Second, Rom. 1:8–12 is typical of several New Testament intercessions in that prayer for others is thought to facilitate an actual meeting between those asking and those receiving so that the gospel may move forward. Thus Paul asks the Romans to strive together with him in "prayers to God on my behalf . . . so that by God's will I may come to you with joy and be refreshed in your company" (15:30–32; see also Phil. 1:19–25; 1 Thess. 3:11; Phlm. 22; and probably 2 Cor. 8:16–17; 9:14). Intercession creates a deep connection with others and a mutual caring that often leads to active ministry. If we pray earnestly for the poor, we are likely to find ourselves feeding and housing them.

This thought suggests another distinctive feature of New Testament intercession. It is primarily for others *as partners in God's saving work.* Jesus prays for Peter's faith so that he can "strengthen [his] brethren" (Lk. 22:32), that is, be a leader in the church. Jesus also urges his disciples to "pray the Lord of the harvest to send out laborers into the harvest" (Mt. 9:38), which is both a request for missionary workers and a declaration of their own readiness to serve ("Here am I. Send me."). Likewise, in his high-priestly prayer, Jesus asks God to grant his disciples a portion of his glory and a profound union with him "so that the world may know that thou hast sent me and hast loved them" (Jn. 17:20–24). In the early church, disciples were commissioned to public ministries with prayer and the laying on of hands (Acts 13:3; 14:23; 1 Tim. 4:14) in the confidence that God would move to strengthen them and bestow the gifts they needed for their various callings. Moreover, those already engaged in active ministries frequently requested the prayer help of others so that God's redemptive cause would prosper through their work (2 Cor. 1:11; Phil. 1:19–20; Eph. 6:19; Col. 4:3). It is not very fashionable these days in the mainline churches or in Roman Catholicism to pray regularly for those who are charged with the missionary proclamation of the gospel. Yet this is where our New Testament writers want the intercessory prayers of their people to be concentrated. Here we contemporary Christians have much to ponder.

One more special characteristic of New Testament intercession ought to be mentioned. As we noted earlier, a significant number of prayers for others begin with the thankful remembrance of these people and then move on to petitions. But the sequence can also be reversed. On occasion, intercessors ask their readers to unite in prayer with them or with one another so that together they can raise a mighty hymn of praise and thanks to God. Two passages from Paul's letters illustrate this intention:

> [God] delivered us from so deadly a peril [probably a Roman sentence of execution] and he will deliver us; on him we have set our hope that he will deliver us again. You also must help us by prayer, so that many will give thanks on our behalf for the blessing granted us in answer to many prayers [2 Cor. 1:11]. May the God of steadfastness and encouragement grant you to live in such harmony with one another in accord with Christ Jesus, that together you may with one voice glorify the God and Father of our Lord Jesus Christ [Rom. 15:5–6].

In the first passage Paul holds up intercession and thanksgiving as roughly equal in importance. Or rather, he seems to have felt that his own liberation, "granted . . . in answer to many prayers," would not be complete until prayers of thanksgiving were offered along with his own. Thanksgiving meant helping the apostle and, more important, increasing the glory of God (see 2 Cor. 4:15). The passage from Romans shows Paul interceding for true community among his readers so that their praise will multiply to enhance God's glory. Behind this text we should probably discern some painful divisions in the Roman church, which were compromising its effective witness to the gospel.[14] Thus the apostle had to pray for a reconciliation among his readers that would allow them to exercise their corporate priesthood more effectively. They and their prayers were the "offering of the Gentiles" which needed to be rendered "acceptable, sanctified by the Holy Spirit" (Rom. 15:16). Here again intercession aims toward the rendering of praise, through which God's redemptive plan can advance (Rom. 15:17–19 in the light of vv. 5–13).

Intercession and Maturity

More than any other form of prayer, it seems, intercession teaches us the sacrificial ways of Christ. He was the man for others in first-century Palestine, and now he "lives to make intercession" for us at the throne of grace (Heb. 7:25). By faith we are joined together with his heavenly work. This is a high calling, almost beyond comprehension; and it is also a humbling experience. When we pray for others in Jesus' name, we are taken up into the greatest and most powerful force for good in the universe, yet we also stand exposed before God with all our faults. What right have we to pray for others, especially when they may seem closer to God than we are? The answer must be that it is not a question of rights at all but of God's grace and love and command. Thus we are bidden to pray as we *can*, not as we *ought*, which in any case we must learn from the Holy Spirit in the midst of our praying (Rom. 8:26). And the Spirit does teach us, once we have made a decision to pray. Our intercession in Christ's name is met by "a winnowing and a cleansing power of separation that can swiftly sort out the self-seeking, manipulative elements in our prayer so that it may become a creative part of a truly redemptive action on the soul and the body of another. P. T. Forsyth once wrote . . . 'our best prayer, broken, soiled, and feeble as it is, is caught up and made prayer in deed and power with God. This intercession prays for our very prayer, and atones for the sin of it.'"[15] To sense and acknowledge such a miracle of grace in the course of our praying is a mark of maturity among Christians. Yet even this consciousness is a gift of the Spirit.

Along with it comes a persistent call to enter ever more deeply into God's work. And this means, for all of us, offering up those parts of our lives that we have not yet allowed God to touch. Precisely in the midst of prayer for others we may hear the exhortation to "yield yourselves to God as those who have been brought from death to life, and your members [i.e., possibilities of attitude and action] to God as instruments of righteousness" (Rom. 6:13). Until we begin to take this road, our discernment of God's will for others must remain quite limited. But when our intercessions are combined with honest self-offering—clearly a lifelong process—they will gain in that boldness and specificity which accompanies all forms of spiritual maturity. The path will be difficult, even perilous at times; but it will not be gloomy, for as we journey farther up and farther in with our interces-sions, the result will always be great joy.[16]

Still another mark of maturity associated with intercessory prayer is a growing ability to take on prayer requests as normal business, which means letting people know what we actually ask on their behalf, and soliciting their prayers for us in return. This is best done in groups, face to face, even as we pray. But it may also happen indirectly, perhaps over the telephone or in letters, with Paul's epis-tolary greetings as our model. Ease in our discourse about prayer is difficult to achieve, for we can mask important issues with the over-use of pious language. Yet it is possible, with humility, to speak about the deep things of God. And it is necessary if we are really to exercise our high calling into Jesus' priesthood. The very recognition that we are always just beginning to pray will help us to move forward.[17]

Finally, our intercession will both demand and grant a costly involvement with those for whom we pray. Gradually the Holy Spirit teaches us to bear one another's burdens in more than an abstract manner. To our communion with God for others we shall be urged to add action with God for others. True, we cannot do this with equal care or effectiveness for all those entrusted to our praying. But the Spirit will guide us, within our intercessions, to those necessary "good works which God prepared beforehand, that we should walk in them" (Eph. 2:10). One of Paul's co-workers can become our model. The apostle tells his Corinthian readers that God is to be thanked for putting "into the heart of Titus the same concern I have for you. For Titus not only welcomed our appeal [to help the Corinthians com-plete their monetary collection for the church in Jerusalem] but he is coming to you with much enthusiasm and on his own initiative" (2 Cor. 8:16–17, NIV). In fact, there are people whose deep needs meet our own deep gifts for ministry, with the result that all parties are strengthened and honored. Intercession that proceeds from (or re-sults in) such blessed connections will usher us toward maturity. And a precious maturity it is. God needs it, for the sake of the world.

CHAPTER EIGHT

Prayers
of Forgiveness
and Healing

TWO BOUNDARY EXPERIENCES that we share most frequently with God's people everywhere are those of forgiveness and healing. They are not exactly the same, although they frequently overlap and reinforce each other. Here, to reflect the usual understanding of healing in the New Testament, we shall think of it as a physical and/or psychic restoration that takes place in individuals without regard to the state of their conscience. Quite often both forgiveness and healing occur "naturally," without prayer, as when two feuding parties simply cool down and let go of their hostile feelings toward each other, or when a cut finger mends over the course of a few days. Lewis Thomas, wise physician and cell biologist, is surely correct in observing that most things are better in the morning. The tendency inherent in all creatures to resolve conflict and regain health is part of God's daily providence. And yet, as we know, this indwelling grace is countered by ominous forces that can skew the process toward well-being or bring it to a grinding halt so that death results. In the New Testament these forces are understood to be the result of sin, although this is not usually thought of as the personal transgression of the individual who is suffering.

Finally, we must all die. But within the span of every lifetime many real victories over sin and death are won. Sometimes we speak a genuine word of forgiveness to others or receive it from them. Sometimes we confess our sin to God and experience the freeing rush of divine pardon. Or we ask God to lift a burden of guilt from a neighbor, and it happens. Healing takes place in analogous ways. Thus our recovery from an illness may be enhanced through the ministrations of others, both by ordinary medical means and by prayer. Or we ourselves may play the role of healer, using all the physical and spiritual resources we can muster.

With both forgiveness and healing, intercessory prayer clearly takes on a profound significance. But in fact prayers of almost every sort (confession, praise and thanksgiving, personal petition, contemplation, etc.) are linked by the biblical writers to events of forgiveness and healing. That is why I have chosen to use the preposition "of" in the title of this chapter. As used here, "of" carries the broad meaning of "associated with," indicating that forgiveness and healing can result from or lead to diverse types of communication in our life with God. We pray not only *for* a release from sin or illness or injury; we also pray *in the midst of* that release, and when it comes to fruition.

The upshot of all this is that prayers of forgiveness and healing turn out to be complex. They involve the exercise not only of our own faith but also the faith of those who pray with or for us. Moreover, such prayers take into account both our personal transgressions and the corporate sin of the various systems to which we belong. Given these variables, we are often tempted to speculate about the quantity of faith required for a particular instance of forgiveness or healing. And what, we ask ourselves, must be the quality of our prayers? To what extent do specific transgressions contribute to our psychic or physical pain? Are there circumstances under which we must repent in the presence of others so as to receive the blessings we desire? Can we in fact *make* the blessings happen, or does God sometimes answer no to even the purest of supplications? How do we tell whether or not to stop asking? These and similar questions frequently torture the souls of believers. Can we gain some clarity about such problems from Jesus and the New Testament authors so that we may learn to pray more wisely and confidently in the face of great suffering?

Causes, Effects, and the Grace of God

As we struggle with our questions, we shall be instructed by the New Testament's most comprehensive statement on the interrelationship of prayer, healing, and forgiveness. It occurs in the fifth chapter of the epistle attributed to James:

13) Are any among you suffering? They should pray. Are any cheerful? They should sing songs of praise. 14) Are any among you sick? They should call for the elders of the church and have them pray over them, anointing them with oil in the name of the Lord. 15) The prayer of faith will save the sick, and the Lord will raise them up; and anyone who has committed sins will be forgiven. 16) Therefore confess your sins to one another, and pray for one another, so that you may be healed. (NRSV)

Here is a glimpse into how the early church has begun to institutionalize the healing ministry of Jesus and the apostles. As far as we know, elders were not chosen for their leadership positions because they manifested special gifts of healing. Nor do we have any indication from the New Testament writings that ordination regularly conferred these gifts. Instead, the presupposition seems to be that because elders have been granted a special authority on behalf of the people (Acts 14:23; 1 Pet. 5:1–3), God works mightily through their intercessory prayers, especially in extreme cases when an official presence of the church is called for outside its normal periods of worship. Nevertheless, God's people as a whole also have authority to pray effectively for one another's healing (v. 16). Here the practice envisioned probably involves prayers of intercession that take place in corporate worship. James may understand these as a means of preventing the emergency case described in the first part of the passage.

But what about sin? James never indicates that the elders ought to enter upon their work suspecting a person of immorality and hypothesizing this as the root cause of the illness. Rather, the impression given is that this healing event will provide opportunities for confession and forgiveness, whether or not the afflicted person is consciously troubled by particular sins. The idea is not to force a confession but to stand ready for disclosures of guilt if these should occur during the course of prayers for healing. We all know how introspective we become when we are crippled by a serious illness or injury and how, as a result, we sometimes need to get certain things off our chest. When we ourselves are unable to initiate such confessions, those who pray for us may be prompted to inquire, gently, about the condition of our hearts. As always, the Spirit leads us (together) in prayer. Here is yet another way of looking at what Paul means when he urges those who are "spiritual" to "bear one another's burdens and so fulfill the law of Christ" (Gal. 6:2).

A firm rule in all such circumstances is provided by Jesus' own healing ministry. Compassion and respect for those who suffer is absolutely paramount. Not once, in all the Gospel stories of those who came to Jesus for help, did he accuse sick people of having caused their illness by their own sinning.[1] On the contrary, when the disciples expressed a common prejudice by asking, "Who sinned, this man or his parents, that he was born blind?" Jesus answered, "It was not that this man sinned, or his parents, but that the works of God might be made manifest in him" (Jn. 9:2–3). In other words, Jesus believed that God had permitted this disability for the sake of a greater good but had not administered it as a punishment. Instead of berating his sick contemporaries for their moral failures, Jesus "went around doing good and healing all that were oppressed by the devil, for God was with him" (Acts 10:38). It is Satan who uses the fallenness of the whole world to oppress people with illness. The Lord raises people up (Jas. 5:15).

On the other hand, it needs to be acknowledged that New Testament writers do sometimes consider illness to be a warning from God or Christ designed to produce repentance on the part of those who are arrogant. In Acts, Luke shows us Paul denouncing Elymas the magician with these words: "You son of the devil, . . . behold, the hand of the Lord is upon you, and you shall be blind and unable to see the sun for a time" (Acts 13:10–11). And Paul announces that the failure of the Corinthians to examine themselves before God and honor the lowly in their midst is producing weakness, illness, and even death (1 Cor. 11:30). Likewise, John hears the risen Christ render this stern judgment on a false prophetess: "I gave her time to repent, but she refuses to repent of her immorality. Behold, I will throw her on a sickbed" (Rev. 2:21–22). In each of these cases it is important to notice that the individuals afflicted are explicitly faulted for thinking of themselves as beyond reproach in God's eyes. They are the very opposite of those who declare their humility and need by calling on God for help.

Luke's story of Paul's conversion in Acts represents a variation on this theme, for it shows what happens when a pious but wrongheaded individual meets with the Lord's judgment in a physical way. Christ struck Saul blind on the road to Damascus, with the result that the future apostle opened himself to divine correction (9:5). Gazing on Saul's remorse, the risen Lord commissioned Ananias to visit him: "Behold, he is praying and he has seen a man named

Ananias come in and lay his hands on him that he might regain his sight. . . . Go, for he is a chosen instrument of mine" (9:12, 15). In his own retelling of the story, Paul remembered that Ananias first healed him and then commanded him to "rise and be baptized, and wash away your sins, calling upon [Christ's] name" (22:16). Here the rite of purification did not come into play until physical restoration was accomplished. It could be argued that Paul's sin of persecuting the church "caused" his blindness (though this is never stated in so many words), but the central message conveyed here is that the gracious call of Christ may wound and heal, convict and forgive more or less simultaneously, thus transcending all our human categories. Stories like this are probably replayed in the lives of believers today far more often than we think or admit.

Like Jesus and the rest of his New Testament interpreters, James assumes that God's baptized people will continue to sin against one another (5:16). But if those sins are regularly confessed and forgiven in conversation with our co-believers, there is no need for compulsive speculation about precise relationships between sin and illness. Prayer on behalf of our neighbors for the forgiveness of sins and healing is a seamless garment (Jas. 5:16). It is an everyday gift to the church that is to be exercised as a normal part of its worship.

The passage from James also tells us something quite essential about the role of faith in prayers for healing. When James refers to the "prayer of faith" that will "save" a sick person, he almost certainly means the faith of the elders who are praying. No direct reference is made to the faith of the sufferer. While that may be important, it is obviously not the chief ingredient here. In fact, as we suggested in chapter 5, the faith associated with healing in the New Testament is often a corporate phenomenon; it is something shared by the person requesting healing, the individual or group ministering directly to that person, the sponsors (if any) who have brought the sick individual, and intercessors both near and far who support the whole process with their prayers.

It is true that Jesus sometimes tells people who seek him out for healing that their faith has "saved" them (Mk. 5:34; 10:52 and parallels; Lk. 17:19), but in each of these narratives the transaction happens solely between Jesus and the individuals healed.[2] There are no intermediaries or intercessors. What is not included in Jesus' pronouncements but must be assumed on the basis of other passages is that his own faith as a healer counts for even more than that of the afflicted ones (see Mk. 7:34; 9:23, and pp. 19, 23, and 56 in chapters 2 and 5). By commending people for their faith, Jesus acknowledged the persistent desire and trust that had led them to approach him with their petitions. Yet his statements do not explain all the workings of each healing event. He, in communion with God, is the real healer. His faith matters most.

Still, some mustard seed of hopeful or desperate seeking was desired by Jesus, especially on the part of those who brought others for healing. Sometimes Jesus discerned a boldness in the sponsors that moved him to action. When four men carried a paralytic friend to him, lowering the invalid through an open roof to create a space in the crowd, Jesus was mightily impressed. He "saw their faith [and] said to the paralytic, 'My son, your sins are forgiven'" (Mk. 2:5). Later Jesus healed the man physically. His quick words of absolution show that he saw how urgently a release from sin was needed *in this case*. He did not say that the man's sin had caused his illness. On another occasion, after jousting verbally with a Syrophoenician woman who had requested healing for her demon-possessed daughter, Jesus was won over by her last word and announced (with some delight?), "For this saying you may go your way; the demon has left your daughter" (Mk. 7:26–30). Likewise, when emissaries from the centurion of Capernaum voiced his trust that Jesus could heal his servant with a single word, Jesus declared to the crowd surrounding them, "I tell you, not even in Israel have I found such faith." And Luke adds that "when those who had been sent returned to the house, they found the slave well" (7:2–10).

Sometimes, however, it appears that Jesus had to stimulate faith in the sponsors and, on one occasion, in the person to be healed. Thus he challenged the anguished father of an epileptic boy with the pronouncement that "all things are possible to one who believes." In response, the man cried out with a prayerful confession: "I believe, help my unbelief!" (Mk. 9:24). Was this faith adequate? Probably not, but brought into the sphere of Jesus' own confidence, it sufficed. Again, as Jesus walked with Jairus toward the house where his daughter lay gravely ill and a servant rushed up to inform them that the situation was hopeless, the distraught father heard these words from his companion: "Do not fear; only believe, and she shall be well" (Lk. 8:50). To what extent was Jairus able to accept this counsel? We do not know. But we do know that he and his wife permitted Jesus to be with them and their lifeless daughter in a terrible moment of loss. And it was enough. Finally, in confronting an invalid who seemed all too content with his illness, Jesus adopted a harsher tone. "Do you want to be healed?" he asked. Paying no attention to the man's excuses (which sound strikingly modern), Jesus issued a simple order: "Rise, take up your pallet, and walk" (Jn. 5:1–9). If the man had little or no faith prior to his encounter with Jesus, he certainly had it now, in the form of obedience and quite possibly some fear.

If the faith of the person being healed and that of the sponsors is as variable as the Gospel stories indicate, then we must use great caution in identifying the human causes of illness. Certainly careless or self-destructive life-styles often speed the development of certain diseases, though even here the evidence is ambiguous. Unfortunately there is no ambiguity attached to the dogma expressed in some New Age circles that individuals are directly responsible for their own maladies and, conversely, for their own healing. One of the most sensible protests I know against this view appeared on the editorial page of the *New York Times*. The author, Barbara Boggs Sigmund, mayor of Princeton, New Jersey, until her death in October, 1990, entitled her short essay "I Didn't Give Myself Cancer."[3] Mayor Sigmund acknowledged that a positive mental state helps us to live productively with our illnesses and may even contribute toward their cure. But this does not mean, she rightly said, that she herself had created her life-threatening malignancy by wrong thinking and could therefore destroy it by a willed change of attitude. Such a message is oppressive and puts more weight on the quality of our inner life than it can bear. Jesus knows that we cannot ultimately control such matters, that healing must come from the outside as well as the inside, and often through others. Sigmund concluded her essay with a wry statement of faith that rings true despite her death: "I'm sticking with the medal of Jesus and Mary around my neck and novenas to St. Jude. It's strictly a utilitarian decision: The data base of success stories is larger by far."

Clearly Jesus and the New Testament writers give us no warrant for *opposing* psychosomatic approaches to healing. These can be and often are an effective part of the divine purpose. But if we employ them as a substitute for interventions by the transcendent God, they can easily degenerate into pseudoscientific formulas. Healing becomes mechanistic; cause and effect become our gods, and despair lies close at hand. By contrast, prayers of healing in communion with Jesus, even when they seem not to accomplish their goal, will always lead us to wholeness.

The Need for Prayer in Forgiveness

But we are getting ahead of our story. Here we must shift our attention backward for a time to that form of human restoration we call forgiveness. It too requires the vigorous exercise of faith, especially as this manifests itself in prayer. Indeed, we learned in chapter 2 that one of Jesus' strongest convictions about prayer had to do with its effectiveness in the overcoming of our mutual estrangements. Following are three of his teachings that make this point:

> If you are offering your gift at the altar, and there remember that your brother or sister has something against you, leave your gift there before the altar and go; first be reconciled to your brother or sister and then come and offer your gift [Mt. 5:23–24]. And whenever you stand praying, forgive, if you have anything against anyone; so that your Father also who is in heaven may forgive you your trespasses [Mk. 11:25]. When you pray, say "Father . . . Thy kingdom come . . . and forgive us our sins, for we ourselves forgive every one who is indebted to us" [Lk. 11:2–4; see also Mt. 6:12, which reads, "as we also have forgiven our debtors"].

What these sayings have in common is the view that problems of guilt will regularly come to consciousness in prayer. The prayers themselves may not initially center on such problems. But in the course of our praying, feelings of need will often arise, both to forgive and to be forgiven. Here, once again, the Spirit leads us in prayer. To this list of passages we may also add Jesus' admonitions to pray for our enemies (Mt. 5:44; Lk. 6:28) and the apostolic variations on this theme (Rom. 12:14–21; 1 Pet. 3:9). These too may give rise to strong feelings of need for forgiveness.

One facet of Jesus' words that we must take care not to misinterpret is the relationship envisioned between our acts of forgiveness and the remission of our own sin by God. The fundamental truth is that we are inspired to forgive others by the magnanimity God shows us (see Mt. 18:23–35). Nevertheless, what we actually sense in much of our everyday life is not release from guilt and shame or empowerment for reconciliation but the demand to be better than we are by simply transcending our resentments toward others. Pastoral counselor John Patton has entitled his recent book *Is Human Forgiveness Possible?*[4] He does not believe that the final answer must be no, but he does want to emphasize how difficult it is for wounded people

(which means all of us) to find genuine resolution in matters of forgiveness. Patton believes that real forgiveness takes place only on the
feeling level and that there is nothing we can do to make this happen.
Just saying the words of absolution is insufficient. In fact, forgiveness
turns out to be not a work or a pronouncement but a discovery that
grows out of our realization that we and the people from whom we
are estranged are not very different after all. I think Patton expresses
an essential truth about forgiveness, one that Jesus himself articulated in his parables. Forgiveness, when it happens, happens by grace.

What resources can prayer offer for the "discovery" of forgiveness?
First, as noted above, we sometimes get messages in prayer about our
need to forgive and be forgiven. To the degree that this happens in
communion with our loving Abba, our need will not be experienced
as a demand to become perfect. Rather, it will be felt as an invitation
to move, with God, toward something grand and luminous, albeit
through suffering. Second, though Patton is right to insist that verbal
formulas as such cannot bring about forgiveness, the New Testament
practice of public prayers for reconciliation (see Jas. 5:16; Col. 3:13–17;
and the Lord's Prayer itself) can function to help our churches become real communities of restoration (Gal. 6:1–2). Praying about
forgiveness, out loud and in the company of other believers, can make
a difference. Surprisingly, the admonition to forgive one another in
public worship is linked by the author of Colossians with the congregation's praise and thanksgiving. If the path to forgiveness frequently
requires us to pray through our anger and sorrow, the exultation of
the community, supporting our struggle, can help us learn new feelings. Third, our intercession for those we need to forgive almost
always results in a more gracious perception of them. Douglas Steere
quotes William Russell Maltby on this matter: "I found that I could
not think of any of these [people] in the presence of God without
some change coming over my thoughts, some stronger sense of their
worth before God, some deeper sympathy with them as hard toilers
in a great sea."[5] Finally, prayers by the church on behalf of estranged
parties may prove effective when ordinary human effort fails. Simon
Tugwell writes: "There is a great ministry here which we can per-
form for one another. Often it is morally impossible for me to forgive
someone who has harmed me; I may want to forgive, but somehow
find it beyond my powers. The support of my brothers and sisters in
Christ, forgiving for me, may well be the means by which eventually
I too can learn to forgive."[6]

Here, as always, God's own timing must prevail over our desire for a quick solution. In one of his letters to Malcolm, C. S. Lewis reports a bit of good news. "Last week," he notes, "while at prayer, I suddenly discovered—or felt as if I did—that I had really forgiven someone I have been trying to forgive for over 30 years. Trying, and praying that I might."[7] Thirty years! That may sound depressing to some of us. But to others it will sound quite realistic. And what if Lewis had not been praying?

In the New Testament view of things, prayer is also essential for those who feel the need to be forgiven. First of all, to the best of our ability, we must recall our misdeeds in the presence of God. We need to confess them not only as wrongs done to neighbors (or ourselves) but also as sins against heaven (Lk. 15:18). Of course such confessions can be empty rituals, but if we have gotten into the habit of communing with a merciful God in other aspects of our life, the Divine Presence will really purge and cleanse us. It is worth noting that in the New Testament those who have confessed their sin most honestly (and therefore felt the release of confession) are precisely those overwhelmed by the magnanimity of God. It was *after* and *because of* a great catch of fish that Peter fell down before Jesus, crying, "Depart from me, for I am a sinful man, O Lord" (Lk. 5:8). And the same holds true for the prodigal son. He was moved to repent of his sin only by recalling the goodness of his father (Lk. 15:17–19). As Rowan Williams has shown, it was Christ in his resurrection majesty who effected the most profound self-judgment among his disciples. Simply by appearing to them as the Risen and Compassionate One, he allowed them to confront their betrayal of him head on, and so to repent.[8]

Particularly vital to the forgiveness of sinners in the New Testament is the prayerful support of the communities to which they belong. Paul urges the Galatians to follow the Holy Spirit's lead in restoring a church member who "is overtaken in [a] trespass." This bearing of the other's burden is to be done in humility, in a spirit of gentleness ("Look to yourself, lest you too be tempted"). Such a process of rehabilitation, among equals and before God, would surely be accompanied by prayer in the Spirit (Gal. 5:22–6:2). In fact, Paul may have been thinking here of his own reception into the church through the prayerful ministrations of Ananias. My hunch is that Rom. 5:5 ("God's love has been poured out in our hearts through the Holy Spirit") represents a personal memory on Paul's part of how it felt to be prayed over for forgiveness and healing. In a related passage, 1 Jn. 5:16, the author tells his readers that whenever they see a believer committing a sin that is not "unto death," they should pray for the person so that God will renew his or her life.[9] This passage and the one from Galatians show that when Jesus, on the evening of his resurrection, granted the Holy Spirit to his closest disciples so that they might "forgive the sins of any" (Jn. 20:22–23), he did not intend to restrict such power to a small group of church officials. All believers are to pray for the recovery of brothers and sisters snared in sin. Twice in the New Testament we find examples of someone praying out loud for his tormenters. These are the extraordinary cases of Jesus on the cross (Lk. 23:34) and Stephen at the moment of his martyrdom (Acts 7:60). Clearly the two narratives are meant to help us emulate these heroic figures, although we must imagine that under less extreme conditions believers would not think to intercede for enemies within their hearing lest this be taken as a prideful claim to spiritual superiority (see Gal. 6:1–2).

The forgiveness of an individual's sin in a community of believers is a delicate affair and often requires a prolonged season of compassionate prayer. The eighteenth chapter of Matthew's Gospel contains a number of sayings by Jesus that deal with community reconciliation. One of them outlines a process through which believers must go when they consider themselves wronged by another:

15) If your brother [or sister] sins against you, go and tell him his fault, between you and him alone. If he listens to you, you have gained your brother. 16) But if he does not listen, take one or two others along with you, that every word may be confirmed by the evidence of two or three witnesses. 17) If he refuses to listen to them, tell it to the church; and if he refuses to listen even to the church, let him be to you as a Gentile and a tax collector. 18) Truly, I say to you, whatever you bind on earth shall be bound in heaven, and whatever you loose on earth shall be loosed in heaven. 19) Again I say to you, if two of you agree on earth about anything they ask, it will be done for them by my Father in heaven. 20) For where two or three are gathered in my name there am I in the midst of them.

Roberta Bondi and Flora Slosson Wuellner both make the important point that we cannot remain closely tied to anyone who sins against us by threatening our very identity in God, for without this true self we cannot serve God or become an agent of reconciliation to others.[10] Thus, painful separations, even among believers, may prove necessary.[11] Judging from Mt. 18:18, it looks as though such events were to be ritualized in prayer on the part of the community. Yet as Wuellner notes, even these heaven-ratified bindings and loosings need not be permanent. Grounding her observations on verses 19 and 20, she writes: "What would happen in a wounded church body if a small group gathered in the name not to complain or blame but to listen in loving, open silence to what the Christ is saying? What would happen in a broken family if a small group of family members gathered in that name not to rehearse history but to share the pain, listen with expectancy to what the living Christ is saying in their hearts, and experience the healing beginning with them?"[12] The only thing that alienated parties or individuals must agree on is a request that Jesus will be present with them. Whether or not complete reconciliation develops from such meetings, real healing will take place.

And here we come to the center of things, for it is finally God, the Holy Trinity, who effects both our forgiveness and our forgiving. As we gather in Jesus' name, he prays with us. And so we no longer live simply in the old, stuck places. Jesus is our advocate and priest at the throne of grace so that we ourselves can "draw near [to] receive mercy . . . in time of need" (Heb. 4:16). True forgiving happens "in the presence of Christ" (2 Cor. 2:10) as the Spirit cries "Abba" to affirm our great worth in God's eyes (Gal. 4:6–7). When our sisters and brothers in the church learn of our need, they too will join the heavenly discourse with their prayers, opening up new networks for the flow of reconciliation. Jesus said that "there is joy before the angels of God over the sinner who repents" (Lk. 15:10). This is not a once-in-a-lifetime event but one that happens "normally," whenever we pray to be forgiven or to let go of our bitterness toward another. Yet the normal is also the extraordinary. With prayer, forgiveness is no isolated, private transaction but a shift in the life of the world.

God's Royal Healing, Granted in Prayer

That is also true of the physical healings and exorcisms performed by Jesus. Once, in casting out a demon, Jesus told a crowd of critics that because he accomplished his act "by the Spirit of God," nothing less than the kingdom of God had broken into their midst (Mt. 12:28). The same interpretation was placed on Jesus' physical healings (Lk. 4:18), at least some of which were seen as a release from evil powers or from Satan (Mk. 9:14–29; Lk. 13:16; Acts 10:38). Thus the cures effected by Jesus and his followers were not thought to be manifestations of God's everyday providence. Instead they were received as special revelations of divine force, signs of God's advent at the end of the age. Again and again in the Gospel narratives verbal proclamations of the kingdom's imminence are accompanied by an outbreak of healings (Mt. 4:23–25; 11:4–5; Mk. 1:21–34; 6:12–13; Lk. 4:14–41).

Moreover, when the early church began to connect Jesus' kingdom message explicitly with his death and resurrection, the healings continued, as a witness to the truth of the gospel (Acts 4:30). Frequently Peter, John, Paul, and other disciples are shown to be healing in the name of Jesus (Mt. 7:22; Mk. 9:38; 16:17; Acts 3:6; 4:10, 30; 16:18; Jas. 5:14). This invocation reflects the earliest faith of the church that Jesus' resurrection had granted him the unique status of *Kyrios,* the chief bearer of God's end-time power. Sometimes Jesus himself is proclaimed as the healer (Acts 9:34; Jas. 5:15). Elsewhere healings are attributed to Christ's gift of the Holy Spirit, as when Paul labels them a "manifestation of the Spirit for the common good" (1 Cor. 12:7–9; see also Rom. 15:19; 1 Cor. 2:4; Gal. 3:1–5). In short, what the early church claimed for its own community life and for the world at large was an extraordinary bestowal of God's power for healing. Now, the gospel says, is a time of royal healing, for God's kingdom has come near.

Physical healings and exorcisms quickly became a hallmark of the New Testament church, and not just among its own members. The four Gospels give the distinct impression that most of those healed by Jesus did not become his disciples but continued their daily life much as before, though perhaps with a deeper faith in God. Surprisingly not one single story in the canonical literature of the early church indicates that healing itself was employed as a means of proselytizing. Indeed, it was offered with no strings attached, apart from interpretations by the healers that God was accomplishing these wonders in the name of Jesus (see esp. Acts 3:6). Those healed were free to believe the message or not. The Book of Acts, certain passages from John's Gospel, and a few rabbinic texts suggest that healing in Jesus' name became a source of controversy between some branches of Judaism and the early church.[13] Such controversy hardly needs to be perpetuated in our day, when every one of the world's major religions is confronted with more cries for healing than it can handle. Indeed, the ministry of healing is a topic of discussion long overdue in our developing ecumenical dialogue.

Whenever Christians return to their New Testament roots, they tend to regard healing as an indispensable feature of the gospel message, a special gift entrusted to the church for the sake of the entire world. The final chapter of Revelation gives us a beautiful symbol of this conviction. In the New Jerusalem presided over by God and the Lamb, the tree of life (Gen. 2:9) reappears; and its leaves are "for the healing of the nations" (Rev. 22:2).

Can we say more about the role of prayer in the healings described by our New Testament authors? As a start, we may observe that every Gospel story of a needy person approaching Jesus is really a statement about prayer. Such vignettes were preserved in the church's oral tradition not only because they magnified Jesus and (occasionally) furnished biographical data about people who later became prominent in the church, but also because they provided models of how we are to offer our supplications. It is hardly an accident that most of these stories turn out to be accounts of healing. We may guess that much of the earliest prayer addressed to Jesus, as well as the ritual invocations of his name, had to do with physical healings and exorcisms (2 Cor. 12:8–10; Acts 3:6; Mk. 9:38–40; 16:17).

In Mark's Gospel Jesus' healings take on a special prominence. This leads us to suspect that one of Mark's purposes was to encourage his readers (probably Romans, living with the memory of Nero's persecution) in their own healing ministry.[14] The longer ending of Mark, often thought to be a later addition to the original manuscript, contains this promise from the risen Christ: "And these signs will accompany those who believe: in my name they will cast out demons; . . . they will lay their hands on the sick, and they will recover" (16:17–18). Then the writer adds that the apostles "went forth and preached everywhere, while the Lord worked with them and confirmed the message by the signs that attended it" (16:20). If these verses are not by Mark himself, they nevertheless represent a faithful interpretation of what his Gospel is about.

In John's Gospel too the disciples are encouraged to pray for the healing of others, though we have to look closely to find this message. According to Jesus, the "greater works" that subsequent believers (including ourselves) are to accomplish will come as the result of prayer in his name (14:12–14). However, an earlier reference to these works occurs in the context of a healing. Just before Jesus restored the sight of a man born blind, he told his disciples, *"We* must work the works of him [God] who sent *me"* (9:4; italics added). This passage is not just a description of Jesus' historical ministry in Palestine but also a prophecy of its continuation through the prayers and actions of his followers in later times (as in Mk. 16:20; Acts 9:34).[15] James describes the church's cooperation with Jesus' healing power in a single paradoxical sentence: "The prayer of faith [by the elders] will save the sick, and the Lord will raise them up" (5:15, NRSV).

Down through the centuries Christians have preserved, adapted, and rediscovered important features of the healing prayers used by Jesus and the earliest disciples. We shall do well to review them and allow them to shape our own practice. One of these details concerns the dimension of partnership in healing. Apart from Jesus himself, who typically worked alone with the disciples standing by as learners, most healing prayer took place through the ministry of groups. The apostles usually went out in teams of two or more to preach and heal (Mk. 6:7; Lk. 10:1). James, writing to a residential community, presupposes both a council of local elders visiting the sick and the whole congregation assembled, praying for one another. In general the New Testament view seems to be that the corporate faith of the church will prove most effective in combatting illness.

Today most of us know of individual Christians who are called to exercise a public ministry of healing (see 1 Cor. 12:9). Yet by and large they too work in concert with the prayers of other believers who accompany or sponsor them. If they do not, they may well arouse our suspicions. Most common today are healing teams, such as those led by Francis and Judith MacNutt, Morton Kelsey, Tilda Norberg and Robert Webber, or Matthew and Dennis Linn and Sheila Fabricant. The writings of these well-known healers testify to the need for group prayer in the daily work of their ministries.[16] The same holds true in many non-Western cultures, where Christians have often taken the healing ministry for granted as a normal part of gospel proclamation. To cite just one example, the Lutheran Church of Madagascar has developed special institutions for combining intercessory prayer with conventional medicine. In these hospital-like camps (called tobys) the healing process is initiated and sustained by services of the Word that include readings, hymns of invocation to the Holy Spirit, opportunities for repentance, and prayers by the congregation, which sometimes lead to exorcisms. At the same time, many of the tobys have also built clinics in order to provide modern medical services.[17]

A second detail to be noted is that prayer for healing must sometimes continue over a period of time. Although Jesus' healings appear to have been mostly instantaneous, Mark tells us that in one case he had to complete a cure with a second laying on of hands (8:22–25). And the admonition of James that we should pray for one another's healing occurs in the Greek present tense, indicating an ongoing activity that does not necessarily bear fruit all at once (see 5:16). Francis MacNutt offers this helpful commentary on the use of prayer in healing today: "There is a time element in most healing. Even in healings that seem instant there is at least a period of minutes in which the change takes place. There is also an element of more or less power, more or less authority in me, since I am not God, but only share in his life, so that the effect of my prayer on the sickness may not completely dispel [it] and bring in the wholeness of life. . . . In consequence, many of the people I pray with are not completely healed but are improved."[18] Sheila Fabricant and the Linns also stress the importance of continued prayers, especially in the healing of memories, family conflicts, and destructive habits.[19] Here, once again, we may recall that one of Jesus' chief teachings on prayer has to do with perseverance.

But in this connection we must also confront a third characteristic of prayers for healing in the New Testament. On some occasions God says no to physical recovery. We see this in a chapter from Paul's life during which he prayed repeatedly that the risen Christ would heal him of an undisclosed bodily illness but never received the answer he hoped for (2 Cor. 12:1–10).[20] Although he later came to understand this trial as a victory of God's grace for the advancement of his ministry, we must suspect that he initially felt great disappointment and anger over being denied what had been granted to many others.[21]

Today prayers for people with advanced illness or those nearing death present a special challenge to faith. The Reverend Paul Anderson, who has taken part in charismatic healing over much of his ministry, writes about these difficulties in narrating the loss of his father to cancer. When persistent prayers did not reverse the disease,

Pastor Anderson and his familiy were thrown into anguish. Gradually, with his father's active participation, family members were led in prayer to release their loved one to God. There was no spectacular revelation of God's will, only a dawning certainty that this was the time to let go. Pastor Anderson writes:

> Faith which accepts healing or the lack of it will soar at the dark moments. Dad's did. Those who cling to healing against God's will and see partners die may struggle with post-mortem guilt and confusion. Ultimately, prayer is not twisting God's arm to do things our way. It is aligning the human will with the sovereign, loving, eternal purposes of almighty God. . . . Will I pray less for healing because we prayed and Dad died? I doubt it. . . . We are commanded to lay hands on the sick; we are not commanded to heal them. We continue to do our part, trusting God for His supernatural part.[22]

Here we may think of those many, many people from the first century onward who have experienced healing through the prayers of believers. But they all died, every last one of them. Finally, we must adopt John Biersdorf's salutary attitude toward the meaning of prayer. What takes place in every true contact with the Divine, he says, is a "healing of purpose" for all parties concerned.[23] Whether we live or die, whether those we pray for live or die, the Holy Spirit is at work, turning everything into good for those who love God (Rom. 8:28).

One more aspect of healing prayer must be noted and pondered, for it presents a great challenge to many contemporary Christians. In our synoptic Gospels the healings accomplished by Jesus and his disciples are often interpreted as exorcisms, that is, the casting out of evil spirits from possessed individuals. Strictly speaking, exorcisms are commands rather than prayers. But when they are done in the name of Jesus (Mt. 7:22; Mk. 9:38; 16:17; Lk. 9:49; Acts 16:18), they tend to resemble prayers for physical healing (Jn. 14:12–14; Acts 3:6; 4:30). Jesus himself connected the two when he told his bewildered disciples that their inability to exorcise a specific demon was due to the fact that "this kind cannot be driven out by anything but prayer" (Mk. 9:29).

What are we to make of all this in the twentieth century? In my view we would be taking a perilous step if we reduced the New Testament understanding of exorcism to our current categories of depth psychology or psychosomatic wholeness, though some of those healed by Jesus and his disciples may well have been suffering from what we now call mental illness. But it is equally wrong, I think, to see the need for exorcism in nearly every illness or conflict situation. Apart from the synoptic Gospels and Acts, New Testament writers do not mention exorcisms, even though they pay grudging respect to the power of Satan and his allies.[24] As the supreme antidote to bondage by demonic forces, Paul holds up the love of God in Christ, poured out in our hearts through the Holy Spirit (Rom. 8:15–16, 31–38; Gal. 4:1–10). It is "devotion to Christ," expressed in our prayers and strengthened by the pastoral care of others, that delivers us from Satan's dominion (1 Cor. 7:26–35; 2 Cor. 11:1–15).

This is hardly to say that exorcisms were rare in the apostolic congregations—Matthew, Mark, and Luke witness to a broad church tradition that continued well into the third century—or that they should not be performed today. Down through the centuries Roman Catholics have wisely retained the office of exorcist in most of their dioceses, and these brave priests have riveting stories of faith to tell. The nineteenth-century German Reformed pastor Johann Christoph Blumhardt was anything but a fundamentalist, but his practice of ministry underwent a radical change in 1842, when he had to deal with a strange nervous disorder suffered by one of the young women in his village. After a long season of prayer with Gottlieben Dittus and her family, a moment of crisis came. The young woman's sister, who herself had begun to exhibit odd patterns of behavior, cried out in a loud voice that did not seem to be her own: "Jesus is victor!" From that moment on, peace and health returned to the whole family. It is not clear that Blumhardt himself commanded a demon to depart, but the event was later interpreted as an exorcism and was followed by a great outbreak of physical, mental, and social healings in the immediate area.[25]

Today in the Pentecostal churches, in the various renewal movements associated with mainline congregations, and in much of non-Western Christianity, exorcisms remain a significant part of the total gospel ministry. When those charged with the performance of exorcisms are at their best, they work cautiously, praying with other believers to discern whether a demonic force is actually present and if so, whether a ritual command to expel it is the appropriate mode of calling forth Jesus' power to heal.[26] Above all, exorcists must resist the temptation to identify suffering people with the evil forces that may be oppressing them. Every manifestation of free choice and personal responsibility on the part of the sufferers must be honored. In chapter 11 we shall have much to say about prayer as warfare against the superhuman forces that oppose God's kingdom.

Here we are led back once more to the themes that introduced this chapter. By God's grace there is a providential tendency toward forgiveness and healing woven into the very fabric of creation. Yet it is constantly thwarted by powers beyond our personal control. Sometimes spiritual death overtakes us in the form of hardheartedness. Always, until the final establishment of God's reign, the forces of decay will succeed in bringing about our physical death. Most of what the New Testament has to say about forgiveness and healing is spelled out against the background of this cosmic, death-dealing evil, which it identifies as sin. What gives us hope in our prayer struggles is the person and work of Jesus; for through him God's kingdom comes near in a decisive new way. The old Latin hymn says it well.

> O love, how deep, how broad, how high,
> How passing thought and fantasy,
> That God, the Son of God should take
> Our mortal form for mortals' sake.
>
> For us he rose from death again,
> For us he went on high to reign,
> For us he sent his Spirit here
> To guide, to strengthen, and to cheer.[27]

When the New Testament authors instruct us in prayers of forgiveness and healing, they do so with a lively sense of this trinitarian drama. Our prayers may help to bring about comfort or recovery for particular individuals, but their larger purpose is to merge our unique soul force with God's ongoing redemption of the whole world. They are truly a boldness and a blessing in the name of Jesus.

CHAPTER NINE

Out
of the Depths
I Cry

ACCORDING TO THE NEW TESTAMENT, every prayer of faith counts for good at the heavenly throne. Thus it not only bears fruit in ourselves and those for whom we intercede but is also taken up into God's cosmic plan for redemption. Yet this all seems hard to believe in moments of distress when the universe seems to shrink in upon us, when personal survival for the next hour or minute is about the only issue we can face. Here are the chaotic, abysmal depths out of which the psalmist cries, "Lord, hear my voice! Let thy ears be attentive to the voice of my supplications!" (Ps. 130:2). And he must literally *cry*, for God does not seem to be present in a saving way. Prayers out of the depths are declarations of faith, or they would not be uttered at all; but they are also expressions of intense isolation, for as we speak them we feel utterly bereft of divine or human comfort. Our normal systems of maintenance, including our prayer life, suffer a major breakdown, and we are reduced to helplessness. Some believers know only a few of these perilous times (for which they are to be neither praised nor blamed). Others experience frequent assaults or live with the almost constant possibility of their onset, perhaps as a form of addiction. Some of us encounter our desperation on a fairly regular basis at four o'clock in the morning.

Perhaps the first thing we need to say about these trials of faith is that they are not alien to the believers of the Old and New Testaments. The biblical writers assume that God allows them to happen, for reasons that humans may or may not come to grasp, in the very midst of redemption. Paul must be referring to them when he enjoins us to "work out your salvation with fear and trembling" (Phil. 2:12).

As always, the life story of Jesus shows that he understands the worst of our depths, because he has been there himself. When he cried out from the cross, "My God, my God, why have you forsaken me?" he felt an emptiness that we can scarcely begin to comprehend. According to the Gospel writers, his relationship with his Abba was more intimate, more trusting than that of any other human being. But then, as he came to a horrible end, the God who had sent him on his mission was nowhere to be found.

In the vocabulary of traditional Christian spirituality the term most often used for such times of absolute loneliness is "desolation." It comes from the Latin verb *desolare*, which means to abandon or forsake someone. Strangely, it can denote either a wet or a dry experience. Like the psalmist, we may seem to be engulfed by mountains of water and dragged down to the very bottom of the sea. Or we may feel physically and spiritually parched, like someone wandering aimlessly in a vast desert. Clearly the term *desolation* is meant to apply to a wide range of mental and bodily states (depression, grief, pain, nausea, rage, shame, weakness). What they all have in common, however, is the definite sensation that no one—especially God—seems ready or able to rescue us from our peril. Out of these depths we nevertheless pray, sometimes as a kind of reflex action involving no thought at all, sometimes with the dimmest of memories that we once enjoyed communion with this now-absent God. What can we learn from the New Testament about such times of abandonment and (more important) the prayers for help that arise from them?

Desolation

Perhaps the simplest and purest form of desolation is an immediate threat to our physical life. The danger is clear, we must face it alone, and we have only a few seconds in which to speak. As it so often happens, the disciples of Jesus provide us with very believable, nonheroic examples of these crisis prayers. "Save, Lord, we are perishing!" they cried out as great waves from a storm on the Lake of Galilee began to crash over the bow of their small fishing boat (Mt. 8:25). And later, when Peter stepped out on the surface of the water to join Jesus but was paralyzed by fear and began to sink, he had no words at his disposal but "Lord, save me!" (Mt. 14:28–30). On both occasions Jesus responded swiftly, and the crises were averted.[1]

115

Many of us have experienced moments that seemed to be our last, and we cried out in terror to God. But the moments passed, and we recovered. If we remember these times at all, it is probably with some embarrassment about the speed with which our fear displaced our faith. On the other hand, many of us have also known relatives or friends who were clearly at peace with God when they died. God's love was absolutely real to them as they breathed their last, and we knew that theirs was a dying to the Lord (Rom. 14:8). Whatever desperation they may have fought through in the process was now behind them. Like those of us who have had our lives handed back to us, they received a positive answer to their prayers from the depths.

But we all know that most of our desolation happens somewhere in between the poles of a renewed life and a holy death. Furthermore, it must often be borne for long periods of time. Mark, for example, tells of a woman who had suffered from a hemorrhage for twelve years before she met Jesus. And here we must understand that her affliction was not simply a physical one, for in the Judaism of Jesus' day such an issue of blood rendered her ritually unclean and resulted in her ostracism by religiously observant people. No wonder she had spent her whole life's savings in search of a cure (Mk. 5:24–26). Perhaps we can just begin to imagine the vast number of urgent prayers she must have offered during her trial. In this connection we also remember the distraught man who informed Jesus that his epileptic son had had to live with his illness "from childhood [and] it has often cast him into the fire and into the water to destroy him" (Mk. 9:21). He too must have prayed often from his pain and frustration.

When believers wrestle with long-term pain or shame, or with the ever-present possibility that a power beyond their control will move, arbitrarily, to annihilate them, every theory of prayer is put to its ultimate test. A few who suffer in these ways manage to achieve extraordinary tranquillity (Paul calls it the peace that passes all understanding). Yet even they tend to experience some periods of hopelessness when existence itself seems unbearable. And they must cry out against the unfairness of it all. Over against life's absurdity, New Testament believers advance the bold claim that with his own prayer of desolation from the cross Jesus somehow embraces every cry of anguish and molds it into a force for redemption that cannot be resisted, either in heaven or on earth. To articulate how this force operates in the prayers of hurting people, we need to look more closely at what the New Testament says about desolation.

One of the most prominent features of early Christian experience was a loss of patience with the status quo of the world. The new creation in Christ had begun, and believers awaited its consummation with great eagerness. Paul and the congregations to which he ministered knew this discomfort as a groaning for the completion of redemption. The apostle writes to the Romans: "We know that the whole creation has been groaning in labor pains until now; and not only the creation, but we ourselves, who have the first fruits of the Spirit, groan inwardly as we wait for [final] adoption, the redemption of our bodies. . . . The Spirit helps us in our weakness; for we do not know how to pray as we ought, but that very Spirit intercedes with sighs too deep for words" (Rom. 8:22–26, NRSV). We ought not suppose that the earliest believers were *constantly* afflicted by this painful sense of the "not yet." Elsewhere we have seen that their daily life was characterized by much joy. But the turbulent depths must have erupted frequently enough for the apostle to include these words of consolation in a basic statement of the gospel.

Of special significance here is the fact that Paul is talking about a kind of holy frustration that could not be sensed at all if the fruits of the Spirit were not already present in our lives. The result of that goodness is that we want more, for ourselves and the world; and we want it soon. It is probably correct to say that this Spirit-induced dissatisfaction provided the original motivation for Christian social action. But what Paul refers to first in this passage is prayer: not a prayer that we control but one that is initiated by the world's groaning and strengthened by the Spirit's help. Somehow, Paul believes, the whole process will hasten God's restoration of the cosmos. When he adds in verse 28 that "all things work together for good for those who love God," we must understand that this love refers above all to our prayerful insistence that every divine promise come to fruition.

Donald Bloesch calls attention to the frequency with which Christian prayer is linked with something like despair. This is not an absolute despair, which always turns to cynicism, but a hope against hope (Rom. 4:18; 8:24–25), a "heartfelt supplication" that protests against our inability to change things for the better and calls upon God to act swiftly.[2] Out of such praying from the depths comes at least the gift that New Testament writers call *hypomonē* (Rom. 5:3; 8:25; Heb. 10:36; Jas. 1:3; Rev. 1:9, among others). The word is usually translated "patience," but in fact it means something closer to a steadfast waiting that is poised to leap at every opportunity God

117

offers. In his pamphlet *Praying with HIV/AIDS*, Randolph Frew focuses on exactly this kind of resolve. One of his collects begins, "Almighty and Most Merciful God, be present and strengthen us in ministry and service among your people. Chasten our timidity and hasten our response in courage and conviction."[3]

Sometimes desolation feels more like bondage than a loss of power. A surprisingly large portion of the New Testament turns out to have been composed by, or with reference to, people in prison. Paul and his associates are the main examples, but Peter was also incarcerated with some frequency, and on several occasions believers in general are told that they must expect to be deprived of their freedom by public officials (Mk. 13:9–11 and parallels; Jn. 16:2; 1 Pet. 4:12–19; Jas. 2:6). In our own time the prison letters of Martin Luther King, Jr., and Dietrich Bonhoeffer come to mind as archetypal Christian writings.

Yet according to the New Testament writers, physical imprisonment, while highly undesirable, is by no means the worst kind. Instead, paralyzing inner conflicts and the loss of choice in determining our behavior constitute the greatest anguish. After confessing that there are times when he does the very opposite of what he wants to do and knows to be right, Paul cries out, "Wretched man that I am! Who will deliver me from this body of death?" (Rom. 7:24).[4]

Here we must think of the experience our society calls addiction. Perhaps we have gone overboard, particularly in the United States, by labeling practically everything that troubles our inner life an addictive behavior or addictive process. One begins to tire of the burgeoning self-help literature on this topic. Yet we know that the best of it describes something real. There are in fact forms of dependence on chemical substances or types of human relationships that result, eventually, in the death of our spirits and/or bodies. To cry out from the depths of such bondage we do not have to wait until we bottom out. God does not insist on our total devastation as a precondition for the answering of our prayers. Psychiatrist Gerald May echoes the New Testament gospel when he tells us that we can even turn to God while we are engaged in addictive behaviors, though sometimes all we can manage to say is "See? This is who I am."[5] Our desire to be seen and known by God in our worst moments amounts to a cry for help that will not be refused. Those who never give voice to their anguish are in worse shape. Saint Augustine says, "How deep in the deep are they who do not cry out of the deep."[6]

It is true that prayer itself can become an addiction. May offers some guidance from his own life to help us separate the wheat from the chaff: "I could tell when this [addiction] happened, because the prayer was not sincere; it was not heartfelt; it was routinized and automatic. . . . I made [it] into my own private technique that eclipsed both God and others. All I could see was myself. . . . Grace was no longer in my vision."[7] May would be the first to admit that we cannot extricate ourselves from this kind of trap by an act of will. What we can do, because God always grants us the power of *hypomonē*, is to watch and wait for the barely opened door, for the slightly bigger space inside us that enables us to receive the Spirit's help.

One more insight from the New Testament may be offered here as an aid to our understanding of addiction. Paul tells us that whenever we cry "Abba" with conviction, it is because the Holy Spirit has prompted our spirits or true selves to do so. Of this Go-Between God the apostle says, "You did not receive the spirit of slavery to fall back again into fear, but you have received the Spirit of adoption" (Rom. 8:15; see also Gal. 4:1–7, where he makes the identical point). Why did Paul take pains to emphasize this? I think it was because he knew that the everyday, "normal" spirit of this age (Is it greed, or deprivation? Or both?) *does* enslave and that we must continue to live in its atmosphere for the rest of our days (Rom. 8:5–8; 2 Cor. 4:4). Authentic freedom, granted through the Spirit and realized in our consciousness when we call God Abba, must walk very close to its opposite. Freedom can degenerate into fear and bondage almost instantaneously when we forget that we are God's own children. Of course Paul was not writing to addicts when he addressed the church in Rome. He was talking about what he considered to be ordinary Christian existence. But his words have a curiously modern ring for anyone who struggles against unhealthy dependencies.[8]

Sometimes our desolation takes the shape of a profound loss coupled with extended grieving. Often we think of such losses in terms of a loved one whom we shall never see again this side of the grave (Jn. 11:32–33; Acts 20:36). But they may also include our jobs, our native land, and even our operative self-images. When Peter heard the cock crow and could no longer hide from the fact that he had betrayed his master, he "went out and wept bitterly"—chiefly for himself (Mt. 26:75). We might say that he had suffered an irreversible loss of innocence. Something analogous happens with Neville Aysgarth, the ambitious clergyman in Susan Howatch's novel *Ultimate Prizes*.

Forced, finally, to confront the disaster of his second marriage and his subsequent tailspin into alcoholism, he could no longer think of himself as a good person, righteously pursuing the noble goals that God had set before him. Now he lived in a wasteland of loss and shame, "where there was no convenient exit marked salvation and no convenient signpost directing one to the spiritual presence of Christ."[9] Of course God wants us to cry out in these moments too, but usually our sense of self has withered to such an extent that we need the help of others who still believe in us and are willing to intercede on our behalf.

On occasion our losses are complicated by a shattering disillusionment. For months after his wife, Joy, had died of cancer C. S. Lewis could hardly bear to raise up his thoughts and words to God. In *A Grief Observed*, his diarylike account of these harsh times, he wrote: "What chokes every prayer and every hope is the memory of all the prayers [Joy] and I offered and all the hopes we had. Not hopes raised merely by our own wishful thinking; hopes encouraged, even forced upon us by false diagnoses, by X-ray photographs, by strange remissions, by one temporary recovery that might have ranked as a miracle. Step by step we were 'led up the garden path.' Time after time, when He seemed most gracious He was really preparing the next torture."[10] During this period Lewis's abiding temptation was not, as we might suppose, to give up his belief in God altogether but to conclude that God had emptied the word *goodness* of all its normal content. In his eyes God was rapidly becoming a "Cosmic Sadist," who delighted in knocking the props out from those who had entrusted themselves to divine mercy.[11]

Eventually Lewis was enabled to give up this loathsome picture of God. But the transformation came slowly, by small increments, and the image of the One who can help us only by hurting us badly never quite faded away. It seems that our own praying in the midst of loss is seldom curative on its own; or at any rate we cannot feel the cure for some time. We need the touching and caring of others. We need to hear the actual words of their prayers in concert with our inarticulate groans.

There is one more form of desolation that we ought to consider. Most of us (I speak for myself) are probably not advanced enough in our faith to have encountered its full force. But it stands in the New Testament record for those who must suffer it, and it should not be ignored. What I mean is the experience of feeling betrayed by God at a critical point in a mission to which we believe God has called us. When Jesus cried out, "My God, my God, why have you forsaken me?" (Mk. 15:34, NIV), he must have thought that his entire ministry, so richly inspired and blessed by the Holy Spirit, was now crumbling into ruins. It is not only loss and grief and doubt (and anger?) that are being expressed here. It is also the total bewilderment of God's Son, who was sure he knew his Abba's will and had submitted to it just a few hours earlier at great personal cost. Jesus had never found it difficult to sense God's presence—until now. On the cross, at this terrible moment, he felt absolutely abandoned by the One to whom he had offered up everything. Was it God's displeasure with him that had caused this withdrawal? Or was it God's own failure in the moment of truth?

Today the great majority of the world's population lives without a vivid experience of companionship with God. This is true even for most Christians. So why, we may ask, should we look to Jesus' suffering as unique or instructive? Here we enter into staggering questions about substitutionary atonement and the resurrection; and we can dare to say only a few things. But some details do emerge with clarity from the New Testament record. For one thing, the earliest believers were united in their conviction that Jesus' loving presence with them after his death signaled God's vindication of everything Jesus had said and done and suffered during his lifetime. Furthermore, because Jesus had returned to them, to the people who had betrayed or misunderstood him, they were led to conclude that his innocent death had somehow accomplished their restitution. Later, with the Spirit's guidance, this embryo theory of atonement grew to include all of humanity. Taken together, these evolving thoughts demonstrate that early on in the New Testament church the events surrounding Jesus' death had acquired a special holiness and a special power to sanctify the lives of all who accepted them as true.

Jesus alone suffered a total separation from God in the midst of his total devotion to God's reign. But the resurrection shows that whenever we struggle through something akin to Jesus' loneliness by committing ourselves to the kingdom, he is right beside us as the pioneer of our salvation (Heb. 6:20; 12:2). When we can only groan in our moments of desperation, his cry from the cross takes over. As we suggested earlier, a profound time of communion with God would have to precede any real feeling of betrayal by God. Yet the first is not inevitably followed by the second. Perhaps this extreme form of desolation will never afflict us. But if it does, even on a small scale, we have an advocate at the throne of grace who also lives in our hearts.

Ways of the Cross

Some Christians can honestly say that God does not call them, regularly, into the wasteland of desolation. But there is one kind of dwelling in the depths that no disciple of Jesus can avoid, or would want to, and that is the sharing of his cross. The command to take up our cross and follow Jesus is issued to everyone (Mk. 8:34–36 and parallels). What does this mean, and what types of prayer can we expect to be associated with it?

The commandment itself is quite open-ended and cannot refer only to physical death for the sake of Jesus. In Luke's version of the saying we are bidden to take up our cross *daily*, as if it were something inside us instead of a life-threatening situation imposed from without (9:23). It is always *our* cross, unique to us. It is never exactly the same as Jesus suffering, though it must be joined with that ("Follow me"). From the very beginning, the word *cross*, as applied to believers, must have taken on a metaphorical sense. Some believers were indeed called to suffer a literal martyrdom, but most found themselves united with Christ's sufferings in a variety of other ways.

One of these was their extraordinary *koinonia*, granted through baptism, with other believers in the Body of Christ. In every congregation each person was to weep with those who wept (Rom. 12:15), for "if one member suffers, all suffer together" (1 Cor. 12:26). Believers were also enjoined to bear one another's burdens—specifically the burdens created by the other person's transgressions (Gal. 6:1–2)—and work for reconciliation between alienated disciples (Mt. 18:15–20). Obviously this kind of activity created emotional pain and required a great deal of intercessory prayer, though not, it is clear, by superiors on behalf of inferiors ("Restore him or her in a spirit of gentleness. Look to yourself, lest you too be tempted"; Gal. 6:1).

Other modes of sharing the cross involved ostracism by one's friends and associates, sometimes with the loss of reputation, income, or property (Phil. 1:28–30; 1 Thess. 2:14; 1 Pet. 3:8–4:19; Heb. 10:32–34; Jas. 2:6–7). In addition, some believers experienced tragic divisions in their families (Mk. 13:12) and a separation from their spouses (1 Cor. 7:12–16). Elisabeth Schüssler Fiorenza is probably correct in hypothesizing that for male heads of household in the ancient world, baptism would have resulted in a diminished social status.[12] All of these situations can be seen as life in the depths if we suppose that they were accompanied by significant grief over what had to be sacrificed for the sake of Christ. Under such circumstances prayer would take the form of repeated self-offerings (see Rom. 12:1–2), quite possibly mixed with mourning. The sorrow would be coming not so much from outside forces as from one's choice to join the Christian movement. For most early believers, baptism itself amounted to a socioeconomic taking up of the cross.

But many New Testament Christians were also visited by crucifixions of a more mysterious sort. These seemed to carry with them an element of divinity that produced inner struggles between an individual and God or Christ over the very nature of faith. Here is Paul, recounting a watershed incident from his life for the benefit of his Corinthian readers:

> I know a man in Christ [i.e., himself] who fourteen years ago was caught up to the third heaven—whether in the body or out of the body I do not know, God knows. And I know that this man was caught up into Paradise—whether in the body or out of the body I do not know, God knows—and he heard things that cannot be told, which humans may not utter. On behalf of this man I will boast. . . . And to keep me from being too elated by the abundance of revelations, a thorn was given me in the flesh, a messenger of Satan, to harass me, to keep me from being too elated. Three times I besought the Lord about this, that it should leave me; but he said to me, "My grace is sufficient for you, for my power is made perfect in weakness." (2 Cor. 12:2–9)

Unlike Jesus on the cross, Paul never lost contact with God or Christ during his time of anguish. His problem was that he was all too aware of a divine presence, an incomprehensible God who not only granted visions and revelations but also caused (or allowed to happen) a wound that virtually took back what was given.

In Paul's case the illness or physical deformity that befell him threatened to compromise his work as a missionary by broadcasting that his gospel was not powerful enough to heal its proclaimer. We can understand why he protested to the Lord in three protracted seasons of prayer. Exactly when and how he heard the voice of the risen Christ he does not tell us. It is quite possible that he received this answer even at the beginning of his supplications, but could not accept it. Whatever happened, he was eventually led to discern a great truth about the cross and to make it a hallmark of his ministry. To share Christ's suffering, especially in the form of particular *stigmata* (see Gal 6:17, where the Greek word occurs with this physical connotation), is not, finally, a deprivation, no matter how painful it may be; it is an empowerment with the grace of God that subverts evil.

The experience of power in the midst of sharing Christ's sufferings is not a side issue for Paul but an integral part of his gospel message (Rom. 8:12–17; 1 Cor. 2:1–5; 2 Cor. 1:8–10; 4:7–12; Phil. 3:8–11). Although he does not expect every believer to visit the third heaven or suffer the indignity of a thorn in the flesh, he does think that all his brothers and sisters in the Lord will find their true peace and freedom and joy, as well as their special gifts of the Spirit for ministry, intertwined with the taking up of Christ's cross. This, to Paul, means a constant dying with Christ to all manifestations of the flesh within us that work to undermine the reign of God (Rom. 8:9–13; Gal. 5:16–26). Much of our communion with the death of Jesus is assumed to be conscious (2 Cor. 4:7–12; Phil. 3:7–16) and thus requires prayer from the depths of our existence. After all, to have one's old self stripped away and replaced by a new one is no casual matter (Col. 3:9–10).

An extraordinary reference to this renewal, which almost certainly describes a kind of contemplative prayer, occurs in one of Paul's letters to Corinth: "While all of us, with unveiled faces, behold the glory of the Lord as in a mirror, we are being transformed in accord with the very image we see, from glory to glory" (2 Cor. 3:18, my translation).[13] This sounds like an altogether pleasant and desirable mystical experience. But when we take into account Paul's insistence that we never meet Christ apart from his cross, we begin to realize that any reception of his glorious image will plunge us simultaneously into ever more intricate configurations of his atoning death. The cross and the crown enter us together as we behold the face of the Lord.

To what might this beholding correspond in our devotional practice today? There is some indication in the context of 2 Corinthians 3 that the mirror Paul refers to means certain portions of the Old Testament, as interpreted by the stories of Jesus' life, death, and resurrection.[14] One would begin to see Jesus' face by quietly meditating on these and allowing the images that appeared to enlarge one's communion with Christ in the inmost self (2 Cor. 4:6). Today we might also fix our attention on representational pictures of Jesus (icons, crucifixes, paintings), as long as these are not allowed to block the visionary richness that comes to us through our inner beholding. We need to understand that "seeing" Jesus from the depths may well surprise or even shock us.[15]

Usually a beholding of the Lord's glory (i.e., his luminous beauty, power, and goodness somehow combined) does not happen when we are crying out to God in the midst of desperate need. Yet sometimes that crying becomes a prelude to contemplation. It is a painful but effective way of emptying ourselves, of declaring ourselves at the end of our rope. Jesus teaches us that we must ask, seek, and knock, sometimes almost violently (like the importunate widow). But then comes a time of letting go so that we can discern God's answer. It took Paul three seasons of anxious petitionary prayer to reach this point. I think he could not have written about the contemplation of Jesus' glory that was available to all believers without first undergoing the personal traumas reported in 2 Cor. 12:1–9. Sometimes we too must hammer on the Lord's door; we must scream out from our depths. And then we shall be ready to hear another sound, from the outside or from a hidden place within us: "Listen! I am standing at the door, knocking; if you hear my voice and open the door, I will come in to you and eat with you, and you with me" (Rev. 3:20, NRSV). The promised meal is a symbol of many things: repentance, reconciliation, communion, and abundance. All of that and more will happen when we meet Jesus face to face in the depths.

Two more facets of the prayerful transformation referred to in 2 Cor. 3:18 deserve our attention. First, the mirror terminology ought to be taken rather literally. We ourselves are reflected in what we discover. Indeed, Paul believed, with many of his contemporaries, that we become what we see. (When applied to our habitual peering into TV screens, computer terminals, and video games, this thought strikes me as frightening.) Thus, when we behold Jesus through the mirror of the gospel, we also see ourselves. We look upon our own faces, blessed and honored by his, held in his loving gaze. And we see ourselves taking on his identity, accepting his cross in our own unique way, and receiving along with it his power to overcome evil with good. This is not a loss of self, for we always retain the freedom to remove ourselves from the process. Instead, the prayer of transformation is a gift of the liberating Spirit (see 2 Cor. 3:17–18) that opens us up to becoming *like* Jesus, to joining his family as younger sisters and brothers (Rom. 8:29; 1 Jn. 3:2).

Second, although we noted above that the images of Jesus surfacing in our contemplation can often surprise us, we have not reckoned with the Lord's freedom to withdraw his image altogether. His face may disappear, though he himself does not. What he tells us then is: "Give up your reliance on images for now. Trust me as I lead you through the void to new ways of perceiving me." If the apophatic (imageless) figure of Christ calls to us, we may initially cry out as if we were being forsaken. But this is not the same thing as desolation.[16] It is an experience of the depths that Paul refers to as "forgetting what lies behind [including that which has been most precious to us] and straining forward to what lies ahead . . . toward the upward call of God in Christ Jesus" (Phil. 3:13–14). This journey too can be painful, can seem, at the beginning, to be only loss. But the sacrifice will turn out to be of no consequence when measured against "the surpassing worth of knowing Christ Jesus [our] Lord," *really* knowing him (see Phil. 3:7–10). Rowan Williams writes, with regard to Christian prayer, that it relies on specific images of Jesus, "yet . . . encourages a deep and fierce suspicion of words, images, particular kinds of experience." In fact, Williams concludes that all prayer inspired by Jesus sooner or later "insists on the need to press on in darkness and formlessness in an absence of obvious meaning (let alone of gratification)."[17] Every step on this road is a form of life in the depths, a way of the cross that brings pain. But it is at the same time a way of holiness, replete with blessings and the praise of God.

Rivers of Living Water

When the depths are experienced as desolation, we may feel engulfed by raging waters or lost in a desert wasteland. There is too much wetness or dryness to sustain life. But when they are joined to the cross of Jesus, the depths become an altogether different sort of reality. According to John, Jesus promises that a singular prophecy by Isaiah will come to fulfillment in every believer: "Out of [each] heart shall flow rivers of living water." And then the evangelist adds, "This he said about the Spirit" (7:38–39). Here is an opening of the depths that threatens neither deluge nor desiccation. The Holy Spirit comes to us as a flowing stream of irrigation, in just the right amount. And it keeps on flowing, from the heart of our being, where Jesus himself has placed it (Acts 2:33; Jn. 14:6–7; Gal. 4:6). This image leads us back once again to the cameo passage from Romans that expresses almost everything that needs to be said about early Christian prayer: "When we cry, 'Abba! Father!' it is the very Spirit, bearing witness with our spirit that we are children of God, and if children, then heirs, heirs of God and fellow heirs of Christ, provided we suffer with him in order that we may also be glorified with him" (8:15–17). Ultimately, our cry from the depths is one of delight and freedom, not anguish.

True to form, the Holy Spirit acts as Go-Between God to sanctify our afflictions, to show us Christ's power for goodness hidden in their midst, and to grant us a share of his life-giving force. It is the Spirit who sustains our transformation in accord with Christ's image (2 Cor. 3:18c), sometimes with our willing cooperation, sometimes in the midst of our protests. We cannot know all the details of God's laboring within us, but of our destiny there is no doubt: "'What no eye has seen, nor ear heard, nor the human heart conceived, what God has prepared for those who love him'—these things God has revealed to us through the Spirit; for the Spirit searches everything, even the depths of God" (1 Cor. 2:9–10).

What are these depths of God? Above all, they are the mysterious workings of mercy that draw us back to our Source no matter how far we stray (Rom. 11:30–36). The author of Ephesians prays that his readers will be "strengthened in your inner being with power through [God's] Spirit, and that Christ may dwell in your hearts through faith, as you are being rooted and grounded in love . . . that you may have the power to comprehend, with all the saints, what is the breadth and length and height and depth, and to know the love of Christ that surpasses knowledge" (3:16–18, NRSV). The Greek word for "comprehend" (*katalambano*) is a strong one. It means not so much "understand" as "grasp to oneself." Here, as in 2 Cor. 3:18, we become what we behold.

This passage from Ephesians also echoes the predominant message of the New Testament that the entire Trinity works in our depths to strengthen our communion with the divine compassion. This happens in prayer, over and over, as the Holy Spirit pours God's love out into our hearts (Rom. 5:5). Following the lead of Bernard Lonergan,

William Johnston aptly characterizes Christian prayer as "being in love."[18] He means by this—correctly interpreting the New Testament, I believe—that when our praying is inspired and upheld by the love of God, we shall in fact *be*. Our thinking, feeling, and acting will acquire real substance, for we shall be living as daughters and sons of God. In the depths of God there is no diminishment of our humanity but rather its fulfillment.

Gerald May uses the words *dignity* and *spaciousness* to describe our encounter with those depths.[19] We are honored by the profundity of God's love and given a new liberty to move about, to choose life over death and (especially in the midst of an addictive process) to cast off the bondage of old behaviors. In New Testament terminology we gain "access" through Christ to God's amazing grace (Rom. 5:2). Because of our great High Priest, we may approach the throne of grace boldly (Heb. 4:14), with the assurance that God will never turn a deaf ear to our requests. Again and again those who cry out to God from the dregs of their soul find blessings for their life and ministry that are far more abundant than all they can ask or think.

Out of the depths I cry. It is clear that believers of the New Testament era passed through virtually every point on the spectrum of life's trials. Despite their newfound freedom in Christ, they were not always happy or tranquil. The same Paul who urged his readers to "rejoice in the Lord always" and to "have no anxiety about anything" (Phil. 4:4–6) also confessed that he and some of his apostolic associates, imprisoned in Asia, had once felt "so utterly, unbearably crushed that we despaired of life itself" (2 Cor. 1:9). Christian faith considers no physical or emotional state to be incompatible with God's grace. Nor does Christian prayer. From the Hebrew Scriptures and from Jesus himself the earliest believers learned that crying out from their depths was a legitimate, even noble, expression of confidence in their Abba. Jesus himself had once been where they now were; in fact he was always there, praying along with their prayer. In his cross even the depths became holy. This did not mean that all of their suffering and frustration were removed but that each petitioner, in his or her own way, could honestly say: "I have been heard. Christ's power is being perfected in my weakness, and all shall be well." Today when we cry from the depths of our being, we may trust that God's ways have not changed.

Prayer
in the
Church's Worship

IN CRYING OUT FROM THE DEPTHS, each of us prays as an individual. God knows us, loves us, and answers each of us one by one, just as we are. By contrast, the common worship of the church requires us to move beyond our individuality for the sake of the whole Body of Christ; and so it may seem to stand at odds with our personal prayers, or even to devalue them. But in fact it does not. One of the bedrock convictions of the New Testament writers is that our most heartfelt conversations with God and Jesus "in secret" (Mt. 6:5–6) will continue to take place, *must* continue to take place, in the public liturgies of the church. We cannot truly pray with others in Christ apart from a personal communion with him. Sometimes this communion helps us contribute to the worship of the assembly. Sometimes it must be awakened or renewed by the praying of our sisters and brothers. How such exchanges occur and what they mean for the life of the whole church is the subject of this chapter. We shall examine it under three headings: (1) rhythm, which refers to the circumstances, times, and postures of our corporate prayer; (2) focus, which has to do with the ways our attention becomes fixed on God and our neighbors; and (3) mission, which describes the church's transition from specific times of prayer to everyday action in the world.

Rhythm

We may begin by recalling that for the New Testament writers corporate prayer includes all those moments when only two or three believers, or just a few more, gather in the name of Jesus (Mt. 18:20). These occasions are quite frequent. The passage from Matthew, probably a summary statement, may refer to a time of prayer during which two people are attempting to overcome their mutual aliena-tion (18:15d), perhaps with the aid of a mediator from the church. Or it may describe a meeting of church representatives who are asking God to guide their decisions and ratify their actions (18:18). In any case verse 19 ("if two of you agree about anything they ask . . . ") is quite open-ended and probably applies to all believers. Paul's mission-ary travels, often with just one or two companions, provided many such occasions for common prayer. The apostle also expected believ-ing husbands and wives to pray together in private, and even to sus-pend sexual relations during particularly intense seasons of prayer (1 Cor. 7:5; see also 1 Pet. 3:7).[1]

Worship groups of a somewhat larger size are referred to in the fol-lowing passages:

> And day by day, attending the temple together, and breaking bread in their homes, [the first believers in Jerusalem] partook of food with glad and generous hearts, praising God and having favor with all the people [Acts 2:46]. Now in the church at Antioch there were prophets and teachers, Barnabas, Simeon who was called Niger, Lucius of Cyrene, Manaen a member of the court of Herod the tetrarch, and Saul. While they were worshiping the Lord and fasting, the Holy Spirit said, "Set apart Barnabas and Saul" [Acts 13:1–2]. Are there any among you sick? They should call for the elders of the church and have them pray over them [Jas. 5:14, NRSV; see also Acts 20:17–38].

The first passage from Acts is one of many New Testament witnesses to what we now call the house church. This fluid institution may have included as many as 120 people (Acts 1:15; 2:1–2; here the house should probably be thought of as adjoining a large, semipublic court-yard). But given what archaeologists tell us about the typical size of private dwellings in the Greco-Roman period, it was usually much smaller. We may guess that the average size came to about 20 or 30 people.[2] If Acts 13:1 is meant to be a complete listing of the people assembled for prayer on this occasion, what we have is a group of five leaders meeting apart from the main body of the church. The author of James gives us a similar picture when he refers to a delegation of elders who visit the home of a sick individual in order to pray

(5:13–15). The account in Acts 15 of an apostolic council deliberating over the status of Gentile believers seems to assume a somewhat larger group of officials, along with the visitors Paul and Barnabas (vv. 6, 12), but not the whole church of Jerusalem. Although the story contains no explicit reference to prayer, there is strong inferential evidence (see "Mission" below) that Luke assumed its presence as an integral part of the decision-making process.

Nearly all the references we have to gatherings of the whole church for worship envision events that were scheduled for a particular time and were subject to repetition.[3] In some cases these gatherings appear to mesh with the Jewish liturgical calendar. Not only did the earliest believers in Jerusalem continue to frequent the temple for regular hours of worship (Acts 2:46; 3:1); they also commemorated the feast of Pentecost at home fifty days after the crucifixion (Acts 2:1) and probably continued to observe a modified version of it in subsequent years to honor the Spirit's first visitation of their worship (see Acts 20:6 and 1 Cor. 16:8).[4] We must further suppose that many Jewish Christians kept up their observance of the Sabbath, although no New Testament texts witness to this. Better attested are assemblies for worship on the first day of the week, Sunday, the day of resurrection (Acts 20:7 and probably 1 Cor. 16:2).[5]

With regard to the hours at which New Testament believers gathered for prayer, we have only a little evidence. Acts 20:7–12 recounts an evening service during which bread was broken in connection with a discourse by Paul; 1 Corinthians 11 provides some details of the Lord's Supper as it was being celebrated by Paul's readers and presupposes a time at the close of the day. Paul Bradshaw calls attention to the probability of some corporate prayer during the night hours: "New Testament references to prayer 'night and day' (Lk. 18:7; 1 Thess. 3:10; 1 Tim. 5:5) would seem to imply its existence. . . . It is not impossible that the custom existed from the earliest days of the Church, especially in the light of [evidence] that this pattern may already have been followed at Qumran and elsewhere in Judaism at this time."[6] The point here is that rhythms of corporate worship were beginning to emerge quite early. They were not the same from church to church, so we must be careful not to see a uniformity of practice where none existed.[7] Nevertheless, as communication grew between churches in the large urban centers of the Roman world, forms of worship that were common to most believers did begin to take shape. Already in the 50s, Paul could cite liturgical etiquette that was held to be normative "in all the churches of the saints" (1 Cor. 14:33).

What can we say about the kinds of prayer that predominated in these early gatherings? And what, if anything, can we learn about the bodily postures or movements that accompanied them? Given the Jewish precedents for prayer at rites of purification and at meals, we may hypothesize that early Christian equivalents grew up around baptism and the Eucharist, even though the New Testament itself gives us no undisputed examples of these.[8] What we do have are clear references to corporate prayers of intercession (Acts 12:5; 2 Cor. 9:14; Eph. 6:18; Col. 4:2; 1 Tim. 2:1–2; Heb. 13:18) and petition (Mk. 11:24–25; Acts 4:24–31; Phil. 4:6), including specific requests for forgiveness and healing (Mk. 11:25; Acts 4:30; Jas. 5:13–16). But what we encounter most often, and in great abundance, are allusions to praise and thanksgiving in the assemblies of believers. Jesus himself sets this tone by telling his followers: "When you [plural] pray, say 'Father, hallowed be thy name'" (Lk. 11:1). And the whole of apostolic literature seems to follow in procession (Acts 2:1–11, 47; 4:24; 10:46; 11:18; 13:2; 16:25; 27:25; 1 Cor. 10:16, 31; 14:16–17; 2 Cor. 8:5; 9:11–15; Eph. 5:18–20; Phil. 4:4–6; Col. 3:16–17; 4:2; 1 Thess. 5:18; Heb. 12:18–29; 13:15–16; 1 Pet. 2:9; 4:9–11; Rev. 7:9–14; chapters 14–15).

Readers who recall our earlier inquiry into the "heartbeat" of praise and thanksgiving will not be surprised by this phenomenon of overflow. But here we need to reemphasize its significance, for it appears to be the case that such prayers formed the very basis of the various New Testament liturgies, however and whenever they occurred. In effect, praise and thanksgiving constituted the common prayer of the church. On many occasions other activities must have preceded or followed, but a reverent acknowledgment of God's presence and the verbal magnification of that presence seem to have been absolutely essential to corporate worship.[9]

Today, when we survey the diverse forms of public worship practiced by Christian churches around the world, we find many services dominated by talk about God. This usually issues from a few leaders and is directed to a more or less passive audience. Churches in which the majority of the worshipers are moved, with some frequency, to offer their personal praise to God aloud may now be in the minority. But their numbers are growing. The base notes of New Testament prayer have begun to sound again as believers rediscover what it means for the Spirit to lead them in prayer.

What can we say about bodily postures of prayer in the New Testament church? Old Testament practices, which must have influenced the Judaism of Jesus' day, allowed for both standing or kneeling; but in both positions "the supplicant's hands were lifted up and spread out toward heaven."[10] This practice seems to be the rule in 1 Tim. 2:1, where the author advises believers to pray by "lifting holy hands without anger or quarreling." Kneeling is the prayer posture referred to most frequently in the New Testament, so frequently in fact that the Greek word *proskyneo* ("bend the knee") becomes virtually synonymous with the general term for worship (see Mt. 2:2, 8; 28:17; Jn. 4:20; Acts 7:43, among others). Bradshaw notes that in the whole New Testament "there is only one explicit reference to standing [for prayer] (Mk. 11:25), although other passages seem to imply this posture (Mt. 14:19; Mk. 6:41; Lk. 9:16; Mk. 7:34; Jn. 11:41; 17:1)."[11]

Additional kinds of bodily movement during prayer can be glimpsed or inferred. The contemplation of Christ's face in 2 Cor. 3:18, which may describe a corporate practice ("And we all, with unveiled face . . ."), could have involved an upward turn of the head toward "the glory of the Lord." On the other hand, rabbinic texts indicate that those who wished to prepare themselves for a vision of God's heavenly throne were to sit with their heads bent between their knees.[12] It is clear that some form of prayer accompanied the distribution of the elements during the Eucharist ("Examine yourselves, and only then eat of the bread and drink of the cup"; 1 Cor. 11:28, NRSV) and may have been manifested in a posture of humility. The "holy kiss" (Rom. 16:16; 1 Cor. 16:20; 2 Cor. 13:12; 1 Thess. 5:16; 1 Pet. 5:14) with which believers were to greet one another appears to have been a kind of embrace, like our passing of the peace, but perhaps it was also an act of blessing. A more formal laying on of hands was practiced in connection with prayers for healing and commissions to ministry (Jas. 5:14; Acts 13:3; 14:23; 1 Tim. 4:14). Finally, the visions of the prophet John in Revelation portray a heavenly worship marked by the waving of palm branches (7:9) and a dramatic gesture of obeisance at the throne of God ("The four living creatures and the twenty four elders fell down before the Lamb, each holding a harp, and with golden bowls full of incense, which are the prayers of the saints"; 5:8). Whether or not these images reflect real practices in the early church is impossible to tell (but see 1 Cor. 14:25). Much of what is set forth here must remain in the realm of speculation.

Yet one feature of corporate prayer in the New Testament pushes us toward interpreting the typical service as a time of exuberance with a considerable amount of physical activity. What I mean is the widespread custom of singing praises ("And do not get drunk with wine . . . ; but be filled with the Spirit, addressing one another in psalms and hymns and spiritual songs, singing and making melody to the Lord with all your heart"; Eph. 5:18–19; see also Acts 16:25; 1 Cor. 14:15, 26; Col. 3:16, and the numerous passages that have been identified as actual hymns of the church to God or the risen Christ).[13] Some of these musical offerings would have been Old Testament psalms or adaptations of them, but others were spontaneous songs of the Spirit (1 Cor. 14:15). Most likely they were accompanied by gestures of the upper body and maybe even by dancelike movements (note the close connection between praise and leaping in Lk. 1:39–55; 6:35; Acts 3:8).[14] Although we need to guard against imposing the image of a modern charismatic prayer meeting upon our historical sources, there is much there to invite the comparison. Paul's critique of the confusion that he perceives to be regnant in worship at Corinth does not include directives to create a somber atmosphere. Instead the apostle simply tells his readers to preserve a sufficient degree of order and intelligibility for the church to be "built up."[15] In Paul's view, quenching the Spirit is the very opposite of true worship (1 Thess. 5:19–20).

Don Saliers underscores a basic feature of New Testament prayer when he observes that the corporate worship of Christians is intrinsically musical. Thus we must constantly attune ourselves "to the pace, the rhythms, and the sound of the hidden music of the liturgy."[16] Saliers does not mean that we are to be constantly singing or performing on instruments but that our hearts must join with the deeper resonances of praise that rise up from our orders of service, even when they are spoken. Yet this happens, he correctly says, only when we can find Christ at the center of our assembly. To that prayerful work of fixing our attention on the Lord we now turn.

Focus

There is a great deal of biblical language available to us for interpreting the corporate worship of the church. Clearly we are to think of it as a pulsating circle of praise and thanksgiving. But we may also see the praying church as a workshop of mutual love and upbuilding (especially in 1 Corinthians 11–14). Gail Ramshaw puts it well when she says that the "eucharistic logic" of Christian worship is to form in us "the mind of praise and the habit of service."[17] Alternatively, we can call upon language from the Gospels to speak of corporate prayers for the kingdom, which will always include our readiness to welcome its appearance precisely in worship (see chapter 4 above). Or we can speak of corporate prayer as a special opportunity for the manifestation of spiritual gifts (*charismata*), not only the spectacular ones like prophecy, tongues, and healing but also those in a lower emotional key like utterances of wisdom and knowledge, administrative acts, generous contributions, the faithful care of the sick and dying, and advocacy for those deprived of their rights (see 1 Corinthians 12 and Rom. 12:1–8).[18] And finally there is the likelihood of conversion. Some of us may look askance at Christians who insist upon ending their sermons or prayers with an "altar call." But Paul believes quite strongly that when outsiders attend a service of the church they may expect to find themselves "convicted" by the prophecies of believers, with the result that "the secrets of their heart are disclosed; and so falling on their face, they will worship God and declare that God is really among you" (1 Cor. 14:25, my adaptation of the RSV). Although Paul here refers to visiting unbelievers, it is also appropriate for us "insiders" to undergo such experiences again and again. Prayer with others often becomes an occasion for expressing our discovery that God is actually present.

And God is *actively* present. Paul presents this trinitarian sketch of how the divine energy shapes our corporate worship: "Now there are varieties of gifts, but the same Spirit; and there are varieties of service, but the same Lord [Jesus]; and there are varieties of working, but it is the same God who inspires them all in everyone. To each is [constantly] given the manifestation of the Spirit for the common good" (1 Cor. 12:4–7). Prayer under these circumstances means that each of us is to be eagerly desiring and seeking a manifestation of the gifts that will contribute most to the upbuilding of our sisters and brothers (1 Cor. 14:1, 12–13). Clearly the praying of the individual is crucial to the integrity of corporate worship.

This holds true at a quite elementary level in that our praying with others must always be at the same time a personal act of "looking to Jesus, the pioneer and perfecter of our faith" (Heb. 12:2). On at least three occasions our New Testament witnesses portray the figure of Jesus praying in the midst of the church. The high-priestly prayer of

John 17 shows us Jesus the Intercessor, who is both with the disciples on the night of the last supper but also, somehow, already in heaven (vv. 1, 11, 12, 24). For Johannine believers this picture was an expression of their confidence that Jesus continued to be present among them, through the Spirit, as they gathered for worship. To overhear his prayer for them was to join that prayer and open themselves to the answer (see esp. vv. 21–24). In two other passages we see Jesus not so much interceding for believers as arousing them to prayer by his own acts of praise. This is how his voice was heard: "Therefore I will praise thee [God] among the Gentiles, and sing to thy name. . . . Rejoice, O Gentiles, with his people [the Jews]. . . . Praise the Lord, all Gentiles, and let all the peoples praise him" (Rom. 15:9–11). "I will proclaim thy [God's] name to my brothers and sisters, in the midst of the congregation [ekklesia] I will praise thee. . . . I will put my trust in him [God]. . . . Here am I, and the children God has given me" (Heb. 2:12–13). These are extraordinary icons of the risen Christ,[19] for they allow us to see him as our worship leader, praying the words of the Hebrew Scriptures so that we can join in.[20] Such a picture can only mean that there was an acute awareness of Jesus' presence in the assemblies of the early believers. Sometimes they actually saw him in visions (Jn. 1:51) or heard his voice through the words of prophecy. Sometimes they discerned him in the Lord's Supper. On many levels they were firmly convinced that he dwelt among them, guiding, comforting, exhorting, and eliciting their devotion.

All of this gives new substance to the phrase "through Jesus Christ our Lord." We offer our supplications quite literally *through* him or *in* his name (i.e., his power and presence) because he stands at the center of our worship. Some such understanding must have given rise to passages like the following:

For all the promises of God find their Yes in [Christ]. That is why we utter the Amen through him to the glory of God [2 Cor. 1:20]. Be filled with the Spirit . . . singing and making melody to the Lord with all your heart, always and for everything giving thanks in the name of our Lord Jesus Christ to God the Father [Eph. 5:18–20]. God has highly exalted him and bestowed on him the name which is above every name, that at the name of Jesus every knee should bow . . . and every tongue confess that Jesus Christ is Lord, to the glory of God the Father [Phil. 2:9–11].

To acknowledge Jesus as God's Yes and our Lord, to pray in his name, is to join his saving work for the glory of God.

How can our corporate prayer today help us move toward this kind of focus on Jesus? One possible answer is for us to allot time in our worship for contemporary stories of Jesus' work in our lives. We give up a great deal when we dismiss such a practice as pietistic emotionalism. In fact we would have no Gospels in our Bible if the earliest believers had not told their Jesus stories to one another with reverence and prayerful reflection. My guess is that Paul was referring to a type of liturgical story telling when he wrote to the Romans: "I long to see you, that I may impart some spiritual gift [*charisma*] to strengthen you, that is, that we may be mutually encouraged by each other's faith, both yours and mine" (1:11–12). Today we need more space in our corporate worship for narrative exchanges of faith. The Anglican contemplative Una Kroll writes movingly of her encounter with Christ in the eucharistic liturgy; but she also notes that some of her clearest insights into redemptive love have come to expression when "men and women . . . gathered to share in informal worship. We have told our life stories to each other, laughed, wept, and comforted each other, and in so doing we have known ourselves touched by the hand of God."[21] The truth is that Christ comes to meet us, in formal liturgies or spontaneous conversations, whenever our stories unite with our prayers.

We may also heighten our sense of Christ's presence in worship by simply calling out to him. The Greek word *epikaleo* bears several meanings, but one of the most prominent has to do with a liturgical voicing of Jesus' name (Acts. 2:21; 9:14; Rom. 10:9–14; 1 Cor. 1:2). Such invocations seem to be both statements of faith (as in the acclamation "Jesus is Lord"; 1 Cor. 12:3) and prayers (as in Ananias's instruction to the newly converted Saul: "Rise and be baptized and wash away your sins, having called upon [Jesus'] name"; Acts 22:16, my translation). In fact the New Testament allows us to be rather specific about what the earliest believers actually said to their risen Master. In addition to the great confession *Iēsous Kyrios*, they certainly cried out with the Aramaic word *Maranatha* ("Our Lord, come"; 1 Cor. 16:22) or "Come Lord Jesus" (Rev. 22:20). Almost as certainly, they prayed such phrases as *Kyrie eleison* ("Lord have mercy"; Mt. 20:31), "Lord, save" (Mt. 8:25), "Hosanna" (Mk. 11:10 and parallels), "Jesus, help" (Mk. 9:22), "Amen" (2 Cor. 1:20; Rev. 3:14), and

"Thanks to you, Lord" (2 Cor. 1:20 in the light of 1 Cor. 14:16 and Eph. 5:19–20).

The picture we get is of many short prayers to Jesus. These would be uttered sometimes by individuals, sometimes by small groups in the assembly, and sometimes by the whole congregation together. Today Christians who are used to fixed liturgies may view this procedure as painfully chaotic and contrary to everything they know as worship. But other believers, who have tried freer forms of expression, can reply that much depends upon their volume and duration and upon how well they are balanced with other parts of the service. Paul advised the Corinthians to do all things "decently and in order," but his notion of order allowed a great deal of freedom for individual expression.[22] His overarching concern was that each believer should be growing toward an "undivided devotion to the Lord" (1 Cor. 7:35), and he was firmly convinced that this would happen through corporate worship.

In his discourse on the celebration of the Lord's Supper, Paul faults his Corinthian readers for neglecting personal acts of devotion. Here the meditations referred to may be silent, but that is not altogether certain. The practice recommended by the apostle is that of "examining" oneself (dokimazo in Greek), while "discerning the body," that is, the Body of Christ assembled to eat and drink from his table (1 Cor. 11:28–29). This is not a privatistic taking of one's spiritual pulse but a new vision of Christ in the self *acting together with* Christ in one's brother and sister believers. To meet the Lord in such discernment is inevitably to worship him, most often with prayers of confession and/or thanksgiving.

In this section we have been exploring the nature of our focus in corporate worship, especially our focus on the presence of Christ among us. Thus it may appear to some readers that the sovereignty of God or the leadership of the Holy Spirit is being neglected. That has been far from my intention; and it was certainly not the intention of the New Testament writers, who were constantly citing the glory of God as the final goal of their worship and naming the Spirit as the instigator of this homage (Eph. 5:18–20 is typical). Nevertheless, in virtually every one of the apostolic sources describing corporate prayer, the figure of Jesus stands out in bold relief. Through him God gives the Spirit for distribution among us. Through him God's sovereignty works for our redemption. Jesus stands at the center of our assemblies, on earth but also in heaven, interceding for us, leading our praises, and uniting our worship with that of the angelic hosts (Jn. 1:51; Heb. 12:22–24). The distinctive mark of corporate prayer in the church is its return, again and again, to the name of Jesus. There are blessings without number in the speaking of that name, by two or three or by ten thousand.

Mission

This truth also holds whenever the church moves, as it must, to share its new life with the broader world. Precisely in mission the earliest believers were never far away from corporate prayer in the name of Jesus. Their proclamation began on Pentecost with praises to God, but it was Jesus who poured out the Spirit to inspire them. Soon the disciples spoke publicly of the One whom God had made "both Lord and Christ" (Acts 2:36), with the result that their continuing praise of God in their homes became a "centripetal mission" of hospitality.[23] The thanking of God through Jesus served to invite people into the church's *koinonia*, helped them to feel that they had come home to God's grace. Some of the Jerusalem authorities were troubled by this renewal movement and arrested its leaders, forbidding them to "speak or teach in the name of Jesus" (Acts 4:18). But the authorities' action turned out to be something like King Canute's attempt to roll back the tide with a royal command. Luke reports that when Peter and John returned to the assembled church after their brief imprisonment, this fervent prayer was offered:

> Sovereign Lord, who didst make the heaven and the earth and the sea and everything in them, who by the mouth of our father David, thy servant, didst say by the Holy Spirit, "Why did the Gentiles rage, and the peoples imagine vain things? The kings of the earth set themselves in array, and the rulers were gathered together, against the Lord and against his Anointed"—for truly in this city there were gathered together against thy holy servant Jesus, whom thou didst anoint, both Herod and Pontius Pilate, with the Gentiles and peoples of Israel, to do whatever thy hand and thy plan had predestined to take place. And now, Lord, look upon their threats, and grant to thy servants to speak thy word with all boldness, while thou stretchest out thy hand to heal, and signs and wonders are performed through the name of thy holy servant Jesus. (Acts 4:24–30)

Luke adds that when this prayer came to an end, "the place in which they were gathered together was shaken; and they were all filled with the Holy Spirit and spoke the word of God with boldness" (4:31).

Acts 4:24–30 is the longest prayer of the church on earth recorded in the New Testament, so we shall do well to give it close attention. Like many other New Testament prayers, it implies a trinitarian experience of God. It is addressed to the Sovereign Lord, the Ruler of Israel and the nations; but it also presupposes the vigorous activity of the Holy Spirit and the presence of Jesus, the holy servant through whose name God was now healing the chosen people and revealing the divine plan in signs and wonders. For our purposes, however, the most striking feature of this prayer is that it shows us the church petitioning God for empowerment in its primal task of speaking the word "with all boldness." Luke probably means to tell his readers that no service of worship is quite complete without such a petition—right down to the infusion of the Holy Spirit that answers it. Jesus himself instructs us that we are to pray to the Lord of the harvest so that laborers will be sent to gather it in (Mt. 9:38). And the clear implication is that we must be ready to become those laborers.

How does corporate prayer help us to move into mission? Today it is probably necessary to begin our answer to this question by looking at a common practice of the modern church that does not contribute very much to our missionary empowerment, and may in fact impede it. I am referring to the subversion of corporate prayer by political agendas. Charles Elliott's extensive work in developing socioeconomic policies from a Christian point of view is well known in England and Africa. Yet he writes about specially prepared "justice" and "aid" liturgies that manage to cripple worship by "engendering (but not dealing with) guilt, thus degenerating into propaganda or newscasting services, indulging in 'heavy' teaching as though the glory of God depended upon his people gaining A level passes in international politics. Some ministers are so anxious to make explicit their commitment to the poor, that the liturgy begins to sound like an ideological closed shop."[24] Of course a similar critique could be directed against churches of the right wing, who show little or no interest in the healing of society and shape their corporate prayers so as to avoid all controversy.

But if this is the wrong way to go, what is the more excellent way? Like the New Testament church, we must always be grounded in praise, for true praise by itself will instruct us in the plan of God and draw us up into it, with thanksgiving. Corporate praise means recounting the saving acts of God, first of all for the sake of God's glory, but also for the benefit of everyone present at worship. We are to *address one another* in psalms and hymns and spiritual songs as we make melody to the Lord (Eph. 5:19). And the author of Colossians adds that we are to "let the word of Christ dwell in [us] richly, teaching and admonishing one another by means of psalms and hymns and spiritual songs as [we] sing with thankfulness to God" (3:16, my translation).

If praise is honest and true to the Bible, it will proclaim the whole range of God's saving acts, including those lodged in Mary's memory ("[God] has scattered the proud. . . . He has put down the mighty . . . and exalted those of low degree; he has filled the hungry . . . and the rich he has sent empty away"; Lk. 1:51–53) and incorporated into the missionary program of Jesus ("The Spirit of the Lord is upon me, because he has anointed me to preach good news to the poor . . . to proclaim release to the captives . . . to set at liberty those who are oppressed"; Lk. 4:18). To say these things to one another in praise is not to heap shame on ourselves for our middle-class lives but to remind ourselves that since God reaches out to all people from an abundance of love and mercy, we can do the same. In praise we begin to take our giftedness more seriously; we begin to see ourselves more clearly as a royal people, "created in Christ Jesus for good works, which God prepared beforehand that we should walk in them" (Eph. 2:10). The path formed by those good works will be specific to each person and congregation. In the praising of God we receive light for the first few steps, and sometimes for the longer journeys that we like to call plans and programs.

Such a revelation of gifts and tasks often came to the earliest believers through words of prophecy. Individuals speaking in the name of the risen Christ would convey simple but powerful messages that were used by the Spirit to transform hearts and change behaviors (see 1 Cor. 14:1–25). Somehow we need to reinstitute this practice in the regular liturgies of our mainline churches. Praise and thanksgiving will almost always generate oracles from God, but they will come forth in a public way only when we are ready to receive them. Of course prophecy itself must be tested according to "the analogy of faith" (Rom. 12:6), that is, the tradition of teaching passed

141

on by Jesus and his chosen disciples. This testing, identified by the Greek words *dokimazo* (1 Thess. 5:21; 1 Jn. 4:1) and *diakrino* (1 Cor. 14:29), is to be done by the whole assembly of worshipers and may itself be thought of as an act of prayer. Some individuals appear to be more gifted than others in discernment (1 Cor. 12:10), but no one is excluded from the process (1 Cor. 14:27–33; 1 Jn. 4:1).

Praise, prophecy, and the discernment of prophecy will work to bring about prayers of self-offering (which is how the New Testament writers often characterize what we now call ethical decision making). Thus Paul calls for the presentation of our bodies as living sacrifices, so that we can "prove [*dokimazo*] what is the will of God" (Rom. 12:2). True to form, his exhortation follows directly upon words of praise for God's mercy (Rom. 11:33–12:2). A similar note is struck when the apostle tells of some exemplary believers in Macedonia. He says that these poor Christians gave monetary gifts beyond their means, "begging us earnestly for the favor of taking part in the relief of the saints [i.e., the collection for Jerusalem administered by Paul] —and this not as we expected but first they gave themselves to the Lord and to us by the will of God" (2 Cor. 8:4–5). What we must imagine here is a gathering for worship during which someone is moved to speak God's word in the form of a gracious challenge to the church's generosity. The result is a new self-offering by the whole congregation, a prayerful act of commitment that results in a major decision about finances. Charles Elliott catches the spirit of this passage in observing that whenever we dedicate our common work and common leisure to God's highest calling, the kingdom itself comes to earth.[25]

As far as I can tell, the earliest churches did not hold business meetings. Instead, their leaders, their programs, and their budgets emerged from times of discernment in corporate worship (Acts 1:15–26; 11:1–18; 13:1–3; 14:23; 1 Cor. 5:1–8; 14:1–5; 2 Cor. 8–9; Col. 3:16–17; Heb. 10:19–25; 13:15–16). In most of these passages prayer, especially praise and thanksgiving, is explicitly mentioned; in the others it is implied.

Yet because God is sovereign and the Spirit blows where it wills, and because we are fallible human beings, no process of discernment can be absolutely tidy or free of controversy. Luke devotes the better part of six chapters in Acts (10–15) to an account of the odd events and strenuous arguments that culminated in a decision by the Jewish church to accept uncircumcised Gentiles as full members. To some believers, it seemed that God had initiated an active outreach to Gentiles. The evidence they cited involved an angelic visit, a vision, and several manifestations of the Holy Spirit. Others felt that these so-called revelations were not sufficient to displace the ancient customs. Throughout this period of uncertainty, people associated with the church or synagogue offered up prayers to God (Acts 10:1-4, 9-15, 30-31, 44-46; 11:18; 12:5; 13:3; 14:23). But in the fifteenth chapter of Acts, when the apostles and elders of the church in Jerusalem finally meet with Paul and Barnabas to determine the status of Gentile believers, we find no clear references to prayer, prophecy, or extraordinary disclosures of God's will. What we do have are personal testimonies by Peter, Paul, and Barnabas, plus a decisive speech by James the brother of Jesus that is based on passages from the Old Testament prophets. In addition we have a passing reference to "much debate" (15:6). This, coming from the irenic Luke, means that what transpired was probably a real donnybrook. It all sounds quite modern.

But what happened to prayer? Perhaps it did not occur at all, in which case Luke's silence might be interpreted as an implicit message to the church of his day on the order of "If they *had* prayed, things would have gone more easily. See that you do better." More likely, however, is the possibility that prayer was offered and answered with a revelation of God's intention, though not with the dramatic signs and wonders that had led up to the council. Here are two hints from the text that urge us toward this conclusion:

1. When Luke states that "the apostles and elders were gathered together to consider this matter" (15:6; i.e., the status of Gentiles in the church), the words for "gather" and "consider" are *synago* and *horao*, respectively. In Acts, the first word usually refers to gatherings of the church where worship would have been the norm; in fact worship is explicitly mentioned in two *synago* passages (4:31; 20:7-8). The verb *horao* literally means "to see" or, in the passive voice, "to appear." But nearly all of its occurrences in Acts (excluding direct quotes from the Old Testament) describe the seeing of a vision or miracle or the deeper meaning of an event.[26] For Luke, *horao* is primarily about receiving a revelation. To "consider this matter" means to look into it prayerfully, in God's presence.

2. When Luke spells out the final action taken by the apostolic council, he does so by quoting a letter, sent from the assembly in Jerusalem to the mixed Jewish-Gentile church of Antioch. This letter contains the sentence "For it has seemed good to the Holy Spirit and to us to lay upon you no greater burden than these necessary things" (15:28). The verb "seem" (*dokeo*) does not indicate uncertainty but the formation of a consensus based on the community's discernment of God's will. Apparently without voting, the participants came "to one accord" over what needed to be done (15:25). Luke does not tell us as much about this process as we would like to know, but the evidence is strong that in his view all the arguments presented, however harshly, were shaped by a reverent attentiveness to the movements of God's Spirit.

For me, this story initially frustrates and then encourages. I would like to have at my disposal a fail-safe formula for the recognition of God's will in corporate worship. But the New Testament does not provide it. What it does give us is a collection of stories and exhortations about struggles informed by prayer, especially prayers of praise. Human reason, risk, and error continue to play their role. There is no way of predicting with any certainty how the plan of God will assert itself in our midst. All we can know for sure is that we must keep our hearts fixed on God, Christ, and the Spirit. And that, to me, sounds real. God is always out ahead of the church and will frequently call us into irregular sessions of prayer, like the council of Jerusalem, in order to help us catch up.

The New Testament shows us that our praying together will exhibit a special rhythm, a distinctive focus on Jesus at its center, and an inherent tendency toward mission. In this chapter we have begun to explore the contours of these three elements. But there is one more axiom of corporate prayer that needs to be stated with emphasis. As in Judaism, the prayers of the people are meant to prepare us for the sanctification of God's name in all the transactions of life. Holy times and places are to produce holy individuals, ready to offer "spiritual sacrifices" wherever they are. For those who worship together regularly, no period of work or play or rest turns out to be quite secular. Dietrich Bonhoeffer understood this well. Commenting on Col. 3:17 ("Whatever you do, in word or deed, do everything in the name of the Lord Jesus, giving thanks to God the Father through him"), he wrote: "Thus every word, every work, every labor of the Christian becomes a prayer; not in the unreal sense of a constant turning away from the task that must be done, but in a real breaking through the hard 'it' to the gracious 'Thou.'"[27] We are unlikely to find a keener insight into the boldness and blessing mediated to us through the church's corporate worship.

Prayer
as Peacemaking
and Warfare

SOME OF THE MOST PRODUCTIVE ENCOUNTERS between the church's worship and the world's aspirations occur in our common search for peace. The very word tends to inspire people of goodwill; and most of them, when pressed, would define peace as something grander than the simple absence of war. The ancient Hebrew concept of *shalom*, which carries with it images of health, well-being, and justice, runs very deep in the human psyche. The church partakes of this as well, for it points in its gospel to a cosmic reconciliation achieved by Christ (Col. 1:20; 2:13–14) and to an ongoing ministry of reconciliation in which all believers are to participate (2 Cor. 5:18–21). According to John, the first words spoken by Jesus to his disciples on the evening of his resurrection were "Peace be with you" (20:19). In a very real way this greeting sums up his work and his victory and his gift to us. Thus it makes perfect sense to expect that both the personal and corporate prayers of New Testament believers would be seen as playing a major role in the establishment of God's peace on earth. And they are, but in a way that will seem strange to us if we equate peace with the normal and tranquil unfolding of human nature.

In fact Jesus and the apostolic writers take a dim view of our potential for creating harmony among ourselves apart from radical interventions by God. Moreover, the language they use to describe these interventions is often far from pacific. To announce that demons are being cast out as the kingdom comes near; to name Jesus as Lord over principalities and powers; to urge that believers put on the whole armor of God when they proclaim the gospel (Eph. 6:11–17)— all this adds up to a worldview in which true peace can be achieved only by means of divine warfare against superhuman forces. For New Testament believers, evil was not adequately described as the shadow side of God or the human spirit. It was, to a large degree, located in "spiritual hosts of wickedness" dwelling "in the heavenly places" (Eph. 6:12). And it was very powerful. What can we say, in the light of this apocalyptic worldview, about the role of prayer in the bringing of peace? We can begin by looking at the peacemaker, the person who longs and works for shalom in communion with God.

Bold and Blessed Are the Peacemakers

The word *peacemaker* occurs just once in the New Testament, in the now-famous pronouncement of Jesus that such people receive a special blessing. Indeed, both now and in the future their blessing will manifest itself in a new name: "For they will be called children of God" (Mt. 5:9, NRSV). Jesus echoes his beatitude just a few verses later in the Sermon on the Mount when he issues a command that, in effect, calls all of us to the vocation of peacemaker: "Love your enemies, and pray for those who persecute you, so that you may be sons and daughters of your Abba who is in heaven" (5:44, my translation). Here we learn that the distinctive way in which we are to work for shalom is by countering hostility with active goodwill and intercession. The principle applies whether enmity is directed against us as victims or whether we are seeking to mediate between two opposing parties. Some of us will prove more charismatically gifted in peacemaking than others, and for this due honor will be shown—above all in praise to God. But in fact the entire church must be constantly about the business of "the things that make for peace" (Lk. 19:41), especially within its own household.

In chapter 8 we looked at a host of New Testament passages that are connected with the realization of mutual forgiveness. And we noted there how frequently prayer is mentioned or implied as the means through which reconciliation comes to pass. Jesus taught that prayer would not only make conscious our need for resolving differences with our adversaries (Mt. 5:23; Mk. 11:25) but would also become

147

the primary means of blessing them (Lk. 6:28). This spirit of peace-making is fleshed out in the fourth chapter of Ephesians, where Paul (or one of his disciples) urges us to "lead a life worthy of the calling to which you have been called . . . with patience, forbearing one another in love, eager to maintain the unity of the Spirit in the bond of peace" (vv. 1–3). "Speaking the truth in love, we are to grow up in every way into him who is the head, into Christ" (v. 16). "Be angry but do not sin; do not let the sun go down on your anger, and give no opportunity to the devil" (vv. 26–27). "Be kind to one another, ten-derhearted, forgiving one another, as God in Christ forgave you" (v. 32). Although some of these admonitions sound almost romantic in their accent on harmony, there are strong hints here (especially in vv. 26–27) that reconciliation among believers will involve a struggle that engages our more heated emotions. The reference to the devil fits with a conviction expressed elsewhere in Ephesians (3:10; 6:10–18) that our everyday behavior toward one another will always serve either God or God's enemy in the great drama of redemption. Prayer keeps us aware of this awesome truth and helps us draw on the power of the Spirit to withstand temptation (2:17–18; 3:14–19; 6:17).

An extended set of directions for peacemaking by believers occurs in Paul's letter to the Romans. Key verses from the twelfth chapter are presented here in the translation by James Dunn:

> Let love be without pretense. . . . Show family affection to one another in brotherly love; show the way to one another in re-spect . . . be aglow with the Spirit; serve the Lord. Rejoice in hope; be steadfast in affliction; be persistent in prayer. . . . Bless those who persecute you, bless and do not curse. Live in harmony among yourselves; do not cherish proud thoughts but associate with the lowly. . . . Repay no one evil for evil. . . . If possible, so far as it depends on you, live at peace with everyone. Do not take your own revenge, beloved, but give opportunity for God's wrath. . . . But if your enemy is hungry, feed him; if he is thirsty, give him to drink; for in so doing you will heap coals of fire on his head. Do not be overcome by what is bad, but overcome the bad with the good (por-tions of vv. 9–21).[1]

Many of these instructions speak to how believers should be treat-ing one another, which itself was a form of worship in Paul's eyes ("Welcome one another . . . as Christ has welcomed you, for the glory of God"; Rom. 15:7). But other parts of the discourse are clearly meant to prepare Christians in Rome for interaction with their neighbors outside the church (e.g., "Bless those who persecute you. . . . So far as it depends on you, live at peace with everyone"; see also 1 Cor. 7:15). Obviously a number of verses could apply to both insiders and outsiders. Dunn is surely right in observing that "Paul did not see a Christian's life as divided neatly into two sets of attitudes and obligations—one to fellow believers, the other to nonbelievers. The same sympathetic concern and positive outgoing love should be the rule in all cases—a love which does not reckon or depend on receiving a positive response in return."[2]

Since love is the reigning thought in this section of Romans, most commentators agree that the striking image in verse 20 of heaping live coals on an enemy's head must be a positive one. Perhaps it alludes to a ritual of repentance well known in the ancient world. William Klassen reminds us that God's wrath (v. 19) is very different from our own, since it is always exercised for the purpose of restoration and is really incited by love. By referring to it Paul would be telling his readers that "the greatest triumph of divine love comes when we get caught up in the celebration of the return to divine love of those who have harmed us in life."[3] Thus, inviting our enemy to eat and drink with us is not a sign of moral superiority on our part but an acknowledgment that God's reconciling power is actually taking effect and needs to be praised in a convivial manner. Of course it is true that enemies may rebuff all our attempts to reach out and become even more hostile. Persecution remains a constant possibility.

To sustain an inner peace that will help us bless the other, no matter what, and overcome every bad deed with a good one, prayer is absolutely essential. In Romans Paul not only encourages us to offer ourselves constantly to God's transforming will (12:1–8; see also 2 Cor. 3:18); he also bids us to "be aglow with the Spirit, serve the Lord, rejoice in hope; be steadfast in affliction; be persistent in prayer" (12:11–12). All of these little commands are summed up in the last one, for each presupposes a conscious, life-giving communion with the triune God. We cannot be peacemakers apart from a graceful relationship with the Author of Peace.

But it is not only the power to love that we need from prayer. It is also honesty. No one who has tried for long to make peace with other individuals or groups can escape the prayer of self-examination. It is incredibly easy to demonize our opponents, to locate all the evil in them so that we do not have to face it in ourselves. The God of peace works to release us from such projections, and sometimes our liberation must come through painful exposures of the phoniness that distorts our peacemaking. On occasion the answer to our prayers for peace will come as a humbling revelation that much of what we take to be noble work for a just cause is really a form of asserting our dominance over others. The more frequently we hold up our motivations to the searching love of God, the less devastating these insights become. Paul considers it a matter of course that whenever "spiritual" people reach out for reconciliation with their erring or warring brothers and sisters, they must do so with a gentleness that proceeds from humility. "Look to yourselves, lest you too be tempted" (Gal. 6:1). The bottom line is that we are more like our enemies than we wish to admit. And we often discover this in prayer.

Paul is probably citing a version of Jesus' own teaching when he says in Romans 12 that we are to bless our persecutors and overcome evil with good (see 12:14, 21, in the light of Mt. 5:39–44; Lk. 6:28). Here both our Lord and his chief apostle to the Gentiles offer us a hard lesson, for they imply that those who initiate a process toward reconciliation must often be precisely those most wronged by the current status quo (see Mt. 18:15–16; Mk. 11:25). We have seen this actually happening in the lives of Ghandi, Martin Luther King, Jr., and several leaders of the anti-apartheid movement in South Africa. Sometimes, of course, the difficult way of active nonviolence cannot be sustained. The erosion happens mostly when practitioners become discouraged and begin to feel that they are changing neither the hearts nor the systems of their opponents and must therefore resort to the same cruel methods being used against them. Since most readers of this book (and its author) have not had to live under totalitarian governments, we need to be very circumspect about judging the feelings and behavior of those who have no other choice.

Perhaps the only way in which persecuted people can bless their tormentors with consistency and integrity is for them to believe deeply in their own self-worth, not only in God's eyes but also (despite all appearances) within the stunted consciences of those who demean them. Jesus knew this when he counseled his hearers not to "resist one who is evil. But if anyone strikes you on the right cheek, turn to him the other also; and if anyone would sue you and take your coat, let him have your cloak as well; and if anyone forces you to go one mile, go with him two miles" (Mt. 5:39–48; see Lk. 6:28–29).

Walter Wink shows that in each of these cases the chief intent of the persecutor is to shame the individual, to break his or her spirit so that future domination will be even easier. The blow to the right cheek, for example, is probably a backhand slap designed to humiliate.[4] In all of these situations what would truly shock an oppressor is the clownlike acceptance of punishment commended by Jesus; for that would mean that the self of the other had not been crushed but was continuing to stand erect.[5] Naturally oppressors retain the option of hardening their hearts and becoming more violent than ever. But many, probably the majority, would begin to move toward a change of heart, particularly if they saw this odd behavior manifesting itself in large groups of people over a period of time. Here is a boldness that transforms our macho definitions of the word. Wink is right to point out that Jesus' words are not absolute rules for every time and place. What they amount to is a brief sketch of the creativity required to love our enemies while at the same time retaining a healthy respect for ourselves.[6]

But here we must turn to a prior question. How can we act in such ways, instinctively, when the person or system in power is heaping shame on us? I suspect that Jesus and the New Testament writers would tell us we can do so only when we have begun to make a habit of offering up our enemies and our hatred of them to the mercies of God. There are two things to keep in mind as we try to sustain this prayer of release. The first is that words and songs of praise (which may seem quite inappropriate to the situation) can grant us a mindset of magnanimity just when we feel bone dry or boiling with rage. Strangely, an act of praise and thanksgiving to God can have the effect of wiping away our shame. This is probably because such acts force us to direct our attention toward the only real Good in the universe, with the result that we discover once again the myriad ways in which God's excellence comes to inhabit us. Over time we are able to feel the grace of the God we are praising; and it makes sense, once again, to do things God's way, by overcoming evil with good. Praise and thanksgiving create honor for both God and ourselves. They are the perfect antidote for shame, not least because they are rendered in the name of him who died shamefully so as to disarm shame.[7]

If this is really true, we have new light shed on the thorny New Testament teaching that we are to rejoice in our afflictions (Rom. 5:3) and persecutions (Lk. 6:22–23; Jas. 1:2–3). We are not asked to feel happy about these sufferings but to offer them up with praise so that

151

we may begin to sense the transforming love of God. And this has everything to do with the vocation of peacemaking. "Rejoice in the Lord always. . . . Let your gentleness be known to everyone. The Lord is near. Do not worry about anything, but in everything by prayer and supplication with thanksgiving let your requests be made known to God. And the peace of God, which surpasses all understanding, will guard your hearts and your minds in Christ Jesus" (Phil. 4:4–7, NRSV). When the peace that comes from rejoicing takes hold in our deepest selves, peace on earth can begin to happen. Anyone who knows Archbishop Desmond Tutu has seen this passage incarnated. With him, boldness, blessing, and joy are effectively rolled into one.

Paul's words to the Philippians help us to formulate a second truth about our prayers for peace in the midst of inner and outer conflicts. "The Lord is near. . . . The peace of God . . . will guard your hearts and minds in Christ Jesus." We do not pray alone. As always, Jesus stands in our midst, leading our petitions and thanksgivings through the power of the Spirit. The author of Colossians urges his readers to "let the peace of Christ rule in your hearts, to which indeed you were called in the one body" (3:15). Behind this passage may be a meditative practice in which believers submitted all the wrongs committed against them, along with their own bitterness, to the reconciling Lord. An extraordinary image of Christ, which could have fueled such prayers, rises up from the second chapter of Ephesians: "For he is our peace; in his flesh he has made both groups [Jew and Gentile] into one and has broken down the dividing wall, that is, the hostility between us. He has abolished the law with its commandments and ordinances, that he might create in himself one new humanity in place of the two, thus making peace, and might reconcile both groups to God in one body through the cross, thus putting to death that hostility. . . . For through him both of us have access in one Spirit to the Father" (Eph. 2:14–18, NRSV).

Through his real presence among us Christ *becomes* our peace, refashioning both us and our enemies. In the trinitarian language we have come to associate with New Testament praying, the author of Ephesians refers explicitly to the overcoming of conflicts between Jews and Gentiles in the church. But by analogy, his words also tell us how Christ works today to demolish the walls between races, sexes, classes, and nations that shout, "I am better than you, but often I feel worse, so I must shield myself against you." True peace comes when the walls disintegrate, as they always do when Christ reigns. True peace reaches out to us in a person. It is achieved on the practical plain by our communion with Jesus. It is also achieved through the cross, a troublesome fact we must now face directly.

Put on the Whole Armor of God

At the end of what is usually called the Colossian Hymn, we read that God has not only deigned to dwell in Christ, but also was pleased "to reconcile to himself all things, whether on earth or in heaven, making peace through the blood of his cross" (1:20). Then, a few verses later, we are informed that this transforming event has brought about forgiveness for every human being. In Jesus' terrible death God was "erasing the record that stood against us, with its legal demands. He set this aside, nailing it to the cross. He disarmed the rulers and authorities and made a public example of them, triumphing over them in it [the cross]" (2:14–15, NRSV).

Many North American Christians today (including, I suspect, some readers of this book) find such a cruciform way of talking about salvation difficult to accept. Lucy Bregman shows us why. In her essay "Two Imageries of Peace: Popular Psychology and Charismatic Christianity" she argues that most of us nowadays find ourselves immersed in one or more versions of the humanistic faith that peace is the normal state of the human being.[8] According to this widespread conviction, tranquillity for both individuals and groups will emerge, like a blossom, from good education, competent psychotherapy, or ancient techniques of meditation. By way of contrast, Bregman spells out the position of today's charismatic Christians, who hold that inward peace and its political manifestations come as a result of divine activity, specifically in the continuing victories of Christ over superhuman forces of evil. Consequently, these Christians believe, the peacemaking of God and of Jesus' disciples must always be seen as a form of spiritual warfare.[9] In Bregman's view (and mine) this way of thinking accounts for the full range of human experience far better than the dominant culture of popular psychology.[10] And perhaps the obvious should also be stated: By and large, charismatic Christianity replicates the central teachings of the New Testament on evil more accurately than the operative theology of today's mainline churches. Given this situation, we might all do well to take a close look at our prayers for peace to determine which traditions are really shaping them.

How can prayer help us take our rightful place in the battle for peace against "the rulers, . . . the authorities, . . . the cosmic powers of this present darkness, . . . the spiritual forces of evil in the heavenly places" (Eph. 6:12, NRSV)? Perhaps the first thing to get clear about is that we are not to pray *against* any person, group, or human institution as such, because none of these is exactly equivalent to the powers named above.[11] Instead we are to intercede for friends and enemies alike—even on the institutional level—that they may be released from bondage to the powers. Above all, we are to pray for our own safety and that of others in the face of threats from Satan, "the evil one" who directs the forces of wickedness. The Lord's Prayer itself is our model here ("rescue us from the evil one"; Mt. 6:1, NRSV), along with Jesus' intercession for Peter ("Satan demanded to have you . . . , but I have prayed for you that your faith may not fail"; Lk. 22:31–32) and for all of us who follow him ("I do not pray that thou shouldst take them out of the world, but that thou shouldst keep them from the evil one"; Jn. 17:15). Indeed, when the Spirit of Jesus moves us to call out to our Abba, this prayer may be interpreted as a battle cry against every satanic "spirit of slavery" (Rom. 8:15; Gal. 4:6). According to the Fourth Gospel, Jesus conferred peace upon his disciples before and after his resurrection, but "not as the world gives" (14:27). Part of his meaning must be that his peace gives no quarter to evil and therefore requires prayers of spiritual warfare.

These prayers are of essentially three types. Many will be requests for protection against the deception of Satan and his underlings. Prayers of watching seem to fall into this category ("Watch and pray that you may not enter into temptation"; Mt. 26:41; "Cast all your anxieties upon [God]. . . . Be sober, be watchful. Your adversary the devil prowls around like a roaring lion, seeking someone to devour"), as do the Lord's Prayer and the high-priestly prayer cited above (see also Acts 4:24–31 and Eph. 6:17–19).[12] To some of us it may seem incongruous or just plain silly to ask for defense against unseen powers of evil as we set about the tasks of peacemaking. Yet according to the New Testament, it is exactly those masters of illusion who want us to keep on demonizing and destroying ourselves. All true efforts toward peace will rouse them to battle. To ask for their binding in the name of Jesus may be the greatest contribution we can make to the cause of world peace. Whenever diplomats of church or state undertake to negotiate an end to hostilities, we need to pray not only for their success but also for their protection.

A second group of prayers against the powers for the sake of peace has to do with deliverance and exorcism. This whole enterprise is extremely difficult for modern Christians to fathom, but such prayers did occur in the common life of the early church and have never really disappeared from it. The Lord's Prayer fits here as well as in the previous category. It is a prayer for deliverance rather than exorcism, since the assumption is that those who offer it are not possessed by an evil spirit.[13] In fact, apart from the synoptic Gospels and a few passages in Acts (8:7; 16:16–18; and possibly 5:16; 19:12), stories of possession followed by exorcism do not occur in the New Testament.[14] Furthermore, as far as I can tell, we are unable to reconstruct any first-century liturgies of exorcism from our available sources. This silence hardly means that exorcism ceased in the church after the ministry of Jesus and the earliest missionaries (see chapter 8). But it may indicate that the actual casting out of demons by means of command tended to be done by specially gifted individuals, apart from the regular worship of the church (see Mk. 8:38–39; Lk. 9:49–50), and that more general prayers of deliverance predominated among New Testament Christians as a whole.

Paul considered those who could not accept the gospel to be blinded by "the god of this world" (2 Cor. 4:4), who is probably Satan. He also called some of his Christian opponents servants of Satan (2 Cor. 11:13–14) because he thought they had deceived and enslaved the Corinthians. Moreover, in Galatians he stings his readers with the accusation that they have deviated from the gospel by submitting to bondage under "weak and beggarly elemental spirits" (4:8–9). And in 1 Corinthians the apostle warns believers who have joined in sacrificial meals at pagan temples that they dare not be "partners with demons" (10:20). Yet nowhere in any of these passages is the practice of exorcism proposed as a remedy. Instead, after naming the powers of evil, Paul blesses his readers or prays for their welfare (1 Cor. 16:23–24; 2 Cor. 13:7–10, 14; Gal. 6:16, 18), even as he prays for the conversion of those blinded to the truth of the gospel (Rom. 10:10). The majority view among our New Testament writers seems to be that most of the time we must both contend against the spiritual powers of wickedness and strive to escape from their influence (see Rom. 12:2; Col. 1:13 and many passages from Revelation). Thus prayers for deliverance can and should be offered by every believer. In contrast, only those singled out for the task by Jesus are to detect and expel the powers that possess.[15]

A third type of battle prayer against the powers is characterized by what we may call discernment and deployment. One New Testament passage stands out from all the others as an exposition of this type. Not surprisingly, it abounds in military metaphors. Paul (or an associate) writes to the Ephesians:

> Finally, be strong in the Lord and in the strength of his power. 11) Put on the whole armor of God, so that you may be able to stand against the wiles of the devil. 12) For our struggle is not against enemies of blood and flesh, but against the rulers, against the authorities, against the cosmic powers of this present darkness, against the spiritual forces of evil in the heavenly places. 13) Therefore take up the whole armor of God, so that you may be able to withstand on that evil day, and having done everything, to stand firm. 14) Stand therefore, and fasten the belt of truth around your waist, and put on the breastplate of righteousness. 15) As shoes for your feet put on whatever will make you ready to proclaim the gospel of peace. 16) With all of these, take the shield of faith, with which you will be able to quench all the flaming arrows of the evil one. 17) Take the helmet of salvation, and the sword of the Spirit, which is the word of God. 18) Pray in the Spirit at all times in every prayer and supplication. To that end keep alert and always persevere in supplication for all the saints. 19) Pray also for me, so that when I speak, a message may be given to me to make known with boldness the mystery of the gospel, 20) for which I am an ambassador in chains. Pray that I may declare it boldly, as I must speak. (Eph. 6:10–20, NRSV)

This is not the place to work out the fuller interpretation these rich images deserve.[16] But we can note the central importance given to proclaiming the gospel in the midst of the battle (see vv. 15, 17, 19, 20, and probably v. 14, since "truth" and "righteousness" are often synonyms for the gospel in Pauline literature). Fighting the powers effectively requires speaking just the right words of good news, which means those given by the Spirit. It is not stated that we are to address the powers directly with God's word.[17] Rather, as we declare the message of grace and peace in Christ to our neighbors, the powers must take note and retreat, though never without a tremendous fight.

Our passage ends with a vigorous summons to prayer as that which undergirds the entire Christian side of the struggle. From his careful work on the grammatical structure of verses 18–20, Clinton Arnold concludes that "the author appears to give prayer a more prominent place than merely the seventh among a list of spiritual weapons. . . . [He] wants his readers to understand prayer as an essential spiritual weapon, but more than a weapon, it is foundational for the deployment of all the other weapons."[18] This means, for example, that when the apostolic writer exhorts us to put on as shoes "whatever will make you ready to proclaim the gospel of peace" (v. 15), he presupposes that we must pray for guidance about what this will be. Praying "in the Spirit" (v. 18), we learn from 1 Cor. 14:15–16, could refer to speaking in tongues; but here in Ephesians it is more likely to mean praising and thanking God in the name of Jesus (see Eph. 5:18–20). As indicated in chapter 6, this "heartbeat" of the church's common life often brings special insights into what God is doing among us right now. Praise is the paramount way to discernment ("Present your bodies as a living sacrifice. . . . Be transformed by the renewing of your mind so that you may discern what is the will of God"; Rom. 12:1–2, NRSV). As such, it constitutes the first line of defense *and* offense against the powers.[19]

Praise also expands, quite naturally, into "every prayer and supplication," especially intercession (vv. 18–19). Here the sole object of prayer is that "all the saints" [believers], but particularly leaders, might be empowered to speak the gospel with boldness, in a way that corresponds exactly to the specific demands of the situation. This "fitting" word of the good news is what confounds the powers. It may come through teaching, preaching, prophecy, or ordinary conversations over coffee. Wherever it happens, it will enter our corporate lives and our individual hearts like the point of a sword (v. 17); and the powers will be forced back. One example of this in Ephesians itself is the everyday reconciliation of believers with one another ("Let all of us speak the truth to our neighbors, for we are members of one another. . . . Be angry but do not sin; do not let the sun go down on your anger, and do not make room for the devil"; 4:25–27). In fact, whenever the New Testament authors symbolize our life in Christ as a battle against the powers, they see that warfare taking place first of all within ourselves and among our immediate friends or enemies over issues of forgiveness. One's personal life in community is the primal "place" for overthrowing the cosmic forces of evil.

That is why Jesus and Paul devote so much of their teaching to these matters. And as we have seen, that is also why they urge us so often to make full use of the resources we have in prayer.

Today the church finds itself engaged in thousands of battles over legitimate demands for peace and justice. Christians have no choice but to join these struggles, because God loves everyone equally, and the gospel is uncompromisingly social. But in each battle the *nature* of the church's engagement requires a clear choice on our part. How much of our time and money and prayer are we going to commit here, or there? And what, exactly, are we going to say in the name of Jesus? One of my major concerns these days is that we appear to be frequently misled by Satan and the powers into fighting our battles at the wrong times, against the wrong enemies with the wrong weapons. Often our approaches to socioeconomic problems do not even touch the powers that are really responsible for troubled relationships and oppressive institutions.[20] We settle for the lowest-common-denominator analyses of "experts," thereby forgetting prayer and the gospel.

Apocalyptic Praying

In his fine book *Love of Enemies: The Way to Peace*, Mennonite scholar William Klassen concludes a chapter on Paul with this short discussion of prayer:

> We speak a good deal about praying for peace. The biblical writers don't put it quite that way. Every greeting, especially the one given the enemy, is for them a prayer for peace. Every blessing is also a prayer for peace. And at least one biblical writer stresses the fact that Christians are to offer petitions, prayers, intercessions, and thanksgivings for *all*; for sovereigns and those in high office, that we may lead a quiet and peaceful life (1 Tim. 2:1–2). We do not pray only for our governments but for *all* who are in authority. Every protest against policies of governments should be . . . bathed with that kind of prayer.[21]

Klassen emphasizes that the prayer he is talking about always assumes "an active and aggressive role in the peacemaking progress." The two belong together. But whether a given moment calls for quiet contemplation or a noisy march, our efforts for peace will be felt as a struggle. The last sentence in Klassen's chapter reads as follows: "It is God's battle, and we are under God's exclusive command."[22]

Here is the point of it all: to find and enter *God's* peacemaking battle, in communion with Jesus, by the power of the Spirit. We do this not as field marshals, directing the strategy, but as lesser ranks who must carry out orders from above. In many cases the first priority in our praying will be to request clarity with regard to how we should formulate our subsequent petitions. The answers may or may not coincide with the priorities set by our national churches, but they will come through a chain of command that is visible to the eyes of faith (1 Cor. 14:37–38).

Some of us may recoil from this military symbolism or find it distasteful. And indeed, it can be used in too facile a manner.[23] Yet nearly every formulation of the gospel in the New Testament presupposes it. We must agree with the hymn writer that it is "not with swords loud clashing, nor roll of stirring drums, but [in] deeds of love and mercy the heavenly kingdom comes."[24] However, these very deeds tend to incite a backlash from the powers that we cannot subdue with our own devices. If Jesus and the New Testament writers are correct, we live on the boundary between "the present evil age" (Gal. 1:4) and the glorious age to come. A balancing act of that sort requires extraordinary tools for survival—weapons in fact. Jesus taught that unclean spirits could be cast out through prayer (Mk. 9:29). But they will never depart altogether from the world order in its current state. They will continue to hover about us, trying their best to poison our atmosphere. Nevertheless, prayer helps in every case. Through it God teaches us and empowers us to proclaim the gospel of peace. In the long and the short run, evil is conquered by good.

The Accomplishments of Prayer in the New Creation

"DO NOT BE OVERCOME BY EVIL but overcome evil with good" (Rom. 12:21). Perhaps these words of Paul are the best we can do to summarize the way of prayer in our struggle against the powers of this age. The words themselves are quite simple, but the task to which they call us is daunting. To pray from the heart in the name of Jesus is not only to find personal renewal and charismatic power to serve; it is also to discover that each of us really matters, matters eternally, in the cosmic plan of God through which all things are being set right.

Jesus and the New Testament authors speak of this plan as the kingdom of God; and Jesus teaches that there is no greater thing we can do, day by day, than to pray on its behalf: "Abba, hallowed be thy name. Thy kingdom come . . ." (Lk. 11:2). God always initiates and completes the inbreaking of the kingdom. Yet neither of these happens to the full satisfaction of God unless we offer up our petitions for the coming of the kingdom and our entry into it. For the sake of God's glory we must want and work for God's rule. In this last chapter we shall focus upon our calling, through and by means of prayer, to be co-workers with God for the world's redemption (see 2 Cor. 5:18–6:1).

The Meanings of New Creation

One term in Paul's letters helps us especially in coming to grips with this stupendous thought. It is *kainē ktisis* in Greek, which we should probably translate as "new creation," since exactly this phrase occurs in some pre-Pauline Jewish writings.[1] Although *kainē ktisis* as such is found only twice in the New Testament, we can point to parallel terms used throughout the Gospels and epistles.[2] The earliest appearance of the phrase itself is in 2 Corinthians, where the apostle writes: "So if anyone is in Christ, there is a new creation. Everything old has come to an end; behold new things have come to be. All things are from God, who has reconciled us to himself in Christ, and has given us the ministry of reconciliation" (5:17–18).[3] The verses surrounding this text make it clear that Paul's intention is twofold. He wants his readers not only to perceive the wonders of God's new order but also to join it at a deeper level of their being and acting. If they do so, they will become, ever more effectively, ambassadors for Christ (5:20) and co-workers with God (6:1) in the ministry of reconciliation.[4]

But the key to all of this desired growth is found in a conditional clause: "If anyone is in Christ . . . " Over the course of this study we have come to see that being "in Christ" means having a close personal relationship with Jesus as Lord. We address him directly; we combine our petitions with his heavenly intercession; we allow his Spirit to guide us, above all in prayer to our Abba (Gal. 4:6). We do this as individuals, though our praying is never solitary; for life in Christ also means being a member of his Body, where mutual supplication for all the saints is the norm.

However, Paul's understanding of *kainē ktisis* goes beyond this axiomatic description of the believer in community. In effect the apostle is saying: "Whenever any one of you realizes your life in Christ as a praying person, a magnificent new world will appear. Again and again you will discover it, as if for the first time. And as you do, you will become, in a manner previously unimagined, an indispensable part of its formation." For Paul, *kainē ktisis* is both "out there," as a space-time continuum where God's righteousness strives to refashion the world order, and "in here," where we and the Holy Spirit struggle against the evil powers by means of prayer. The *kainē ktisis* is not finished, and will not be until Christ's visible return. Up to that moment our praise and petition, our intercession and confession must unite with compassionate action to prepare the way of the Lord.

Although "everything old" (i.e., all the devious systems through which death tries to enslave us) has in one sense come to an end, it has not been destroyed. *Kainē ktisis* describes the new order aborning, in us as sinners and in the midst of this present evil age. The new creation displaces the old powers, compressing them into a smaller and smaller domain until a great bursting of the world order occurs, and God's kingdom comes with finality. Some of Jesus' prophecies and the Revelation of John warn that this will be a time of severe tribulation from which only the worshipers of the true God will emerge. Indeed, it will be precisely their worship that enables God to purge the world of its lust for the enslaving powers (Rev. 8:1–5).

Yet Jesus and the majority of the New Testament authors say relatively little about this final period. Their emphasis lies upon our vocation now to exercise our freedom and power in the Spirit for the advancement of God's rule. This note is sounded in Paul's other use of the term *kainē ktisis*. Toward the end of his letter to the Galatians he writes: "Far be it from me to glory except in the cross of our Lord Jesus Christ, by which the world has been crucified to me, and I to the world. For neither circumcision counts for anything nor uncircumcision, but a new creation. Peace and mercy be upon all who walk by this rule" (*kanōn* in Greek; Gal. 6:14–16). The apostle's strange language about crucifixion to the world and vice versa does not mean detachment from the material order but liberation from the "elemental spirits of the world" (Gal. 4:3–5). These Paul thinks of as the quasi-personal forces undergirding what we now call ideologies, that is, explanations of how the world works that demand total homage. We are released from slavery to such powers by receiving a new Lord, by having our existence made over from the inside: "I have been crucified with Christ; it is no longer I who live, but Christ who lives in me" (Gal. 2:20).

Here too the language can be deceptive. Paul hardly means that our self just disappears when Christ comes to dwell within us. William Johnston gets closer to Paul's intention with this paraphrase of the verse: "He [Christ] will be in you and act through you: not through your little ego but through your big universal self."[5]

Once again Paul is speaking of prayer. To be crucified with Christ, to know Christ as our true life, is to be in deep communion with him so that authentic freedom and loving purpose can well up from our hearts. And once again, the whole Trinity is involved. "Because you are sons and daughters, God has sent the Spirit of his Son into our hearts, crying 'Abba! Father!'" (Gal. 4:6, my translation). Walking by the rule of the new creation is none other than walking by the

Spirit according to the law of Christ (5:16–6:3). And this amounts to behavior informed by prayerful attention to the Spirit's leadership (5:25).

When Paul juxtaposes the new creation with disputes over circumcision and uncircumcision, he is telling us that all the conflicts of our day over what is right and wrong in social relationships must be constantly reframed within us by the Spirit of Christ. Yet the effect of that reframing is always much more than a personal change of mind. God's new creation alters the very structure of the universe in that many of its highest values are rendered not very important by the redeeming cross of Jesus. Through our prayer communion with Jesus, we enter into his reconciling mission at ever-deeper levels. We and our efforts are never the center of the new creation, for God is always out ahead of us giving life to the dead and calling into existence the things that do not exist (Rom. 4:17). But without the heart-work of our prayers, God's plan will suffer loss. Indeed, our sanctified consciousness must become a vital part of that plan.

In expanding upon his definition of new creation for the Corinthians, Paul casts further light on the nature of our cooperation with God:

> 18) All this [newness] is from God, who through Christ reconciled us to himself and gave us the ministry of reconciliation; 19) that is, in Christ God was reconciling the world to himself, not counting their trespasses against them, and entrusting to us the message of reconciliation. 20) So all of us believers are ambassadors for Christ, God making his appeal through us. We are beseeching [the world] on Christ's behalf: "You [world], be reconciled to God." 21) For our sake God made Christ to be sin, who knew no sin, so that in him we might become the righteousness of God.
>
> 1) And as we all work together with God, we [apostles] strongly urge you not to accept the grace of God in vain. (2 Cor. 5:18–6:1; in 5:20 and 6:1 my own translation differs from that of the RSV)[6]

The constant refrain we hear in this passage is "in (or through) Christ" (vv. 18, 19, 21). That is how God operates, and that is how we cooperate with God. When the apostle states that we are "ambassadors for Christ" (v. 20), this does not mean just "on his behalf" or "in his place" but also "with the full authority of Christ."[7] But to receive and carry out Christ's authority we must be in regular, personal contact with him through prayer.

The "ministry [*diakonia*] of reconciliation" is a synonym for new creation. It is always introduced and directed by God, Christ, and the Holy Spirit (see 2 Cor. 3:7; 4:1); but it is also given to us (v. 18), primarily as "message" (*logos*; v. 19). This is the fitting word of the gospel that we hear in our hearts and articulate with our lips as a result of prayer in the Spirit (Eph. 6:17–18). Speaking the good news effectively, it seems, is the most important thing we are called to do as co-workers with God in the new creation. The rest of ministry is crippled without it. But of course we must also emphasize that the same prayer that issues in speech leads simultaneously to loving action. Even as we proclaim the gospel we are to *become* God's righteousness (2 Cor. 5:21) and walk, that is, behave, according to the rule of the new creation (Gal. 6:14–16). Bearing in mind this necessary unity of speech and action, can we be more specific about what is actually accomplished through our prayerful creating with God? What are the perceivable contours of the good that overcomes evil?

The Fruits of Our Labor in Prayer

We can say two things right at the beginning of our probe. First, it is not always given to us to see the results of our praying. God's plan remains a mystery to us no matter how closely we cooperate with the throne of grace. One person sows the seed in prayer; another waters it with devotion. But God alone brings forth the harvest (1 Cor. 3:6–7). And it may be that neither the sower nor the gardener will be around to partake of this abundance. With prayer, as with much else, we walk by faith and not by sight. Second, and in marked contrast, everyone who prays from the heart in the name of Jesus can expect to experience what Paul calls the fruit of the Spirit: "love, joy, peace, patience, kindness, goodness, faithfulness, gentleness, self-control" (Gal. 5:22–23). This does not mean an absence of conflict or the end of negative feelings but rather a felt addition to these things, a Something or Someone More, whose goodness deprives our trials of their ultimacy. It really happens, and our deepest selves know it to be so.

But there is much else to say about the accomplishments of our prayer as the New Testament writers understand them. Perhaps the best way of drawing them together in this last chapter is to review the various outcomes of each prayer type examined above. Readers who have followed our whole discussion will not be surprised that we begin our list with the genre of prayer that grounds all others in the New Testament.

PRAISE AND THANKSGIVING

Because of the abundant life experienced by Jesus' first disciples, praise and thanksgiving are in fact the "common prayer" of the New Testament church. The respected missionary bishop Lesslie Newbigin identifies several traits in a congregation that would aspire to follow the call of Jesus today. At the top of his list is this statement: "It will be a community of praise. That is, perhaps, its most distinctive characteristic."[8] With the wisdom of his experience, Newbigin gives top priority to what we have called the heartbeat of New Testament praying.

Even when we do not feel God's abundance (for feelings vary and do not always give us accurate readings of reality), we are called to offer praise for God's sake. And the happy discovery is that this offering reeducates our feelings so that our words and songs begin to take on authenticity. Praise helps us join God's cause with joy. It strengthens God's hand to bring the kingdom near—which is why the Lord's Prayer begins "Abba, hallowed by thy name" (see also 2 Cor. 4:15). In praise we stand with the hosts of heaven at the throne of grace, and this great assembly of adoration makes a difference in how God acts upon the world (Rev. 7:9–8:5). Paul writes that all things work together for good for those who love God (Rom. 8:28). Indeed, we believe that because of Christ all things work together for the good of *everyone.* But when we express our love for God in praise and thanksgiving, we begin to *see* that this is so and that our devotion helps to make it so. Like no other form of prayer, praise leads us into formulations of the gospel that correspond to the real needs of our burdened neighbors.[9]

Praise also instructs us in righteousness, for when we begin to voice the specific qualities of God that deserve our love and the particular blessings from God that enrich our lives, we are drawn into the divine goodness and inspired to act. Two works of righteousness that are directly linked with praise are welcoming our estranged

165

neighbors "to the glory of God" (Rom. 15:7) and sharing our goods with the needy, "for such sacrifices are pleasing to God" (Heb. 13:16; see also 2 Cor. 9:13). Theodore Jennings develops this line of thought nicely:

> To give praise and thanksgiving is to recognize that there is "more than enough." But such a recognition places us in direct conflict with the social, economic, and political structures of our world, which are based upon "scarcity.". . . What happens when we begin to act as if there were more than enough? Obviously, we will be unable to take the structures and institutions as seriously as they take themselves. . . . We will be unable to restrain ourselves from debunking these structures, and they will begin to totter.[10]

In another variation on the theme, Charles Elliott reminds us of a kingdom parable by Jesus that ends this way: "The earth produces of itself, first the blade, then the ear, then the full grain in the ear. But when the grain is ripe, at once [the sower] puts in the sickle, because the harvest has come" (Mk. 4:28–29). The point, Elliott recognizes, is that prayer (I would say especially prayers of praise) will enable us to see where and when God's harvest has ripened and how we are to reap this plenitude for the sake of the kingdom.[11] We ourselves become the harvesters we have petitioned God to send (Mt. 9:38).

What happens in praise and thanksgiving is the discovery of God's abundance when others are saying that only poverty, oppression, and impossibility exist. When that perception forms, we can act with real intention. Praise calls forth charismatic gifts in ourselves and impels us to search for their emergence in our neighbors (Rom. 12:1–8). Praise mobilizes the power of God for transformation. As such, it is eminently practical, not only in the church but also in the world.

PETITION

The New Testament is quite straightforward about our need to ask for God's blessings, a need that does not diminish as we mature in faith. But even asking can be creative. Every time we pray "Thy kingdom come" we are bidding God to restructure the world by introducing fresh forms of the good. And we are also saying as we pray, "Let us here and now be ready to take up new roles in your everchanging ministry of reconciliation."

Even our crude and selfish prayers may become channels for God's redemptive creativity. A few qualifications are placed on Jesus' promise that we shall receive whatever we ask for in prayer, but not many. That is so because God wants us to approach the throne of grace in total honesty. The Spirit will reform our inadequate petitions even as we offer them (Rom. 8:26). There is no need to hang back or suppress our prayer for fear that it will not be worthy of God's hearing. Again and again as we pray, the Spirit helps us cry Abba, reminding us in our deepest selves that we are God's own dear children (Rom. 8:15–16). To experience this renewed identity is to move from our lesser desires to the desires of the Spirit, which are the ways of God. In our best moments, the "you" of "whatever you ask for in prayer" includes the high-priestly intercession of Jesus for all humanity.

Over time, we learn that even when individual petitions meet with a negative answer, the sum total of our requests is honored by responses from God that prove far more abundant than all that we ask or think (Eph. 3:20). Our basic calling is to perseverance. Therefore we ask: sometimes creatively, in ways that support (or alter) God's will, sometimes stupidly. Yet the cumulative effect of our praying will be a gain for the quality of the world's life. One person, honestly seeking God's reign and gifts, will change the shape of the universe. Jesus did it, and we who belong to his Body are expected to follow him in this vocation.

Often our petitions will be answered with a command to take up our crosses, and when we obey, the healing of the world will be enhanced. To deal with our pain before God is to open our imaginations toward the positive use of that pain. Like Paul, we shall hear the risen Lord say, "My power is being made perfect in your weakness" (2 Cor. 12:9). And wherever the power of Christ comes to fruition, cosmic good will triumph over cosmic evil.

INTERCESSION

The New Testament writers think of intercession as our communion with God for the sake of others. Here, more than in any other form of prayer, the otherness of our neighbors is stressed and honored. Of course we are to pray first of all for our own family, friends, and members of our immediate circle, but precisely as those who have their own integrity before God, which is beyond our control. Intercession cannot be coercive; otherwise evil would not be conquered by good. At their best, our prayers serve "to lower the threshold in the person prayed for and to make the besieging love of God . . . slightly more visible and more inviting."[12] This honoring of the other's freedom applies especially to those who differ from us most noticeably in culture, race, or philosophy, and above all to those whom we think of as our enemies. On behalf of all such people we are to ask that the fullness of blessing that God intends for them may actually come to pass. Our intercession creates a channel for God's abundance.

In the New Testament, intercession often carries an implied call. Because we cannot pray equally for all people in need, we shall be guided by the Spirit to shape our requests according to God's will for specific situations, groups, and individuals. These become our "prayer burdens" (see Gal. 6:2), our unique assignments within Christ's heavenly intercession for the whole world. Most often mentioned in the New Testament as requests for others are those having to do with reconciliation, forgiveness, and healing. These benefits of the gospel are clearly meant for all humanity. They are granted through the church for the sake of the world, and we should expect them to happen on a daily basis (Acts 2:43; 4:29–30). At the same time, however, believers are urged to pray zealously for the continued sanctification of their sisters and brothers in Christ, and especially for the strengthening of those charged with the public proclamation of the gospel.

According to the New Testament, our prayer burdens will typically draw us into costly involvement with the lives of others, and we shall be moved to act on their behalf. Nearly everyone who prays regularly for another person or group can recount "coincidences" that have had the effect of producing real contacts with these people, often face to face. Such encounters lead to profound exchanges of gifts and new forms of partnership that can change the shape of the world.

I like Walter Wink's claim that "history belongs to the intercessors, who believe the future into being."[13] When seen in the light of the gospel, this is not a boast about the autonomous power of our believing but a promise that our faithful cooperation with God in prayer will in fact speed the kingdom's coming. We groan with and for everything that is not fully redeemed, for that which remains enslaved to the principalities and powers (Rom. 8:22–23). But our very groaning gives voice to the Holy Spirit, who wells up in our consciousness, seeking articulation through prayer and prophecy. Then *God's* defining of the issues comes to expression, and we shall be ready to receive exactly those charismatic gifts and tasks that go to the heart of the matter. Then abysmal powers that we cannot understand by rational analysis alone will fall back into retreat.

Sometimes in our interceding we are blessed with a glimpse into the larger providence of God (see Rom. 9–11). Bishop Gottfried Forck of the Evangelical Church in Berlin-Brandenburg writes that

> intercessory prayer services and vigils for people who had been arrested played an important role in the transformation of the [East German] state. Many non-Christians also participated; the services were for them initially only a sign of protest, but they became increasingly an opportunity for reflection. Demonstrations, demanding the release of those arrested, developed out of these worship services in Leipzig, a model which was taken over by other cities in September and October, 1989. One can truly say that these intercessory services played an important role in the peaceful development of the demonstrations.[14]

Intercession is inherently political, if we allow God to define that term (see Mt. 5:14; Phil. 3:20). It aims at nothing less than subduing the powers of evil with the gospel of peace (Eph. 6:10–20).

CONFESSION AND REPENTANCE

The confession of sins, one to another, was a regular part of corporate worship in the New Testament church (Col. 3:13–16; Jas. 5:16; 1 Jn. 1:9). But there may be little similarity between that activity and the brief rituals that still survive in our contemporary liturgies. Usually in the New Testament the word *confession* refers to a bold acknowledgment, a statement of faith that God in Christ is really present among believers as the ruler of the world. Like so many other prayers of the earliest church, confessions were couched in praise and frequently occurred in hymns. Philippians 2:11 is a notable example: "Therefore God has highly exalted [Jesus] and bestowed on him the name which is above every name, that at the name of Jesus every knee should bow, in heaven and on earth and under the earth, and every tongue confess that Jesus Christ is Lord to the glory of God the

Father." The language here is unusually celebrative, but the substance of it is found in many other passages where the confession of Jesus' name is understood to be the primal act of faith.[15]

What this means is that confessions of *sin* are derived from faith. They grow out of real encounters with the living God and the Lord Jesus. They are prayerful responses to the Ultimate Good. When Isaiah was overwhelmed by a vision of God "sitting upon a throne, high and lifted up," he had to cry out: "Woe is me! For I am lost; for I am a man of unclean lips, and I dwell in the midst of a people of unclean lips" (Isa. 6:1, 5–6). It is not that Isaiah and the people of Israel were so terribly evil. Yet in the presence of God's holiness they were brought very low.

Similar events happen in the New Testament. When the newly discipled Peter witnessed a great catch of fish that Jesus had caused to happen, he was virtually forced into a confession: "He fell down at Jesus' knees, saying 'Depart from me, for I am a sinful man, O Lord'" (Lk. 5:9). God's abundance and mercy brought Peter's own poverty to light, and he had to express it. Paul, writing to the Corinthians, predicts that whenever someone visiting their worship chances to hear their prayers and prophecies one to another, "the secrets of the unbeliever's heart are disclosed [and] that person will bow down before God and worship him, declaring, 'God is really among you'" (1 Cor. 14:25, NRSV).

Confession is prayer because it responds directly to God's holiness, God's power to bring forth plenitude, and at the center of it all God's burning love for us. Our confession of sin happens when we try to put holiness, plenitude, and love together and come up short. The sin that resides in us is exposed and overcome by God's goodness. Sometimes this happens quite dramatically, as in the stories narrated above. Usually it occurs more quietly. It evolves as the Spirit leads us in prayer and persistently confronts us with the desires of our "flesh," that is, the aspects of our self that still want to be ruled by the powers of this age (Gal. 5:16–21).

Repentance means the change of mind and heart that comes from recognizing God's mercy to be incomparably greater than our flesh. This good news produces a peace inside us that permits us to choose God's ways over our own sefish and destructive behaviors. "Now after John was arrested, Jesus came into Galilee, preaching the gospel of God, and saying, 'The time is fulfilled, and the kingdom of god is at hand; repent and believe in the gospel'" (Mk. 1:14–15). To repent and believe is to see a whole new world opening up before us, and to enter it. Confession and repentance count as basic prayer in the New Testament (see Lk. 15:17–19; 18:9–14). They happen frequently because they are intermingled with all of our other prayers, both personal and corporate. As we walk through straight and narrow passages into God's light, or as we open the door of our heart to let God in (Rev. 3:20), we engage in a creative act. Something of cosmic proportions happens, for "there is joy before the angels of God over one sinner who repents" (Lk. 15:10).

But does this personal act accomplish anything real in the socio-political order here and now? At least one social scientist thinks it does. In his challenging book *The Political Meaning of Christianity*, Glenn Tinder devotes a long chapter to prayer and meditation as forces for just action in the world. Tinder believes, as I do, that all of our action is tainted by sin (especially pride and false dominance when the action "works"). This, however, is no reason for inaction, which can be even more sinful. What prayer does is to bring forth honesty. Through it "one . . . resigns the ascendancy gained in action." Prayer becomes the vehicle for confession and repentance; it "reflects a faith in God as the origin of all [just] deeds" and thereby defeats the ever-present temptation to take all the credit ourselves.[16] Precisely when our action bears much fruit, we must acknowledge that at some level it has violated agape love and sown the seeds of future discontent. In prayer we confess that "only through humility, through awareness of these moral and practical limitations, does action have spiritual integrity."[17]

On the other hand, prayer also leads us to repent of inaction: "Hopelessness is sin, unwillingness to anticipate anything not comprehensible to the human mind and assured through human power. We are drawn into the sin of hopelessness by fear, and fear arises from pride. In our pride we are fearful unless all things are under our control. But they are not, and the eventual failure of control fans the flames of our fear."[18] The prayer of confession that God and Christ are in control, quite apart from our best or worst efforts, frees us to act boldly as junior partners in the new creation. We do not have to hold out for a perfect action that does everything right without hurting anyone. It does not exist. Instead we bring all of our actions, by confession and repentance, into the embrace of God's righteousness, so that we and they may be set in tune with the kingdom. Does this prayerful communion with the God of history really make a difference in the world? Faith says yes, and there are firm indications that reason can agree.

SELF-OFFERING

That is particularly so when reason has been offered up to God for renewal. The apostle writes: "I appeal to you therefore, brothers and sisters, by the mercies of God, to present your bodies as a living sacrifice, holy and acceptable to God, which is your spiritual worship. Do not be conformed to this world, but be transformed by the renewing of your minds, so that you may discern what is the will of God—what is good and acceptable and perfect" (Rom. 12:1–2, NRSV). There is no mind-body dualism here. Reason and physicality together comprise the offering of our selves. To the degree that a duality exists, we find it in the evil forces of this age, which oppose God's will. We get out from under these powers, get into the knowing and loving and doing of God's will, when we offer up our entire personhood. Earlier, in 2 Corinthians, Paul had characterized this as the transformation according to Christ's death and resurrection that we undergo when we behold the Lord's glory in contemplative prayer (3:18). He repeats the theme in Romans 6, which is a sermonic interpretation of our baptism. Because we have died with Christ in the water and now walk with him in newness of life, we must yield our whole selves to God, again and again, and our "members" (all our physical and spiritual potentialities) as *hopla* (tools or weapons) of righteousness (6:13).

All of this is both prayer language and new creation language. In fact, self-offering is the proper completion of that archprayer of the new creation we call praise. We offer ourselves most naturally when we taste and acknowledge the sweetness of God's mercy (Rom. 11:30–12:1). But self-offering can and does occur in combination with all kinds of prayer. Often it develops out of petition and intercession as we begin to hear God's answer to our requests. As we pray for what we want or what we desire for others, the Lord may well respond by saying: "And what are *you* willing to do about this? Take up your cross. Leave your old baggage behind. Come, follow me, and we shall work together for the true fulfillment of your longings. Walk with me, and you will receive far more than you ask for or think possible."

In some cases our prayer of self-offering may be one of flat-out surrender. In perilous times we must simply give our lives over to God, crying out from the depths because we have no other choice, apart from self-destruction. Addicts of all sorts know this prayer well, but every believer has some acquaintance with it. Though it may seem to be a desperate act, it is just as honorable as all other self-offerings, and perhaps more productive of joy in heaven than most.

Self-offering also counts mightily for the redemption of the world. Paul seems to be thinking along these lines when he holds up the example of some poor believers in Macedonia who "gave themselves to the Lord" as the initial part of their decision to contribute "beyond their means" to a collection of money for the church in Jerusalem. And this collection, Paul believed, would powerfully advance God's gracious plan for the world (see 2 Corinthians 8–9).

Today ethical analysis, decision making, and action may well be the arena in which prayers of self-offering make the most sense to us. Both as individuals and communities we need something more than information and job training to be God's people in the world. We need to know where God is and how we can join Christ as co-workers. We need to know which tools we can use to build people up and which weapons we can deploy to drive back the powers of this age. Above all, we need to open ourselves to the Spirit's leadership so that we can speak fitting words of the gospel in moments of crisis.

None of this will happen without fervent prayer, especially the prayer of self-offering. It is no accident that Paul follows his appeal for the presentation of our bodies with a discourse on God's grace coming to expression in our charismatic gifts and tasks (Rom. 12:3–8). By offering up our selves, we take a first big step toward the working out of our salvation (Phil. 2:12–13). But to work out salvation means that we shall be well equipped to enact *God's* choices when it comes to creating programs for the just reform of society. And this in turn means abundant life on a grand scale.

Boldness and Blessing in the Name of Jesus

In his prison cell John the Baptizer hears rumors of how Jesus is conducting his ministry. These rumors perplex him, because the military work of the messiah does not seem to be getting done. Matthew continues the story: "[John] sent word by his disciples and said to [Jesus], 'Are you the one who is to come, or are we to wait for another?' Jesus answered them, 'Go and tell John what you hear and see: the blind receive their sight, the lame walk, the lepers are cleansed, the deaf hear, the dead are raised, and the poor have the good news brought to them. And blessed is anyone who takes no offense at me'" (Mt. 11:2–6, NRSV; see also Lk. 7:18–23). As usual, Jesus' words pose a kind of riddle. He does not say straight out, "Yes, I am the Coming One." Instead he tells John to evaluate the works he does, to discern in them that evil is being conquered, but conquered by healing and hope rather than brute force. And he ends with a curious promise: "If you [including you the reader!] can stay by me as I do these things, you will be blessed."

Already in Jesus' own ministry we find a preview of what Christian prayer will come to be. Finally it is nothing other than a blessed relationship with him in service to God's kingdom. This is confirmed by the mystery of the resurrection and by the powerful movement of God's Holy Spirit among the earliest believers. In the Spirit they joyfully called upon God as Abba and Jesus as Kyrios. And they did mighty works in Jesus' name, all the while confessing that God and Jesus were the real force behind their accomplishments (Mk. 16:17–20; Jn. 14:12; Acts 4:30; 9:34; Rom. 15:17–19; 1 Cor. 12:5–6; Jas. 5:15).

In this ongoing confession, which is also a song of praise and thanksgiving, resides the real boldness of the New Testament believers. They did not simply wield power. They received it from and attributed it to the One God, who met them in three Persons. They testified to this saving threeness of God. They preached it as good news. And much of their prayer revolved around their calling to be its witnesses (Acts 4:24–31; Rom. 15:30–32; Eph. 6:18–20; Col. 4:2–4). The distinctive nature of their communion with God at the turn of the ages compelled them to speak and teach in the name of Jesus (Acts 4:17–20), not as a figure of nostalgia but as a living Lord.

In the contemporary church we are often tempted to locate our boldness and blessing exclusively in the exercise of power (usually understood as right or privilege). Thus we tend to forget Jesus, the Coming One who intrudes upon all our pretensions (Rev. 3:17–20). New Testament prayer reminds us that there is no power worth having apart from a transformative relationship with him. Paul gets things in the right order when he tells the Philippians: "I regard everything as loss because of the surpassing value of knowing Christ Jesus my Lord. For his sake I have suffered the loss of all things . . . in order that I may gain Christ and be found in him, not having a righteousness of my own that comes from the law, but one that comes through faith in Christ. . . . I want to know Christ, and the power of his resurrection and the sharing of his sufferings by becoming like him in his death" (Phil. 3:8–11, NRSV). Knowing Jesus takes priority over acquiring power. Or, better stated, it is the only way into the true exercise of power, for it always includes the cross. But knowing Jesus requires fervent and regular prayer in his presence.

Boldness and blessing are inherent to the Christian life. God wants us to experience them in the fullest possible manner. Yet access to them is carefully defined—by a Person (Rom. 5:1–2). Yes, there is a new creation. Yes, we are God's co-workers in overcoming evil with good. But only "in Christ" do we accomplish this (2 Cor. 5:17–21). The author of Hebrews urges us on: "Since, then, we have a great high priest who has passed through the heavens, Jesus, the Son of God, let us hold fast to our confession. For we do not have a high priest who is unable to sympathize with our weaknesses, but we have one who in every respect has been tested as we are, yet without sin. Let us therefore approach the throne of grace with boldness, so that we may receive mercy and find grace to help in time of need" (4:14–16 NRSV). The writer of this passage is talking about a boldness and blessing that we can bring to prayer, and he grounds it in Jesus' perpetual intercession for us at God's right hand. But such a prayer also *receives* boldness and blessing. When the beleaguered young church in Jerusalem petitioned God for strength to carry out its ministry in Jesus' name, Luke reports that "the place in which they were gathered together was shaken; and they were all filled with the Holy Spirit and spoke the word of God with boldness" (Acts 4:31).

Do things like this still happen today? In the burgeoning churches of Africa they most certainly do. And I believe we can also discern them in pockets of the more established churches, scattered throughout the world. In fact, some of our own prayer experiences are best understood as shakings of the foundation by the power of the Spirit.

Could it be that we are just now witnessing a new return to the basics in mainstream Christianity? Is New Testament prayer once again claiming its rightful place at the center of the church's life? Only God knows. What I know is that sometimes, by grace, we are able to rediscover in the biblical record an elemental wisdom for the renewal of the church and the redemption of the world. Surely, New Testament prayer fits into this category. Surely, praise God, all we need to do is try it.

Notes

PREFACE

1. From Part 3 of J. S. Bach's *Christmas Oratorio*; my free translation of the German.

CHAPTER ONE

Communion with God at the Turn of the Ages

1. I have in mind here, for example, the monumental Classics of Western Spirituality project that has been coming into print through Paulist Press. Most of the volumes are devoted to Christian authors, but some contain Jewish, Islamic, and native American writings. In addition, Dharma Publishing has made great quantities of Buddhist literature, especially from Tibet, available to English-speaking readers. Comparable outpourings of Hindu spirituality can be found, and the Christian Book Distributors of Peabody, Massachusetts, should be mentioned as a ready source of time-honored volumes on prayer from the evangelical wing of the church.

2. A recent cover story from *Newsweek* (December 17, 1990) documents the rise in North America of a free-form spirituality characterized by very tenuous affiliations with traditional religious groupings or none at all. See "And the Children Shall Lead Them: Young Americans Return to God," 50–56. Similar trends can be read from some of the Gallup polls of the last few years. See, in addition, the analysis of American religion presented in *Habits of the Heart: Individualism and Commitment in American Life* by Robert Bellah, et al. (Berkeley: Univ. of California Press, 1985).

3. Jacob Needleman, a philosopher sympathetic to many of the teachings found in the various New Age movements, is nevertheless critical of their adherents on just this matter. See "In the Spirit of Philosophy: An Interview with Jacob Needleman," by D. Patrick Miller, *Free Spirit* 7, 6 (1989): 27–33.

4. "Prayer and Action," *A Primer on Prayer*, ed. Paul R. Sponheim (Philadelphia: Fortress Press, 1989), 98.

5. "How Do Pastors Worship?" *Action Information* (a publication of the Alban Institute), May/June 1990, 5.

6. The book was first published in London by Hodder & Stoughton.

7. Published in Philadelphia by Westminster Press in 1984.

8. Nielsen, *The Bible*, 92f.

9. Nielsen, *The Bible*, 94.

10. "Wasting Time with God," *Weavings* 4, 3 (March/April 1989): 32.

11. In 2 Cor. 11:2–3; Eph. 5:25–32; Rev. 22:17 (and probably 3:20) believers are related to Christ as bride to bridegroom. But the sexual overtones here are minimal when compared, say, with the prayer language of certain medieval mystics and eighteenth-century protestant pietists.

12. In the passages cited Paul argues by way of reminder. He is not introducing new information, nor does he need to explain what it means or how it feels to know God and be known by God.

13. In his classical treatment of prayer, *The Communion of the Christian with God*, Wilhelm Herrmann stresses that "the moral activity of the Christian forms part of his communion with God. For the Christian such occupation is not foreign service . . . it is, itself, worship." I am quoting from the second German edition as translated by J. Sandys Stanyon and reprinted by Fortress Press (Philadelphia, 1971), 298.

14. See (in order) 2 Cor. 5:17; Gal. 6:15; Rom. 3:26; 8:18; 11:5; 2 Cor. 8:14; 2 Cor. 6:2; 1 Cor. 10:11; Gal. 4:4; Jn. 12:31.

15. See *Abba: Meditations Based on the Lord's Prayer* (London: Longmans, Green, 1940), 1.

16. That the title *Kyrios* is applied simply to Jesus rather than to Jesus Christ or Christ means that the earliest believers were most awed by the fact that their friend and leader, the historical prophet from Nazareth, was now reigning at God's right hand.

17. *Addiction and Grace* (San Francisco: Harper & Row, 1988), 8.

18. *Being in Love: The Practice of Christian Prayer* (San Francisco: Harper & Row, 1989), 31.

CHAPTER TWO

Jesus, Our Teacher and Priest

1. Scholars are divided as to whether these verses were part of Luke's original manuscript. The current Nestle-Aland Greek text of the New Testament includes them but places them in brackets.

2. This is one of Joachim Jeremias's strongest arguments that the term *Abba* was taught by Jesus to his disciples as a distinctive prayer word for their own use. It seems far more likely that Jesus himself introduced this culturally unusual address to God among his earliest followers than that it originated in the post-Easter worship of the church. It continued in the life and liturgy of the Greek-speaking congregations *because it came from Jesus*. See *The Prayers of Jesus*, trans. J. Bowden and C. Burchard (Philadelphia: Fortress Press, 1967), esp. 9–65.

3. See Geza Vermes, *Jesus the Jew: A Historian's Reading of the Gospels* (New York: Macmillan, 1973), 58–82.

4. Some of the Beatitudes appear to be conditional, "If you do thus and so, you will be blessed" (see Mt. 5:6–9). But the whole context for the Beatitudes in Matthew and Luke, which is one of grace, suggests that even these verses are more likely to be simple statements of fact than demands for improvement. The Matthean Beatitudes especially are inclusive; they are meant to reach out to everyone.

5. I have provided a short interpretation of this event in *New Testament Hospitality: Partnership with Strangers as Promise and Mission* (Philadelphia: Fortress Press, 1985), 28.

6. See his instructive book by this title, published by Harper & Row (San Francisco, 1987).

7. The image recalls Jacob's dream (Gen. 28:10–17) in which the patriarch sees angels moving up and down a ladder that reaches to heaven. According to Jesus, Nathanael will see the angels making their transit "upon the Son of Man," that is, himself. But in the Greek the promise "you will see" refers to a *plurality* of viewers. What seems to be intended for Nathanael alone is actually extended to all of Jesus' followers. In his ground-breaking work *History and Theology of the*

Fourth Gospel, rev. ed. (Nashville: Abingdon, 1979), J. Louis Martyn has demonstrated that John fashioned his Gospel so as to present a "two-level drama." On one level the historical Jesus speaks to the people of his day. On another level the risen Christ simultaneously addresses all of his later disciples down through the centuries.

CHAPTER THREE

How the Spirit Leads Us in Prayer

1. *The Go-Between God: The Holy Spirit and the Christian Mission* (New York: Oxford Univ. Press, 1979), 17f.
2. Larry W. Hurtado, *One God, One Lord: Early Christian Devotion and Ancient Jewish Monotheism* (Philadelphia: Fortress Press, 1988), 124. One of Hurtado's main points is that these confessions of and prayers to Jesus as a divine figure issued precisely from Jews who thought they were remaining true to the one God of Israel.
3. Donald G. Bloesch, *The Struggle of Prayer* (Colorado Springs: Helmers & Howard, 1988), 61.
4. Here Jesus is probably using Semitic exaggeration to magnify the goodness of God. On the other hand, he was not at all romantic about human nature. See Mt. 5:21–32; Mk. 7:20–23.
5. See James D. G. Dunn, *Romans 1–8, Word Biblical Commentary,* vol. 38a (Dallas: Word Books, 1988), 252–54.
6. "Born Anew," *Theology Today* 44, 2 (July 1987): 189–96. See esp. p. 194, where Schneiders writes that "the Spirit is the one of whom we are *born* spiritually in the waters of baptism just as we are born physically of our mothers in the waters of natural birth. . . . Jesus was not speaking here [Jn. 3:3–6] of being 'engendered' by God, as of a male principle, but of being 'born' of God, as from a female principle."
7. See Phyllis Trible's illuminating discussion of these passages in *God and the Rhetoric of Sexuality* (Philadelphia: Fortress Press, 1978).
8. It is important to emphasize that we dare not isolate the feminine aspects of God in the Spirit so as to contrast them with masculine ones located in the Father and the Son. The Father and the Son are just as feminine as the Spirit. Thus Julian of Norwich and other medieval mystics addressed Jesus as Mother. But it is clear that in doing so, they were not attempting to deny his maleness. See Caroline Walker Bynam, *Jesus as Mother: Studies in the Spirituality of the High Middle Ages* (Berkeley and Los Angeles: Univ. of California Press, 1982).
9. In the New Testament these anthropological terms are roughly synonymous.
10. "Gathered in That Name," *Weavings* 5, 4 (July/August 1990): 13.
11. From earliest times one can distinguish two modes of devotion practiced by Christians. One is the kataphatic way of praying with images. Much of the New Testament manifests this approach. The other mode is the apophatic, which means "apart from images."
12. For Paul, the term *flesh,* when used pejoratively, denotes all those forces of fallenness that inhabit human beings. They reveal themselves in sinful behavior, both physical and psychic, but do not constitute the heart or physical body of the individual (Rom. 7:13–18:13; Gal. 5:16–24). In these, however obscured, God's image persists.
13. The hymn text is by Frank von Christierson and is designated no. 698 in *The Hymnal 1982 According to the Use of the Episcopal Church* (New York: Church-Hymnal Corp., 1985). Deborah Dunn called my attention to the appropriateness of this prayer. Though we find no direct addresses to the Holy Spirit in the New

Testament, there are instances of hearing the Spirit's prayer as our own (Gal. 4:6) and requests to God for the Spirit's aid (Lk. 11:13). Prayer to the Holy Spirit is a legitimate development within the devotional life of Christians, but if we wish to maintain continuity with the believers of the New Testament, the Spirit will not become the chief focus of our imagistic praying. That will always be Jesus.

14. James Dunn, who himself identifies with charismatic elements in the church, doubts that 8:27 is a "specific allusion to glossolalia." See *Romans 1–8*, 478.

15. *Romans 9–16, Word Biblical Commentary*, vol. 38b (Dallas: Word Books, 1988), 860.

CHAPTER FOUR

Thy Kingdom Come

1. See esp. Mt. 25:1–13; Mk. 13:24–27; Lk. 12:35–40; 21:25–28; 22:28–30.

2. The Greek word for "take [it] by force" (*harpazein*) can denote this brutal act, especially when it happens in wartime.

3. John A. Sanford's popular book *The Kingdom Within: The Inner Meaning of Jesus' Sayings* (New York/Ramsey: Paulist Press, 1970) errs in this direction. He holds that "the kingdom [as taught by Jesus] was not something coming upon man from outside of himself, but was a reality within himself, the very foundation of his personal existence" (42). This inside-outside opposition does not accurately reflect Jesus' words about the kingdom.

4. "Entering into the Kingly Power of God," *Journal of Biblical Literature* 107,4 (1988): 667.

5. Marcus, "Entering into the Kingly Power," 668.

6. "Entering into the Kingly Power," 674.

7. *New Testament Hospitality*, 27f. Note also festal passages like Mt. 11:16–19; 25:14–30; Mk. 2:15–22; 6:30–44; Lk. 15:3–10, 11–32, where the kingdom is not mentioned as such but is surely implied.

8. In Lk. 14:24, which concludes a parable about a great banquet, the Greek word for "you" is plural. This means that the scene has shifted from a fictional master, addressing a single servant, to Jesus himself, telling his hearers about "my banquet," i.e., his ministry.

9. A Christian document called the *Didache* ("teaching"), which comes from the first or early second century, juxtaposes instruction on the use of the Lord's Prayer with directions for celebrating the Eucharist (see chapters 8–9). This suggests, but does not prove, that the two were already connected in the church's liturgy. Arland Hultgren believes that there is good evidence for the use of the Lord's Prayer by the first-century Johannine community and that it was prayed "in eucharistic and other gatherings." See "The Bread Petition of the Lord's Prayer," in *Christ and His Communities: Essays in Honor of Reginald H. Fuller*, ed. Arland J. Hultgren and Barbara Hall (Cincinnati: Forward Movement Publications, 1990), 51.

10. *Praying the Kingdom: Towards a Political Spirituality* (New York/Mahwah: Paulist Press, 1985), 30f.

11. *The Struggle of Prayer*, 168.

12. *Letters to Malcolm: Chiefly on Prayer* (New York: Harcourt, Brace & World, 1964), 24.

13. Gerhard Lohfink, *Jesus and Community: The Social Dimension of Christian Faith*, trans. J. P. Galvin (Philadelphia: Fortress Press; and New York/Ramsey: Paulist Press, 1984), 14f.

14. See J. Jeremias, *The Prayers of Jesus*, 100f., and my *New Testament Hospitality*, 44f.
15. "Fear Not, for Behold . . . ," *The Urban Oasis*, Winter 1989, 1 and 7.

CHAPTER FIVE
Whatever You Ask for in Prayer

1. Sharyn Echols Dowd, *Prayer, Power, and the Problem of Suffering; Mark: 11:22–25 in the Context of Markan Theology*, SBL Dissertation Series 105 (Atlanta: Scholars Press, 1988), 161, n. 39.
2. *Prayer, Power, and the Problem of Suffering*, 121.
3. *Commands of Christ: Authority and Implications* (Nashville: Abingdon Press, 1972), 63.
4. The idea is that the widow's adversary is trying to prove, legally, that she does not deserve to retain certain rights or items of property. When the widow cries, "Vindicate *me* against my adversary" (18:3; italics added), we see that her very self is being threatened.
5. Mk. 8:34 and 9:29 show that Jesus himself used prayer in order to heal.
6. In his book *The Struggle of Prayer*, Bloesch demonstrates how the verb in this title applies to most forms of prayer.
7. Cited by Bloesch, *The Struggle of Prayer*, 79.
8. See *Welcome Holy Spirit: A Study of Charismatic Renewal in the Church*, ed. Larry Christenson (Minneapolis: Augsburg, 1987), 236.
9. Dowd, *Prayer, Power, and the Problem of Suffering*, 65.
10. Other factors are considered by the New Testament authors. James says that we may not receive what we ask for because we ask "wrongly" (4:3), intending to squander the object of our petitions. Such activity dishonors God and Christ and compromises our love for one another (1 Jn. 3:22–23). See Sophie Laws, *A Commentary on the Epistle of James* (London: A. & C. Black, 1980), 173. Still another reason for prayers to go unanswered would be the inability of the believing community or its authorized representatives to unite in their requests (Mt. 18:18; Jas. 5:14–16).
11. Yet "seeing" God's glory does diminish suffering by adding something more real than the pain. Besides, as God wills, some human suffering will indeed be done away with in this present life. See chapter 8.
12. New Testament scholars are divided as to whether the apostle himself wrote this letter or whether one of his followers composed it after his death from recollections and notes. Given the literary climate of the first century, this second possibility would not be seen as an attempt to deceive.
13. See *The Hymnal 1982*, no. 636. These words come from stanza 3 of the hymn "How Firm a Foundation Ye Saints of the Lord," attributed to the anonymous author "K" in John Rippon's 1787 *Selection*.
14. Geza Vermes, *Jesus the Jew*, 75. Cited from Bab Talmud Ber. 34b and Jer Talmud Ber. 9d.
15. *Letters to Malcolm*, 60f.
16. *With Christ in the School of Prayer* (Springdale, PA: Whitaker House, 1981), 81.
17. The citation is from her *Sometimes I Feel Like a Blob* (Glendale, CA: Regal Books, 1965), 67–70. It is quoted by Stanley J. Grenz in his *Prayer: The Cry for the Kingdom* (Peabody, MA: Hendrickson Publishers, 1988), 90f.
18. *The Hymnal 1982*, no. 693, stanzas 1 and 2. For details of Charlotte Elliott's life, see F. Colquhoun, *A Hymn Companion: Insight into Three Hundred Christian Hymns* (Wilton, CT: Morehouse Barlow, 1985), 164f.

19. Arland J. Hultgren, "Expectations of Prayer in the New Testament," in *A Primer on Prayer*, ed. Sponheim, 35. Hultgren found this reference in David M. White, *The Search for God* (New York: Macmillan, 1983), 127.

CHAPTER SIX

The Heartbeat of Praise and Thanksgiving

1. "Eucharistic" comes from the Greek word *eucharistia*, which means "thanksgiving." Today the term "eucharist" usually denotes a celebration of the Lord's Supper, but in the New Testament era it had not yet acquired this technical meaning, at least not in the church as a whole. Its earliest occurrence in this sense seems to be the *Didache*, chapters 9 and 10.
2. Other reasons are cited by Paul F. Bradshaw, *Daily Prayer in the Early Church* (New York: Oxford Univ. Press, 1982) 14ff, and Thomas J. Talley, "From Berakah to Eucharistia: A Reopening Question," *Worship* 50, 2 (March 1976): 115–37.
3. *The Lutheran*, November 23, 1988, 19.
4. Probably the best-known representative of this position is Merlin R. Carothers. See especially *Power in Praise: How the Spiritual Dynamic of Praise Revolutionizes Our Lives* (Plainfield, NJ: Logos International, 1971).
5. C. S. Lewis, *Letters to Malcolm*, 90.
6. It was well known among the earliest believers that Jesus, in a manner not typical of first-century Judaism, began some of his most important pronouncements with the words "Amen, I say to you" (see Mt. 5:18; Mk. 14:25; Lk. 4:24; Jn. 1:52 as prime examples).
7. Hans Dieter Betz, commenting on 2 Cor. 4:15 and 9:11–15, interprets Paul's meaning as follows: "The more thanksgiving occurs, the more grace has been bestowed and received, . . . the greater the power of God." See *2 Corinthians 8 and 9: A Commentary on Two Administrative Letters of the Apostle Paul* (Philadelphia: Fortress Press, 1985), 119.
8. Daniel W. Hardy and David F. Ford, *Praising and Knowing God* (Philadelphia: Westminster Press, 1985), 82. The phrase comes from Herbert's poem "Providence."
9. Herbert wrote at least three poems entitled "Praise," and many of his other works fall into this category, either as descriptions or as actual prayers.
10. Jaroslav Pelikan, *Bach Among the Theologians* (Philadelphia: Fortress Press, 1986), 140.
11. See my article, "The Knowing of Glory and Its Consequences (2 Corinthians 3–5)" in *The Conversation Continues: Studies in Paul and John in Honor of J. Louis Martyn*, ed. Robert T. Fortna and Beverly R. Gaventa (Nashville: Abingdon Press, 1990), 158–69. Here I attempt to show that the chief consequence of apprehending God's glory in Christ is enlistment, at ever-deeper levels, in the ministry of reconciliation.
12. C. S. Lewis, *Reflections on the Psalms* (New York: Harcourt, Brace & Co., 1958), 97.
13. *Power in Praise* seems to be based on the view that praise will bring forth results when all other forms of prayer have failed. See esp. 101–4.
14. *Power in Praise*, 8.
15. Here the person "in the position of an outsider" is probably any member of the church who is not capable of blessing God along with the tongues-speaker because he or she cannot comprehend what is being offered up. See Gordon D. Fee, *The First Epistle to the Corinthians* (Grand Rapids, MI: Wm. B. Eerdmans, 1987), 673.
16. *Praising and Knowing God*, 76.
17. This point is made with regard to the earthly temple in Ps. 9:11, 14; 48:1–2, 11; 65:1, etc. Isa. 12:6 and 40:9 probably refers to an ideal Zion at the dawning of God's absolute reign.

18. The Book of Common Prayer (1979). See "The Holy Eucharist, Rite II."
19. Carothers, *Power in Praise,* 101. Carothers does not tell us about his acquaintance with this woman, if any, or how he came to hear her story. He does mention that she was later healed of her arthritic pains at a prayer service. His interpretation seems to be that this happened because her praise experience had rendered her "free to believe" (102). On the role of faith in prayers for healing, see chapter 8 of the present study.

CHAPTER SEVEN
Our High Calling to Pray for Neighbors

1. This raises the important question of efficacious praying by non-Christians. Does prayer have value only as it goes "through" Jesus? This question is never addressed directly by the New Testament writers. But of course Jesus assumed that Jewish prayer was valid, and Luke believes that the prayers of well-meaning Gentiles will be heard by God even when those offering them do not know Jesus as Messiah (Acts 10:1–5, 34–35; 17:22–28).
2. This translation is by Harold W. Attridge in *The Epistle to the Hebrews* (Philadelphia: Fortress Press, 1989), 206. Attridge interprets the verse as follows: "Christ, because of his 'inviolable' priesthood, is able to offer complete salvation, that is, salvation that involves participation in the same transcendent sphere of which he is a part" (210). This would mean, among other things, sharing in Christ's priesthood.
3. *Lutheran Book of Worship* (Minneapolis: Augsburg, 1978), no. 299, stanza 7.
4. L. William Countryman, *The Mystical Way in the Fourth Gospel: Crossing over into God* (Philadelphia: Fortress Press, 1987), 106–8.
5. *With Christ in the School of Prayer,* 198f.
6. *With Christ in the School of Prayer,* 195.
7. C. S. Lewis, *Letters to Malcolm,* 70.
8. Douglas V. Steere, "Intercession: Caring for Souls," *Weavings* 4, 2 (March/April 1989): 19f.
9. *The Hymnal 1982,* no. 602.
10. *New York Times,* June 10, 1990, "Week in Review," p. 5.
11. Steere, "Intercession," 20.
12. See Gal. 3:1ff; 4:19f.
13. Larry Christenson, *The Gift of Tongues* (Minneapolis: Bethany Fellowship, 1963), 18; and Dennis J. Bennett, "Is Speaking in Tongues Necessary?" *Acts 29,* May/June 1990, 8.
14. Koenig, *New Testament Hospitality,* 55–57.
15. Steere, "Intercession," 21.
16. See Bloesch, *The Struggle of Prayer,* 88. Yet it would be a mistake (not made by Bloesch) to conclude that the deep joy given by God (Jn. 17:13; Rom. 5:1–5) simply displaces our sorrow and depression. These somber aspects of life may persist or recur, but they need not dominate our hearts.
17. See the fine little book by Anthony Bloom, *Beginning to Pray* (New York/Paramus/Toronto: Paulist Press, 1970).

CHAPTER EIGHT
Prayers of Forgiveness and Healing

1. Mk. 2:5 does not really constitute an exception to this rule. The man is both paralyzed and a sinner, but no causal sequence is articulated by Jesus. The most

natural interpretation of this verse is that Jesus perceives the man's moral suffering to be particularly acute and thus moves swiftly to relieve it.

2. The Greek word *sozein* also means to "deliver, release, or heal" and is the same one used in Jas. 5:15.

3. *New York Times*, December 30, 1989, sect. A, p. 25.

4. *Is Human Forgiveness Possible? A Pastoral Care Perspective* (Nashville: Abingdon Press, 1985), esp. 174–77.

5. Steere, "Intercession," 24f.

6. Simon Tugwell, *Prayer: Living with God* (Springfield, IL: Templegate Publishers, 1975), 90.

7. *Letters to Malcolm*, 106.

8. *Resurrection: Interpreting the Easter Gospel* (New York: Pilgrim Press, 1984), 7–51.

9. Raymond E. Brown understands the sin unto death as apostasy from the community. Only this willful act of self-exclusion will remove someone from the church's prayer list. See *The Epistles of John*, The Anchor Bible, vol. 30 (Garden City, NY: Doubleday, 1982), 612–18, 636. Brown thinks that the author is actively discouraging all prayer for apostates, but the text does not seem to require this interpretation.

10. See Bondi, "Becoming Bearers of Reconciliation," *Weavings* 5, 1 (January/February 1990): 6–17; and Wuellner, "Gathered in That Name," 14.

11. When Jesus says, in Mt. 18:17, "Let him be to you as a Gentile and a tax collector," three features of the text ought to be noted. First, in the Gospels Gentiles and tax collectors are prime candidates for repentance because Jesus seeks them out in love. Second, the little word *as* suggests the meaning of "not really, not for all eternity." Third, the pronoun *you* in this saying is singular, which means that the offended one may have to break off the relationship, but the church as a whole need not do so.

12. "Gathered in That Name," 15.

13. J. Louis Martyn demonstrates that the controversies surrounding healing in Jn. 5:1–18 and chapter 9 would have been understood by the Gospel's first readers as a two-level drama. That is, the stories were taken to be not only incidents from the time of the historical Jesus but also allusions to recent events in the life of the Johannine congregation where an unnamed Christian healer had experienced hostile responses to his or her activity. See *History and Theology in the Fourth Gospel*, revised and enlarged ed. (Nashville: Abingdon Press, 1979), esp. 24–72 and the rabbinic texts cited on 31.

14. Several of the healing stories in Mark's Gospel contain traces of what we might call directions for how to do it (see 5:9, 41; 6:12–35; 7:31–35; 8:22–26; 9:14–29). More than in any other Gospel Jesus lays hands on those he heals (6:5; 7:32–35; 8:22–26; and 9:27 are unique to Mark). In 13:34 Jesus says that as his disciples wait for the coming of the Son of Man, they will be like servants, "each with his work." The word for "work" in Greek is *exousia*, which literally means "authority." But elsewhere in Mark the only *exousia* conferred on disciples is for casting out demons (3:15; 6:7) and healing (6:12).

15. See n. 13 above.

16. See especially Francis MacNutt, *The Power to Heal* (Notre Dame: Ave Maria Press, 1977); Matthew Linn, Sheila Fabricant, Dennis Linn, *Healing the Eight Stages of Life* (New York/Mahwah: Paulist Press, 1988); and Tilda Norberg, Robert D. Webber, *Stretch Out Your Hand: Exploring Healing Prayer* (New York: United Church Press, 1990).

17. Peri Rasolondraibe, "Healing Ministry in Madagascar," *Word and World* 9, 4 (Fall 1989): 344–50, esp. 348f.

18. *The Power to Heal*, 33.

19. *Healing the Eight Stages of Life*, 3–22.

20. Scholars disagree about what Paul's illness or "thorn in the flesh" actually was. But the context surrounding his most extensive allusion to it (2 Cor. 12:1–11) suggests that it was something visible and unpleasant, something that appeared to compromise his authority as a minister of the gospel. Gal. 4:12–15 points to the possibility of an ocular disorder that repelled people.

21. We shall be wise to heed the reminder of Robert Llewelyn that the nonhealing of diseases during the apostolic period was not necessarily cause for great concern about the efficacy of prayer. He writes: "Timothy's digestive problems presumably remained . . . and Paul had to leave his friend Trophimus sick at Miletus" (1 Tim. 5:23; 2 Tim. 4:20). *Prayer and Healing* (Norwich, England: Julian Shrine Publication, n.d.), 13. Though prayers for healing are not mentioned in either of these passages, it is reasonable to assume that they were offered. On this topic see also Arland J. Hultgren, "Expectations of Prayer in the New Testament," in *A Primer on Prayer*, ed. Sponheim, 23–35.

22. "'When God Doesn't Heal," *International Lutheran Renewal*, no. 111, February 1989, n.p.

23. John E. Biersdorf, *Healing of Purpose: God's Call to Discipleship* (Nashville: Abingdon Press, 1985).

24. In sharp contrast to the synoptic writers, John tells no stories about exorcisms. Yet he clearly conceives of Jesus and his followers as engaging in battle with "the evil one" (17:15) who is "ruler of this world" (12:31).

25. See *Thy Kingdom Come: A Blumhardt Reader*, ed. Vernard Eller (Grand Rapids, MI: Wm. B. Eerdmans, 1989), xviif.

26. Note the sensible comments on ministries of deliverance in *Welcome Holy Spirit*, Christenson, ed., 341–46, and *Deliverance Prayer: Experiential, Psychological, and Theological Approaches*, ed. Matthew and Dennis Linn (Mahwah, NJ: Paulist Press, 1981). With regard to M. Scott Peck's *People of the Lie* (New York: Simon & Schuster, 1983), which relates several incidents that fall into the categories of possession and exorcism, I tend to agree with the assessment of Walter Wink that the book "is flawed by [Peck's] refusal to see the parents of his patients themselves as the victims of parents who were victims, *ad infinitum*. As a consequence he demonizes people." See *Violence and Nonviolence in South Africa: Jesus's Third Way* (Philadelphia and Santa Cruz: New Society Publishers, 1987), 93, n. 40.

27. *The Hymnal 1982*, no. 449, stanzas 1 and 5.

CHAPTER NINE

Out of the Depths I Cry

1. This was also true with Paul, whose prayers in the midst of a life-threatening storm at sea were answered with the appearance of an angel promising deliverance to him and his shipmates (Acts 27:21–26). Though Stephen had to die, he was comforted in the moments just prior to his martyrdom by a vision of the heavenly Jesus, standing at God's right hand as if to welcome him (Acts 7:54–56).

2. *The Struggle of Prayer*, 67.

3. Randolph Lloyd Frew, *Praying with HIV/AIDS: Collects, Prayers and Litanies in a Time of Crisis* (Cincinnati: Forward Movement Publications, 1990), 10.

4. I find James Dunn to be on the right track in interpreting this verse. He writes "We may assume that it is not so much an anthropological tension which evokes the cry, but the eschatological tension of being caught between the two epochs of Adam and Christ, of death and life. . . . That this *can* be the cry of one who already *has* the Spirit . . . is sufficiently evident from 8:23 and 2 Cor. 5:2–5." See *Romans 1–8*, 396f. The "body of death" does not refer to an evil inherent in matter but to a current existence in which one's good physicality is headed for death because of sin's power.

5. *Addiction and Grace*, 168.

6. Quoted by Bloesch, *The Struggle of Prayer*, 68. His source is cited as *Saint Augustine: Sermons on the Liturgical Seasons*, trans. Sister Mary Sarah Muldowney (New York: Fathers of the Church, 1959), 85f.

7. May, *Addiction and Grace*, 167.

8. With reference to Paul's thorn in the flesh (2 Cor. 12:7–10), May notes that although we cannot be sure what affliction the apostle suffered from, "the words [of his description] speak superbly to the problem of addiction." See *Addiction and Grace*, 183, n. 20.

9. *Ultimate Prizes* (New York: Ballantine Books, 1989), 183.

10. *A Grief Observed* (London: Faber & Faber, 1961), 26f.

11. *A Grief Observed*, 32.

12. See *In Memory of Her: A Feminist Theological Reconstruction of Christian Origins* (New York: Crossroad, 1983), 217. Schüssler Fiorenza observes that "the baptismal declaration of Gal. 3:28 runs counter to the general acceptance of male religious privileges among Greeks, Romans, Persians, and also Jews in the first century C.E." She then proceeds to offer strong evidence from relevant texts that this is so.

13. My view of this passage is that Paul meant to accent the constancy of the process—the Greek present tense is used—rather than the spiritual improvement of the believer day by day. See the parallel in 2 Cor. 4:16–17. In the ancient world mirrors were thought to be both reflectors and revealers of hidden truth.

14. Note the references just before and after chapter 3 to opponents who seem to be advocating a form of scriptural interpretation that Paul denounces as peddling and tampering with God's word (2:17; 4:2). 2 Cor. 3:7–18 is itself a mystical exegesis of the Moses story in Exodus 34. It may well be based on ideas promoted by the teachers Paul is trying to refute.

15. Not all the images of the risen Jesus presented in the New Testament are personal. Note, for example, the Ladder, the Bread of Heaven, the Light of the World, the Way, the Truth, and the Life, the Door to the Sheepfold, the Lamb, the Lion of Judah, and the Root of David, all of which are found in the Johannine writings. In Revelation, precisely the personal images of Jesus are fierce and frightening (1:12–17; 19:11–16).

16. William Johnston offers us wise counsel regarding such experiences when he writes: "You can say with Paul that your life lies hidden with Christ in God. And this painful sense of absence is an excellent prayer. Remain with it. Do not feel obliged to think about Jesus or pray to Jesus. Just be! And you will find that Jesus reveals to you the Father who is present, though not objectified, in the depths of your being." See *Being in Love: The Christian Practice of Prayer*, 80.

17. *Resurrection: Interpreting the Easter Gospel*, 92.

18. *Being in Love*, 12; 15f.

19. *Addiction and Grace*, 169–71, 175f.

CHAPTER TEN

Prayer in the Church's Worship

1. Gordon Fee, *The First Epistle to the Corinthians*, 282.

2. Robert Banks, *Paul's Idea of Community: The Early House Churches in Their Historical Setting* (Grand Rapids, MI: Wm. B. Eerdmans, 1980), 41f.

3. This is indicated by expressions like the following: "And whenever you [plural] stand praying . . . " (Mk. 11:25); "When you [plural] pray, say 'Father, hallowed be thy name . . . ' " (Lk. 11:2); "they went up to the upper room, where they were staying . . . [and] with one accord devoted themselves to prayer" (Acts 1:13–14); "And they were all together in Solomon's Portico [in the temple]" (Acts 5:12); "On the first day of the week when we were gathered together to break bread . . . " (Acts 20:7); "The cup of blessing which we [repeatedly] bless, is it not a participation in the blood of Christ . . . " (1 Cor. 10:16, my translation); "When you are assembled as a church . . . " (1 Cor. 11:18); "For as often as you eat this bread and drink this cup, you proclaim the Lord's death . . . " (1 Cor. 11:26); "When you come together, each one has a hymn, a lesson, a revelation . . . " (1 Cor. 14:26); "Let each [speaker in tongues] keep silence in church [*en ekklēsia*] and speak to himself and God" (1 Cor. 14:18); " . . . not neglecting to meet together as the habit of some is, but encouraging one another" (Heb. 10:25); "If a man with gold rings and in fine clothing comes into your assembly . . . " (*synagōgē*; Jas. 2:2); "Therefore confess your sins to one another and pray for one another . . . " (Jas. 5:16). Less certain, but still probable references to regular assemblies of the whole church for worship are 1 Cor. 5:4; 16:2; Eph. 5:18–20; Phil. 4:4–7; Col. 3:15; 1 Thess. 5:16–22; 1 Tim. 2:1, 8; Heb. 12:22–24; 13:15; 1 Pet. 4:9–11. The special events described in Acts 1:15–26; 4:24–31; 12:5; 14:23; and 1 Cor. 5:3–5 may have occurred during regular times of worship involving the whole church, but it is impossible to be certain about this.

4. Fee, *The First Epistle to the Corinthians*, 280.

5. Paul E. Bradshaw, *Daily Prayer in the Early Church: A Study of the Origin and Development of the Divine Office* (New York: Oxford Univ. Press, 1982), 40f.

6. *Daily Prayer*, 26.

7. The *Didache*, which may come from the first century, contains directives on prayer that do not appear in the New Testament. For example, the author insists that the Lord's Prayer should be offered three time a day (8.3) and provides the actual words of a long prayer that is to be said at the Eucharist (chapters 10 and 11).

8. *Didache* (as noted above) does transmit a eucharistic prayer, while the New Testament provides only the "words of institution" (Mk. 14:22–25 and parallels; 1 Cor. 11:23–26). Gal. 3:27–28; Rom. 6:1–11; and 1 Pet. 2:1–10 probably contain fragments of a baptismal liturgy, but strictly speaking they are not prayers.

9. Of course baptism and the Eucharist must have been prominent in the services of the church, but we simply do not know how often they took place. Almost certainly there were gatherings of the local church for worship that did not include them. See Bradshaw, *Daily Prayer*, 40. While it goes without saying that some type of gospel proclamation would have graced every corporate service of the church, this need not have happened via Scripture readings, teachings, or sermon-like addresses. Only one of these is even mentioned in Corinthians 14, our best piece of evidence for a New Testament community at worship (see the *didachē* or "lesson" in 14:26). When Paul and his followers name the activities that "build up" the church in its worship, what they mention most often are prophecy (1 Cor. 14:1–32; 1 Thess. 5:19) and praise and thanksgiving (Eph. 5:18–20; Col. 3:15–17; 1 Thess. 5:16–18). These are assumed to be effective statements of the good news in and of themselves.

10. Bradshaw, *Daily Prayer*, 18. He cites as evidence from the Old Testament, 1 Kgs. 8:22, 54; 2 Chron. 6:12–13; Ez. 9:5; Ps. 28:2; Isa. 1:15; Lam. 2:19.

11. *Daily Prayer*, 27.

12. Moshe Idel, *Kabbalah: New Perspectives* (New Haven: Yale Univ. Press, 1988), 78f.

13. See chapter 6, 66, 77.

14. Philo of Alexandria, a contemporary of Jesus and Paul, tells of a Jewish monastic community in Egypt—like the Shakers it was composed of both men and women—who sang hymns to God in a kind of choric dance. See *On the Contemplative Life*, XI, 83–87.
15. Fee, *The First Epistle to the Corinthians*, 652.
16. "When in Our Worship God Is Glorified: The Music of Liturgy and Life," *Weavings* 4, July–August (1989), 10.
17. "Living the Eucharistic Prayer," *Weavings* (see above), 29.
18. J. Koenig, "Vision, Self Offering, and Transformation for Ministry (Rom. 12:1–8)" in *Sin, Salvation, and the Spirit*, ed. Daniel Durken, O.S.B. (Collegeville, MN: Liturgical Press, 1979), 320f.
19. See Dietrich Bonhoeffer, *Life Together*, trans. John Doberstein (New York: Harper & Row, 1954), 45f, and Richard B. Hays, *Echoes of Scripture in the Letters of Paul* (New Haven: Yale Univ. Press, 1989), 72f.
20. Most of the prayer words in Rom. 15:9–11 and Heb. 2:12–13 are direct quotes from or allusions to the psalms and the prophets.
21. "Liturgy and Life: Christ's Redemptive Work," in *Christian Living for a Change*, May/June 1990, 7.
22. Fee, *The First Epistle to the Corinthians*, 684, 698.
23. See Koenig, *New Testament Hospitality*, 138, for Mortimer Arias's use of this phrase.
24. *Praying the Kingdom*, 126.
25. *Praying the Kingdom*, 138.
26. Acts 2:3, 17; 4:20; 7:2, 30, 35, 44, 55; 8:18, 23; 9:12, 17, 27; 10:3, 17; 11:5, 6, 13, 23; 13:12, 31; 14:9; 16:9, 10; 22:14, 15, 18; 26:13, 16; 28:26f.
27. *Life Together*, 71.

CHAPTER ELEVEN
Prayer as Peacemaking and Warfare

1. J. D. G. Dunn, *Romans 9–16*, 736f.
2. *Romans 9–16*, 756.
3. *Love of Enemies: The Way to Peace* (Philadelphia: Fortress Press, 1984), 119.
4. *Violence and Nonviolence in South Africa*, 15.
5. *Violence and Nonviolence in South Africa*, 16, 34.
6. *Violence and Nonviolence in South Africa*, 26. When Jesus gives his instructions in Mt. 5:39–41, the "you" of the hearer is consistently singular. It is as if he says, "You here might be called on to do something like this; on the other hand, you there might respond as follows."
7. See Hardy and Ford, *Praising and Knowing God*, 94.
8. *Horizons* 16, 1 (1989): 79–86.
9. "Two Imageries of Peace," 83–92.
10. "Two Imageries of Peace," 95f.
11. In *Naming the Powers* Walter Wink spells out his view that the spiritual powers referred to in the New Testament are not "separate or heavenly or ethereal entities but . . . the inner aspect of material or tangible manifestations of power." Thus "the principalities and powers are the inner or spiritual essence, or gestalt, of an institution or state or system [while] 'demons' are the psychic or spiritual power emanated by organizations or individuals or subaspects of individuals whose energies are bent on overpowering others." See *Naming the Powers: The Language of Power in the New Testament* (Philadelphia: Fortress Press, 1984), 104. All such cosmic powers reside "in the heavenlies" (a literal translation of Eph. 1:20; 3:10), which Wink takes to be "the transcendent 'within' of material reality" (118). Wink's concern to retain the material dimension of the powers and thus to avoid a fundamental

dualism in the cosmos is laudable. Still, I cannot help thinking that his definitions move too far in the direction of rendering the powers plausible to the dominant culture of psychotherapy. Maybe they are just more than we can comprehend
with our modern categories. Wink seems to admit as much when he notes that
"we have no unmediated access to the 'within' of a system, or institution, or even
another person. . . . That is where faith and prayer come in" (127).

12. In the passage from Acts, Jerusalem believers may seem to adopt a rather belliger-
ent stance over against the officials who are restricting their freedom. But in fact
they are mostly offering up their hurt and anger to God and asking that the
wrongs done to them be overcome with healing and with a bold proclamation of
the gospel. They hold the civil and religious authorities to be deluded (see Acts
3:17) but not in themselves demonic.

13. Some groups within the contemporary charismatic movement think of deliverance as virtually synonymous with exorcism. Others find this identification
problematic and prefer to distinguish between possession and oppression (partial
bondage). For Matthew Linn, deliverance prayer would apply to the latter. See
Deliverance Prayer, 8, and the discriminating essays by Dennis Hamm (49–71),
Robert Faricy (72–85), and John B. Healy (86–106), in which great care is taken not
to overinterpret the biblical and experiential data.

14. Acts 10:38 and 26:18 refer to release from Satan's oppressive power, not to possession and exorcism as such.

15. Mk. 16:17 might seem to imply that Jesus gives all believers the power to cast out
demons; but the most natural way to read this passage is as a prophecy that the
diverse signs accompanying believers will be distributed (as in 1 Cor. 12:11) in accord
with the divine will. Thus, some will cast out demons, some will speak in new
tongues, some will pick up deadly serpents, and so on. It is really Jesus who works
these signs (16:20). He chooses when, where, and by whom.

16. For more extensive expositions of the symbolic armor, see Wink, *Naming the
Powers* 84–89, and Clinton Arnold, *Ephesians: Power and Magic. The Concept of
Power in Ephesians in Light of Its Historical Setting* (Cambridge: Cambridge
Univ. Press, 1989), 109–12.

17. Exorcism, of course, would require such words of command, but the practice is
not dealt with in Ephesians. Wink has come to the conclusion that Eph. 3:10
describes a proclamation by the church specifically directed to the powers. This,
however, is unlikely. See the critique of Wink's position by Arnold, 62–64.

18. See *Ephesians: Power and Magic*, 112.

19. Wink and Arnold agree that the weapons mentioned in Eph. 6:1–20 are offensive
as well as defensive. See Wink, *Naming the Powers*, 86–89, and Arnold, *Ephesians: Power and Magic*, 119–21.

20. Wink, *Naming the Powers*, 110f.

21. Klassen, *Love of Enemies*, 128f.

22. *Love of Enemies*, 128f.

23. Bregman finds herself "deeply ambivalent over the cheery and breezy use of military imagery in a Christian context." She thinks that it needs to be supplemented
(but not replaced) "by [New Testament] alternatives drawn from . . . farming or
domestic life." See "Two Imageries of Peace," 80 and 90.

24. *The Hymnal 1982*, no. 555.

CHAPTER TWELVE

The Accomplishments of Prayer in the New Creation

1. See Jubilees 4:26; 1 Enoch 72:1. The substance of the term also occurs in the
Qumran writings (1QS iv.25; 1QH xi.10–14; xii.11–12) and in the prophetic

visions of Second Isaiah 42:9; 43:18–21; 48:8; 65:17–25; 66:22), which provide the basis for all these passages.

2. To a large extent, "kingdom" overlaps in meaning with "new creation"; but in the case of the latter more emphasis is placed on the immanent and abiding character of God's redemptive activity, as opposed to its nearness or arrival. A closer parallel in Jesus' language might be the "new wine" of his ministry, which bursts through old wineskins (Mk. 2:22). With Paul, such expressions as "the present time" (Rom. 3:26; 8:18; 11:5; 2 Cor. 8:13), "the appointed time" (1 Cor. 7:29), "the ends of the ages" (1 Cor. 10:11), and "the day of salvation" (2 Cor. 6:2) come very close to "new creation." The Gospel of John is full of new creation terms and images, though the exact phrase does not occur.

3. This translation, which seems to me closest to the the Greek, is by Victor P. Furnish. See *II Corinthians*, Anchor Bible 32A (Garden City, N.Y.: Doubleday & Company, Inc., 1984), 306.

4. John Koenig, "The Knowing of Glory and Its Consequences," in *The Conversation Continues*, ed. Fortna and Gaventa, 162–65.

5. *Being in Love*, 120.

6. See the exegetical basis for this in "The Knowing of Glory," 164f.

7. Furnish, *II Corinthians*, 339.

8. *The Gospel in a Pluralistic Society* (Grand Rapids, MI: Wm. B. Eerdmans, 1989), 227. Newbigin makes two additional points about the importance of praise. One is that it delivers us from an obsessive devotion to the hermeneutic of suspicion. The other is that "in Christian worship [of praise and thanksgiving] the language of rights is out of place except when it serves to remind us of the rights of others. . . . We acknowledge that if we had received justice instead of charity we would be on our way to perdition" (see 228f).

9. See Acts 2:1–42; 4:31; Eph. 5:18–20; 6:17–20, where prayer in the Spirit, dominated by praise and thanksgiving, generates apt and powerful words of the gospel.

10. *Life as Worship: Prayer and Praise in the Name of Jesus* (Grand Rapids, MI: Wm. B. Eerdmans, 1982), 119–21.

11. *Praying the Kingdom*, 88–90.

12. Douglas V. Steere, "Intercession: Caring for Souls," 19f. See above, chapter 7, n. 8.

13. "Prayer and the Powers," *Sojourners*, October 1990, 12.

14. See *Word and World* 10, 3 (Summer 1990): 272.

15. See Mt. 10:32; Lk. 12:8; Jn. 9:22; 12:42; Rom. 10:9–10; 2 Cor. 9:13; Heb. 3:1; 4:14; 1 Jn. 2:23; 4:2–3, 15; 2 Jn. 7.

16. *The Political Meaning of Christianity: An Interpretation* (Baton Rouge and London: Louisiana State Univ. Press, 1989), 214.

17. *The Political Meaning of Christianity*, 218.

18. *The Political Meaning of Christianity*, 232f.

General Index

Biblical Index

OTHER ANCIENT LITERATURE